Operating Systems, Cloud Computing, and Linux
Second Edition

Larry Sanchez

ISBN-13: **979-8-8692-8484-6**

DISCLAIMER

The names 'AWS', "Azure", "GCP", "Amazon", "Microsoft", "Google", "Linux", "Unix", "Ubuntu", "Windows", "Mac", and "iOS" are registered trademarks and belong to their respective owners. The use of these names in this book is for reference and educational purposes only and is not intended to imply endorsement by the trademark owners. The author and publisher of this book do not claim any ownership or affiliation with these trademarked names. All rights belong to their respective owners.

NOTICE OF LIABILITY

The author and publisher have made every effort to ensure the accuracy of the information herein.
However, the information contained in this book is sold without warranty, either express or implied.
Neither the author nor the publisher will be held liable for any
damages to be caused either directly or indirectly by the instructions
contained in this book, or by the software or hardware products described herein

CONTENTS

Chapter 1: Introduction to Operating Systems

Chapter Learning Outcomes

1.1 Explaining the operating system's role in managing computer hardware and software resources.
1.2 Describing how operating systems have evolved over time to meet changing technology needs.
1.3 Explaining why operating systems are essential in computer systems.
1.4 Explaining how operating systems are utilized in cloud environments.
1.5 Providing examples of operating system functions that control hardware components.

1.1 Definition of Operating Systems

An Operating System is a collection of software that manages computer hardware resources and provides common services for computer programs. It is the interface between the computer hardware and software, providing an environment in which programs can run efficiently and securely.

1.1.1 Types of Operating Systems

There are several types of operating systems. This section surveys a few of them.

Single-user operating systems: these are designed for use by a single user on a personal computer, such as earlier versions of Windows or MacOS.

Multi-user operating systems: these are designed to allow multiple users to access the system simultaneously, such as modern Windows or Mac OS. They are usually accessed through a network and allow multiple users to share resources such as storage, printers, and servers.

Real-time operating systems: these are designed for systems that require immediate response times, such as those used in aircraft or medical equipment. These operating systems are designed to process data in real-time, which means that they have very low latency and high throughput.

Embedded operating systems (EMS) are tailored for resource-constrained devices like smart home gadgets and Internet of Things devices. EMS prioritize stability and reliability, which are essential for remote devices. A key feature is customizability to match specific hardware platforms, streamlining functionality. EMS also incorporate robust security to protect sensitive data, making them indispensable for secure, efficient operation of modern embedded devices.

Network operating systems: These are designed to manage and control network resources, such as servers, printers, and network storage. They provide a centralized administration interface and allow users to access resources from different locations. Examples of network operating systems include Novell NetWare and Windows Server.

Mobile operating systems: These are designed for use on mobile devices, such as smartphones and tablets. They have specific features that make them suitable for use on small, portable devices, such as touch screen support and battery life optimization. Examples of mobile operating systems include iOS and Android.

Review Question 1.1
What is the primary function of an operating system?
A) To provide a graphical user interface (GUI) for users.
B) To manage computer hardware resources and offer common services for applications.
C) To connect multiple computers in a network.
D) To develop software applications efficiently.

Review Question 1.2
Which type of operating system is suitable for systems requiring immediate response times, such as aircraft control systems or medical equipment?
A) Multi-user operating systems
B) Single-user operating systems
C) Real-time operating systems
D) Network operating systems

Review Question 1.3
What is a key feature of embedded operating systems (EMS)?
A) Network administration
B) Touch screen support
C) Robust security
D) Centralized resource management

Review Question 1.4
Which type of operating system is optimized for use on smartphones and tablets?
A) Real-time operating systems
B) Multi-user operating systems
C) Network operating systems
D) Mobile operating systems

Review Question 1.5
What is the primary purpose of a network operating system?
A) To provide a graphical user interface (GUI) for users.
B) To manage computer hardware resources and offer common services.
C) To connect multiple computers in a network and manage network resources.
D) To optimize battery life on portable devices.

Review Question 1.6
What does the operating system interface connect?
A) Software and servers
B) Hardware and software
C) Drivers and applications
D) Firmware and drivers

1.1.2 Major Functions of Operating Systems

An operating system performs several functions that make it an essential component of any computer system. These functions can be classified into four categories: process management, memory management, device management, and file management.

Process Management: An operating system manages the execution of various processes. A process is a program in execution. The OS is responsible for starting, stopping, and scheduling processes. The OS creates a process when a user runs a program. It allocates system resources such as memory, CPU time, and input/output (I/O) devices to a process. The OS schedules processes to ensure that each process gets a fair share of system resources. It also provides mechanisms for interprocess communication and synchronization.

Memory Management: An operating system manages the allocation and deallocation of memory. It also provides a mechanism for virtual memory, which allows a process to access more memory than it actually has. The OS is responsible for swapping processes between main memory and secondary storage (hard disk) to ensure that there is enough memory for running processes.

Device Management: The operating system manages the various hardware devices connected to a computer, including input devices like keyboard and mouse as well as output devices such as printers and displays. The OS provides software drivers that enable applications to access these devices by abstracting away hardware complexity. Drivers act as translators between generic device commands from apps and device-specific instructions understood by hardware.

File Management: Operating systems handle the organization and storage of data in an efficient hierarchical file system. This involves maintaining file directories to logically structure data, as well as keeping track of physical disk space allocation. Some key responsibilities include facilitating opening, reading, writing and closing of files by applications, allocating disk blocks when files are created, managing free and used storage space, and mapping files to their physical location on disk. The file system also implements access protections in the form of file permissions based on user access rights.

Review Question 1.7
What is the primary responsibility of an operating system in process management?
A) Managing file directories
B) Allocating memory to processes
C) Creating user accounts
D) Designing networking protocols

Review Question 1.8
What is a process in the context of operating systems?
A) A type of memory allocation
B) A file storage structure
C) A program in execution
D) An input/output device

Review Question 1.9
Which function of an operating system involves maintaining file directories and managing disk space allocation?
A) Memory management
B) Device management
C) File management
D) Security and access control

Review Question 1.10
What is the purpose of an operating system's memory management function?
A) Allocating CPU time to processes
B) Managing input/output devices
C) Ensuring secure network connections
D) Allocating and deallocating memory

Review Question 1.11
What mechanism allows a process to access more memory than it actually has?
A) Virtual memory
B) Buffering
C) Encryption
D) RAID configuration

Review Question 1.12
What is the role of device drivers in device management?
A) Allocating memory to devices
B) Managing file permissions
C) Abstracting hardware complexity
D) Monitoring network traffic

Review Question 1.13
Which of the following is a process in relation to an operating system?
A) A program that is loaded into memory
B) A program in execution
C) A set of instructions
D) A memory location

Review Question 1.14
Virtual memory in an OS allows ________.
A) Faster access to RAM
B) Access to more memory than physically available
C) Secondary storage to act as main memory
D) Caching of frequently used data

Review Question 1.15
Which function does the OS NOT perform?
A) Compiler design
B) Memory management
C) File management
D) Process scheduling

1.2 History and Evolution of Operating Systems

The history of operating systems is a journey that traces back to the earliest days of computing. This section will delve into the fascinating world of early computer operating systems, exploring their development, features, and contributions to the field of computing.

1.2.1 The Early Development of Operating Systems

In the early decades of electronic computing, from the 1940s to 1950s, the earliest computers were enormous machines that filled entire rooms. These large-scale devices, such as the Electronic Numerical Integrator and Computer (ENIAC) developed by J. Presper Eckert and John Mauchly at the University of Pennsylvania in the 1940s, were designed primarily for scientific calculations and military applications.

Remarkably, these pioneering computers functioned without the type of operating systems we are familiar with today. Instead, programming the ENIAC required manually resetting hardware configurations and switch settings to execute each new task. This method was time-consuming and limited the computer's flexibility.

A key advancement came with the introduction of the Universal Automatic Computer I (UNIVAC I) by Eckert and Mauchly's company Remington Rand in 1951. As one of the first commercially viable computers, UNIVAC I featured a rudimentary operating system to manage hardware resources. Although primitive compared to modern systems, this represented the genesis of operating system technology.

As computer technology improved, it became increasingly important to use resources more effectively. This need led to the creation of batch processing systems, a significant development. Batch processing involves loading a series of computational tasks into the computer's memory and then processing them automatically in sequence. This automation increased productivity by eliminating the need for manual task loading.

The UNIVAC I operating system introduced pioneering concepts such as automatic program sequencing and program libraries for storage. Despite such innovations, user interactivity remained restricted compared to contemporary standards. Jobs were submitted in batches and executed sequentially in a predefined order. Still, batch processing indicated significant progress in operating system capabilities.

The emergence of batch processing systems and early operating systems like that of the UNIVAC I laid the groundwork for more sophisticated, interactive systems that would ultimately transform computing. This pioneering era established foundational operating system concepts still reflected in modern designs.

Review Question 1.16
Which of the following accurately describes the state of operating systems during the era of the ENIAC computer?
A) Operating systems with graphical interfaces were prevalent.
B) Programming the ENIAC required manual configuration changes.
C) The ENIAC used virtualization extensively.
D) Batch processing systems were the norm.

Review Question 1.17
What was the significance of the Universal Automatic Computer I (UNIVAC I) in the history of operating systems?
A) It introduced advanced virtualization techniques.
B) It featured a modern graphical user interface.
C) It was the first computer to use batch processing.
D) It included a rudimentary operating system to manage hardware resources.

Review Question 1.18
What is batch processing in the context of operating systems?
A) Manually executing each task one at a time.
B) Sequentially processing computational jobs automatically.
C) Parallel processing of tasks for maximum efficiency.
D) Distributing tasks to multiple processors for speed.

1.2.2 The Operating Systems for Mainframe Computing

Mainframes emerged as powerful, robust computers designed for demanding computational tasks. Mainframes excel at processing vast data volumes and performing complex calculations, making them critical for research, industry, and business.

IBM's 1964 System/360 mainframe family introduced standardized interfaces for hardware and software, enabling software portability across models. This innovation allowed programs to run on different mainframe configurations, shaping operating system evolution.

Mainframes are defined by robustness, reliability, and sophisticated resource management. With redundant components and rigorous error checking, mainframes provide consistent uptime for mission-critical applications. Their operating systems expertly allocate CPU time, memory, and peripheral devices, enabling multitasking and multi-user environments.

IBM's OS/360 pioneered a layered architecture, dividing the operating system into modules with distinct functions. This improved modularity and maintainability, influencing modern operating system design.

Time-sharing systems like IBM's TSS/360 allowed multiple users to access mainframe resources simultaneously and interactively by efficiently allocating time slices. This transformed mainframes into collaborative environments.

Mainframes explored parallel processing, using multiple CPUs collaboratively for faster computation. This increased speed for applications like simulations and modeling. Mainframes also introduced virtualization, allowing one system to host multiple virtual machines for efficient resource utilization.

Mainframes remain vital for critical systems in sectors like finance and healthcare due to unmatched reliability and performance. Concepts like virtualization and layered architectures conceived on mainframes shaped modern operating systems. Mainframe resource management techniques remain integral for allocating resources in today's complex computing environments.

Review Question 1.19
What distinguishes mainframes in terms of their computing capabilities?
A) They are known for their compact size.
B) They excel at processing vast data volumes and complex calculations.
C) They are primarily used for gaming purposes.
D) They have limited multitasking capabilities.

Review Question 1.20
What was the significant contribution of IBM's System/360 mainframe family to operating system evolution?
A) It introduced virtualization technology.
B) It emphasized graphical user interfaces.
C) It developed real-time operating systems.
D) It introduced standardized interfaces for hardware and software.

Review Question 1.21
What does the layered architecture of IBM's OS/360 entail?
A) Dividing the operating system into modules with distinct functions.
B) Running multiple operating systems in parallel.

C) Creating virtualized mainframes.
D) Implementing real-time processing.

Review Question 1.22
What did time-sharing systems like IBM's TSS/360 enable?
A) Running multiple operating systems in parallel.
B) Virtualizing mainframe resources.
C) Simultaneous and interactive access to mainframe resources.
D) Robust error checking.

Review Question 1.23
What is the purpose of parallel processing in mainframes?
A) Running multiple operating systems in parallel.
B) Dividing the operating system into modules.
C) Collaborative use of multiple CPUs for faster computation.
D) Enabling virtualization technology.

Review Question 1.24
Why are mainframes essential for critical systems in sectors like finance and healthcare?
A) They offer extensive gaming capabilities.
B) They have a modern graphical user interface.
C) They excel at multitasking.
D) They provide unmatched reliability and performance.

Review Question 1.25
What is the key contribution of mainframes to modern operating systems?
A) Introduction of virtual reality technology
B) Emphasis on real-time processing
C) Development of gaming applications
D) Shaping concepts like virtualization and layered architectures

Review Question 1.26
What is a notable characteristic of mainframes in terms of multitasking and user interaction?
A) Limited multitasking capabilities
B) Sequential processing of tasks
C) Single-user environments
D) Support for multitasking and multi-user environments

1.2.3 Personal Computer Operating Systems

In the evolution of computing, the emergence of personal computers marked a significant turning point that brought technology directly into the hands of individuals. At the core of these machines, personal computer operating systems took center stage, shaping the user experience and democratizing access to computing power.

The origins of personal computing can be traced back to the 1970s, when microcomputers began to make their presence felt. A pivotal moment in this era was the introduction of the Altair 8800. However, these early personal computers lacked integrated operating systems, leaving users to manually input machine code instructions to execute tasks.

Amidst this landscape, CP/M (Control Program/Monitor) emerged in 1974, thanks to Gary Kildall. CP/M stands as one of the first popular operating systems tailored for microcomputers. Notably, CP/M provided a standardized platform for software development, establishing a foundation that would influence the evolution of personal computer operating systems.

The ascent of personal computer operating systems was closely intertwined with the rise of graphical user interfaces (GUIs). A pivotal contributor to this shift was Xerox's Palo Alto Research Center (PARC), which introduced the Alto computer. This innovative machine brought forth elements of the graphical user interface, including icons, windows, and mouse input. These pioneering GUI concepts, laid down by the Alto, paved the way for the modern GUI-based operating systems we rely on today.

Subsequently, the introduction of the Apple Macintosh in 1984 revolutionized personal computing with its iconic GUI-driven operating system. Not to be outdone, Microsoft's Windows 3.0, released in 1990, brought the power of GUI capabilities to IBM-compatible PCs, triggering a wave of GUI democratization.

The realm of personal computer operating systems flourished with diversity. MS-DOS (Microsoft Disk Operating System) became a household name, providing a command-line interface for IBM-compatible PCs. It was soon complemented by various versions of Windows, each evolving to offer a more user-friendly and visually engaging experience.

Meanwhile, the influence of Unix, born in the 1970s, extended to personal computers through different variants like BSD and Sun's Solaris. An even more notable development was the advent of Linux in 1991, conceived by Linus Torvalds. Linux gained prominence as a free and open-source Unix-like operating system, igniting a movement that brought together a community of dedicated developers.

In today's digital age, personal computer operating systems have achieved unprecedented levels of sophistication and functionality. Microsoft's Windows series, with its numerous versions, has established itself as a leading player, providing a variety of operating systems designed to cater to diverse user requirements. Windows 11, the most recent version, blends traditional interface components with modern innovations, focusing on compatibility and user experience. This new version introduces features like intuitive navigation, faster performance, and an AI-powered intelligent assistant, Copilot. It was released on October 5, 2021, succeeding Windows 10, and is available for free for any Windows 10 devices that meet the new Windows 11 system requirements.

Apple's macOS, built upon a Unix foundation, boasts a sleek graphical interface and seamless integration with Apple hardware and software, offering a premium computing experience.

Meanwhile, the Linux ecosystem thrives with its diverse distributions (distros), catering to a wide spectrum of users, from casual enthusiasts to seasoned developers. This open-source spirit has nurtured a dynamic and collaborative community that drives innovation and adaptability.

As we continue to journey through the digital age, personal computer operating systems remain integral to our daily lives, enabling us to navigate a complex and interconnected digital landscape with ease and confidence.

Review Question 1.27
What marked a significant turning point in the evolution of computing, bringing technology directly to individuals?
A) Mainframe computers
B) Personal computers
C) Supercomputers
D) Embedded systems

Review Question 1.28
What is the significance of personal computer operating systems in the evolution of computing?
A) They introduced the concept of mainframes.
B) They facilitated communication between devices.
C) They shaped the user experience and democratized access to computing power.
D) They were primarily used for gaming purposes.

Review Question 1.29
Which microcomputer is considered a pivotal moment in the emergence of personal computing?
A) Apple Macintosh
B) Altair 8800
C) IBM System/360
D) ENIAC

Review Question 1.30
Which operating system brought the power of GUI capabilities to IBM-compatible PCs?

A) Windows 3.0
B) MS-DOS
C) Linux
D) Unix

Review Question 1.31
What is a key characteristic of MS-DOS?
A) Graphical user interface
B) Command-line interface
C) Open-source license
D) Unix-like architecture

Review Question 1.32
What role did Unix play in the evolution of personal computer operating systems?
A) It introduced the concept of GUIs.
B) It shaped the user experience of mobile devices.
C) It extended to personal computers through various variants.
D) It focused on gaming applications.

Review Question 1.33
What impact did Linux have on the development of personal computer operating systems?
A) It introduced graphical user interfaces.
B) It provided a proprietary operating system.
C) It ignited a movement of free and open-source operating systems.
D) It introduced mobile operating systems.

1.2.4 Mobile and Embedded Operating Systems

The proliferation of mobile devices and the integration of technology into various aspects of our lives have led to a paradigm shift in the way we interact with the digital world. At the heart of this transformation lie mobile and embedded operating systems, which enable the seamless operation of devices ranging from smartphones and tablets to specialized embedded systems.

The turn of the 21st century witnessed a technological revolution with the introduction of smartphones and tablets. These portable devices redefined the way we communicate, access information, and perform everyday tasks. At the core of these devices are specialized operating systems that cater to the unique demands of mobile computing.

Smartphones brought forth a wave of operating systems designed to optimize user experience on smaller screens. Platforms like Apple's iOS, Google's Android, and Microsoft's Windows Phone (later evolved into Windows 10 Mobile) revolutionized the concept of mobile computing, offering touch-friendly interfaces, app ecosystems, and seamless integration with online services.

Apple's iOS is renowned for its elegant design, seamless integration with Apple hardware, and curated app ecosystem. Its focus on security and user privacy has made it a popular choice among consumers. Google's Android, characterized by its open-source nature, offers versatility and customization. It caters to a wide range of devices and manufacturers, contributing to its widespread adoption. While iOS and Android dominate the market, alternative mobile operating systems like KaiOS and Ubuntu Touch cater to niche segments, providing distinctive features and user experiences.

The fusion of computing with everyday objects has given rise to the Internet of Things (IoT), a network of interconnected devices that communicate and share data. Embedded operating systems form the backbone of this interconnected ecosystem. Embedded operating systems power a myriad of devices, ranging from smart home appliances and wearables to industrial machinery and medical devices. These operating systems are designed for efficiency, stability, and real-time performance in resource-constrained environments.

Embedded operating systems prioritize real-time responsiveness, making them suitable for applications requiring instantaneous decision-making, such as robotics and industrial automation. Embedded systems often operate in challenging environments. Embedded operating systems are engineered for robustness, ensuring stable and dependable performance even under adverse conditions.

From smartphones and tablets that have become extensions of our lives to the intricate web of interconnected smart devices in the IoT, mobile and embedded operating systems have emerged as the linchpins of this interconnected era. As we continue to embrace the transformative potential of these systems, they will shape the future of computing, enabling us to navigate a world where technology is not only at our fingertips but seamlessly integrated into every facet of our lives.

Review Question 1.34
What has led to a paradigm shift in how we interact with the digital world?
A) Proliferation of desktop computers
B) Integration of technology into various aspects of our lives
C) Rise of supercomputers
D) Focus on mainframe computing

Review Question 1.35
What technological revolution occurred with the introduction of smartphones and tablets?

A) Development of supercomputers
B) Integration of IoT devices
C) Emergence of mobile and embedded operating systems
D) Redefining communication and everyday tasks

Review Question 1.36
What is a distinguishing feature of Apple's iOS?
A) Open-source nature
B) Curated app ecosystem
C) Versatility and customization
D) Compatibility with various manufacturers

Review Question 1.37
What is a key characteristic of Google's Android operating system?
A) Closed-source nature
B) Limited app ecosystem
C) Focus on security and user privacy
D) Open-source nature and versatility

Review Question 1.38
How do alternative mobile operating systems like KaiOS and Ubuntu Touch cater to the market?
A) By offering advanced security features
B) By focusing on gaming experiences
C) By providing distinctive features and user experiences
D) By targeting high-end smartphones

Review Question 1.39
What do embedded operating systems power in the context of the Internet of Things (IoT)?
A) Desktop computers
B) Wearables and smart home appliances
C) Supercomputers
D) Industrial machinery and medical devices

Review Question 1.40
What is a significant advantage of embedded operating systems in resource-constrained environments?
A) Compatibility with traditional desktop applications
B) Focus on high-definition graphics
C) Real-time responsiveness
D) Ability to run multiple virtual machines

Review Question 1.41
What is a key characteristic of embedded operating systems in terms of performance under adverse conditions?
A) Lack of stability
B) Focus on graphics-intensive tasks
C) Robustness and stable performance
D) Emphasis on gaming applications

Review Question 1.42

What role do mobile and embedded operating systems play in the interconnected era?
A) They focus on mainframe computing
B) They enhance gaming experiences
C) They shape the future of computing by seamlessly integrating technology into everyday life
D) They prioritize compatibility with traditional desktop applications

1.3 The Need for Operating Systems

In the intricate tapestry of modern computing, the role of an operating system stands as a cornerstone that orchestrates the complex interactions between hardware, software, and users. The question arises: why is an operating system essential? This section embarks on a journey to unravel the fundamental reasons behind the necessity of an operating system, exploring the ways it facilitates efficient resource management, enhances user experience, and provides a platform for software development.

At the heart of any computing device lies a myriad of hardware components, each with its unique functions and intricacies. An operating system acts as a bridge between users and the underlying hardware by providing a layer of abstraction. This abstraction shields users and applications from the complexities of hardware, enabling them to interact with standardized interfaces and commands. An operating system provides a standardized platform for software development. By offering a consistent set of APIs (Application Programming Interfaces) and libraries, it abstracts the underlying hardware details, allowing developers to create software without having to worry about the intricacies of different hardware configurations.

One of the primary functions of an operating system is to manage the allocation and utilization of crucial resources such as central processing units (CPUs), memory, storage, and peripheral devices. By regulating access to these resources and ensuring fair distribution, an operating system maximizes efficiency and prevents conflicts among various software components vying for the same resources.

An operating system acts as an intermediary through which users interact with a computer or computing device. Through intuitive user interfaces, such as graphical user interfaces (GUIs) or command-line interfaces (CLIs), users can initiate actions, access files, launch applications, and configure settings. The operating system's user interface simplifies the complex underlying processes, making computing accessible and user-friendly.

In the modern computing landscape, multitasking has become a norm, allowing users to perform multiple tasks simultaneously. An operating system enables this by efficiently managing processes and threads. Multitasking ensures that different applications can run concurrently, facilitating seamless context switching and resource allocation to maintain responsiveness.

Operating systems play a vital role in ensuring compatibility across a wide range of software applications. By providing a consistent environment, an operating system ensures that software developed on one system can run on another with minimal modifications. This compatibility fosters a thriving software ecosystem, enabling users to choose from a diverse array of applications to meet their needs.

An operating system serves as the guardian of system security, implementing various mechanisms to safeguard against unauthorized access, data breaches, and malicious software. By enforcing access controls, user authentication, and encryption, an operating system mitigates potential threats and ensures the integrity and confidentiality of user data.

From abstraction and resource allocation to providing a cohesive user experience and fostering software compatibility and security, an operating system plays an indispensable role in orchestrating the symphony of computing. As technology continues to advance, the need for operating systems remains unwavering, anchoring our digital world and empowering us to navigate the complex realms of modern computing with efficiency, ease, and security.

Review Question 1.43
What is the primary role of an operating system in modern computing?
A) Enhancing hardware complexity
B) Managing software development
C) Orchestrating interactions between hardware, software, and users
D) Focusing on peripheral device management

Review Question 1.44
How does an operating system shield users and applications from hardware complexities?
A) By emphasizing direct hardware control
B) By providing standardized interfaces and commands
C) By promoting hardware customization
D) By minimizing resource allocation

Review Question 1.45
What is a primary function of an operating system in terms of resource management?

A) Removing conflicts among software components
B) Ignoring allocation of peripheral devices
C) Maximizing efficiency and preventing resource conflicts
D) Focusing on hardware customization

Review Question 1.46
How does an operating system enhance user interaction with a computer?
A) By introducing hardware complexity
B) By providing a layer of hardware abstraction
C) By exclusively using command-line interfaces
D) By emphasizing software development

Review Question 1.47
How does an operating system support software development?
A) By limiting the use of APIs and libraries
B) By focusing on hardware intricacies
C) By providing standardized APIs and libraries
D) By discouraging software compatibility

Review Question 1.48
What does operating system compatibility ensure?
A) Software developed on one system can run on any system
B) Software can only run on the system it was developed on
C) Compatibility with hardware configurations
D) Incompatibility between different software applications

Review Question 1.49
What is a fundamental reason for the unwavering need for operating systems?
A) Simplifying hardware complexity
B) Enhancing software development
C) Fostering hardware customization
D) Navigating peripheral device management

Review Question 1.50
What role does an operating system play in the realm of modern computing?
A) It is optional and not essential for daily tasks.
B) It acts as a barrier between users and hardware complexities.
C) It is responsible for hardware customization.
D) It orchestrates computing interactions, resource management, and security.

1.4 Cloud Computing and Operating Systems

In the dynamic landscape of modern computing, the emergence of cloud computing has reshaped how we conceive, access, and utilize computing resources. At the nexus of this transformation lies the interaction between cloud computing and operating systems. This section delves into the symbiotic relationship between cloud computing and operating systems, exploring how operating systems have evolved to support cloud environments, and how cloud computing has revolutionized the way we deploy and manage operating systems.

1.4.1 The Convergence of Cloud Computing and Operating Systems

Cloud computing has revolutionized the way computing resources are delivered and consumed. It offers on-demand access to a shared pool of configurable computing resources, including networks, servers, storage, applications, and services. This paradigm shift has profound implications for operating systems.

Virtualization technologies, such as hypervisors, form the bedrock of cloud computing. These technologies enable the creation of virtual machines (VMs) that run multiple instances of operating systems on a single physical server.

Cloud environments have embraced containerization, facilitated by technologies like Docker (containerization technology) and Kubernetes (container orchestration platform). Containers encapsulate applications along with their dependencies, making them portable across different cloud platforms and operating systems.

Review Question 1.51
What paradigm shift has cloud computing brought to the delivery and consumption of computing resources?
A) Decreasing accessibility to computing resources
B) Limiting the sharing of configurable resources
C) Offering on-demand access to a shared pool of resources
D) Focusing on physical server utilization

Review Question 1.52
How do containers differ from virtual machines (VMs) in cloud environments?
A) Containers cannot encapsulate applications and dependencies.
B) Containers run only a single instance of an operating system.
C) VMs are not portable across different cloud platforms.
D) Containers encapsulate applications along with their dependencies and are portable.

Review Question 1.53
What role do hypervisors play in cloud computing?
A) They provide on-demand access to computing resources.
B) They encapsulate applications and dependencies.
C) They enable the creation of virtual machines (VMs) on a single physical server.

D) They manage network connections in cloud environments.

Review Question 1.54
How have operating systems evolved to support cloud environments?
A) They have become less relevant due to cloud technologies.
B) They have stopped running on virtual machines.
C) They have become less complex to adapt to cloud platforms.
D) They run as instances on virtual machines or containers.

Review Question 1.55
Which technology is used for containerization in cloud environments?
A) Hypervisors
B) Kubernetes
C) Virtualization technologies
D) Docker

1.4.2 The Impact of Cloud Computing on Operating Systems

The advent of cloud computing has profoundly impacted the landscape of operating systems and introduced new paradigms in operating system design. By providing on-demand access to vast pools of configurable computing resources over the internet, cloud computing has enabled greater flexibility, scalability, and cost-efficiency. This has led to the prominence of lightweight operating systems designed specifically for cloud environments.

Unlike traditional operating systems focused on managing local hardware resources, these cloud-based operating systems emphasize abstracting infrastructure complexities. For instance, Linux variants like CoreOS provide only essential functionality needed to run applications inside containers orchestrated by container managers like Kubernetes. This container-centric approach aligns with the cloud philosophy of treating infrastructure as code.

Cloud operating systems also utilize auto-scaling capabilities to dynamically allocate resources based on application demands, optimizing efficiency. Furthermore, cloud operating systems leverage virtualization to create isolated, secure environments for running applications while masking underlying hardware differences.

By simplifying deployment across diverse, distributed infrastructure, virtualization enabled the very concept of the cloud. Other innovations in cloud operating systems include serverless computing models where resources are provided dynamically as a service without users managing servers at all. By reducing hardware dependencies, cloud computing has shifted the role of operating systems away from low-level resource control and toward enabling applications to harness the elasticity and agility of the cloud.

Serverless computing represents the pinnacle of how cloud computing has shifted operating system responsibilities away from developers. In serverless platforms like AWS Lambda and Azure Functions, developers simply deploy functional code without provisioning servers or managing any operating system. The service provider automatically handles all server and operating system administration under the hood. This allows developers to focus solely on writing code, without worrying about configuring and maintaining infrastructure.

The operating system functionality is abstracted into the serverless platform itself, which dynamically manages the OS and server resources required to run each function. When a function is triggered, the provider rapidly provisions a runtime container to execute the code. Containers are ephemeral and exist only during function execution, then disappear. This auto-scaling container model maximizes resource efficiency. The developer is completely shielded from operating system tasks like patching, upgrading, or scaling. Anything required for OS management is handled automatically by the serverless platform.

By fully decoupling code from infrastructure, serverless represents the next evolution in cloud computing's impact on operating systems, where OS responsibilities dissipate entirely into the background, liberating developers to simply deploy pure business logic.

Review Question 1.56
What is the primary goal of lightweight operating systems designed for cloud environments?
A) Managing local hardware resources
B) Emphasizing abstracting infrastructure complexities
C) Enhancing low-level resource control
D) Focusing on virtual machine management

Review Question 1.57
Which technology allows cloud operating systems to dynamically allocate resources based on application demands?
A) Auto-scaling
B) Containerization
C) Hypervisors
D) Virtualization

Review Question 1.58

What is the primary advantage of using virtualization in cloud operating systems?
A) Reducing application complexity
B) Centralizing data storage
C) Masking hardware differences
D) Enhancing container management

Review Question 1.59
What is the key concept of serverless computing models?
A) Manual server provisioning
B) Direct OS control by developers
C) Auto-scaling container management
D) Code deployment without managing servers

Review Question 1.60
In serverless platforms like AWS Lambda and Azure Functions, what aspect is automatically handled by the service provider?
A) Hardware provisioning
B) OS administration
C) Function execution
D) Code writing

Review Question 1.61
What is the purpose of runtime containers in serverless platforms?
A) Managing networking
B) Providing persistent storage
C) Executing functional code
D) Isolating hardware resources

Review Question 1.62
How does the auto-scaling container model in serverless computing benefit resource efficiency?
A) By increasing hardware capacity
B) By reducing code complexity
C) By minimizing server downtime
D) By optimizing resource usage

Review Question 1.63
What role does serverless computing play in terms of operating system responsibilities?
A) It enhances low-level resource control.
B) It fully eliminates the need for operating system management.
C) It centralizes OS patching and upgrading.
D) It automates virtualization processes.

Review Question 1.64
What is the main benefit for developers in the context of serverless computing?
A) Simplified container orchestration
B) Reduced code deployment complexity
C) Direct control over hardware provisioning
D) Increased focus on infrastructure management

1.5 Computer Hardware and Operating Systems

In the intricate interplay of modern computing, the hardware and operating system of a computer form a symbiotic partnership that underpins the entire computing experience. This section delves into the essential relationship between computer hardware and operating systems, exploring how hardware components interact with the operating system to execute tasks, manage resources, and facilitate user interactions.

1.5.1 Hardware Abstraction and Interaction

Computer hardware consists of many different components that work together to enable computation and data processing. At the core is the central processing unit (CPU), which executes program instructions and performs calculations. The CPU relies on main memory modules like RAM to temporarily store data and instructions while they are actively being used. For longer-term storage, hardware includes disk drives, solid state drives, and other persistent storage media. Input and output (I/O) devices allow users to interact with the computer and connect it to the outside world. Examples include keyboards, mice, monitors, printers, and network interface cards.

Each hardware component has its own unique characteristics, data formats, and control mechanisms. This complexity makes it challenging for software developers to directly interface with hardware. The operating system provides an abstraction layer that hides the specifics of the underlying hardware. For example, the operating system manages memory allocation and mapping virtual memory addresses to physical RAM locations. Drivers are software components that manage and facilitate the interaction between the operating system and various input/output (I/O) devices connected to a computer system. File systems organize data on disk drives into hierarchical directories and files.

By providing standardized application programming interfaces (APIs) and system calls, the operating system creates a consistent interface for software to leverage hardware capabilities without needing to understand device-level details. The operating system handles all the interactions with hardware at a low level, while presenting an abstract virtual platform for applications. This greatly simplifies software development and enables portability across different hardware configurations. The role of the operating system is crucial in enabling hardware resources to be utilized efficiently for computation and data processing while insulating software from underlying complexity.

Review Question 1.65
What is the main purpose of the operating system's abstraction layer in relation to hardware?
A) To expose device-level details to software
B) To create unique APIs for each hardware component
C) To simplify hardware interactions for software developers
D) To eliminate the need for hardware components

Review Question 1.66
Which hardware component performs calculations and executes program instructions?
A) RAM
B) Disk drive
C) CPU
D) Network interface card

Review Question 1.67
What is the primary role of drivers in the context of an operating system?
A) Managing RAM allocation
B) Executing program instructions
C) Communicating with I/O devices
D) Creating hierarchical directories and files

Review Question 1.68
What is the function of main memory modules like RAM in a computer?
A) To provide long-term storage
B) To perform calculations
C) To temporarily store data and instructions
D) To facilitate user interactions

Review Question 1.69
How does the operating system enhance software portability across different hardware configurations?
A) By providing unique APIs for each hardware component
B) By eliminating the need for hardware interactions
C) By presenting a consistent interface through APIs and system calls
D) By focusing on low-level hardware details

Review Question 1.70
What is the benefit of the operating system's abstraction of hardware complexities?
A) It eliminates the need for device drivers
B) It enhances hardware performance
C) It simplifies software development and portability
D) It replaces the need for RAM

1.5.2 Resource Management and Allocation

The central processing unit (CPU) executes instructions and performs computations, serving as the "brain" of the computer. The operating system manages how CPU time is distributed via scheduling algorithms. It allows multiple processes and threads to share the CPU transparently and efficiently. The scheduler determines which process runs at a given time, for how long, and switches context from one process to another. This provides the illusion that each process has full access to the CPU. In reality, the CPU rapidly switches between processes. The scheduler aims to utilize the CPU optimally, providing reasonable response times and throughput. Common scheduling algorithms include first-come, first-served, shortest job first, priority-based, and round-robin approaches. Advanced schedulers support preemption, where higher priority processes can interrupt lower priority ones. Overall, the OS scheduling function coordinates CPU activities for optimal usage.

Memory, or RAM, is used to temporarily store code and data needed by running processes. The operating system manages memory, allocating portions to specific processes. It does this via virtual memory techniques, using page tables to translate virtual addresses used by processes to actual physical RAM addresses. This provides each process with the illusion of a large, contiguous memory space. The OS optimizes physical memory usage by swapping less active pages to disk and tracking which pages haven't been recently used. It deallocates memory from terminated processes and provides mechanisms to request additional memory. Overall, the OS memory manager coordinates allocating the right amount memory to processes to optimize utilization.

Storage devices provide long-term data storage capacity. The operating system manages filesystems, which organize data into files and directories. It coordinates reading/writing data, keeping track of storage usage, and mapping physical storage blocks. The OS manages access permissions and data integrity. It facilitates sharing data between users and applications. The OS optimizes retrievals by caching frequently accessed data in memory. It manages virtual memory swapping activities with disk. The storage manager role is critical for reliable, efficient data storage and retrieval operations.

Review Question 1.71
What is the role of the operating system in relation to the central processing unit (CPU)?
A) The operating system manufactures CPUs
B) The operating system executes CPU instructions
C) The operating system manages CPU distribution and scheduling
D) The operating system physically connects CPUs to other hardware

Review Question 1.72
How does the operating system manage memory (RAM) allocation for running processes?
A) By storing all process data in physical memory

B) By allocating memory only to high-priority processes
C) By using virtual memory techniques and page tables
D) By swapping memory between processes continuously

Review Question 1.73
What is the primary purpose of an operating system's memory manager?
A) To physically manufacture RAM modules
B) To allocate memory only to the operating system itself
C) To ensure each process has a contiguous memory space
D) To optimize memory allocation and utilization for processes

Review Question 1.74
What is the function of an operating system's storage manager?
A) To design storage devices like hard drives
B) To manufacture storage devices like solid state drives
C) To organize data into files and directories on storage devices
D) To physically connect storage devices to the CPU

Review Question 1.75
How does the operating system optimize data storage and retrieval?
A) By using slow storage devices exclusively
B) By avoiding the use of filesystems
C) By caching frequently accessed data in memory
D) By storing all data on physical storage blocks

Review Question 1.76
What role does the operating system's scheduler play in CPU management?
A) It manufactures CPUs
B) It executes CPU instructions
C) It physically connects CPUs to other hardware
D) It determines which process runs on the CPU and for how long

1.5.3 User Interaction and Interface

Hardware devices like keyboards, mice, printers, and network cards enable user input/output but communicate using device-specific protocols. The operating system includes driver software that acts as translators between devices and applications. Each driver encapsulates the details of a specific hardware device. It implements functions for initializing the device, reading/writing data, and controlling device behavior. Drivers present a consistent software interface that other parts of the OS and applications use to access the device. This enables portable high-level operations like "print file" without needing device specifics. The driver handles the low-level instructions for that printer model. By abstracting device complexities, drivers provide a smooth user experience.

The user interface (UI) facilitates interactions between the user and computer. Graphical UIs provide a visual environment with elements like windows, icons, menus, and pointer controls. This makes the system intuitive and easy to use. The OS manages display output, interprets mouse/keyboard input, and renders the visual interface. Command line UIs accept text-based commands that perform operations. This allows automation and more advanced use. Both styles of UI help users harness the capabilities of computers in an accessible way thanks to OS interfaces. Whether menu-driven or command-driven, the OS plays a central role in adaptation of the computer system to user needs. UI and drivers allow the OS to act as an intermediary between users and hardware.

Review Question 1.77
What is the primary role of driver software in an operating system?
A) To manage the physical hardware components
B) To translate device-specific protocols into readable data
C) To create user interfaces for applications
D) To handle memory allocation for processes

Review Question 1.78
What is the purpose of driver software for hardware devices in an operating system?
A) To manufacture the hardware devices
B) To encapsulate the details of specific hardware devices
C) To design graphical user interfaces for the devices
D) To physically connect the devices to the computer

Review Question 1.79
How do drivers contribute to a smooth user experience in operating systems?
A) By eliminating the need for hardware devices
B) By simplifying the operating system's user interface
C) By abstracting the complexities of hardware devices
D) By creating device-specific user interfaces

1.5.4 Bootstrapping and Initialization

When a computer powers on, the CPU has no software to execute. The operating system code is stored on disk. So a special bootstrapping process must occur to load the OS. This bootstrap sequence is handled by the computer's firmware built into the motherboard. The firmware initializes CPUs, memory, and hardware. It locates the bootloader on disk and executes it. The bootloader loads the kernel, which contains core OS functions. The kernel initializes device drivers for hardware access. It mounts the filesystems containing other OS files. Useful background services and daemons are launched. Finally, the login prompt is presented to the user. This boot process brings the system from inert hardware to an interactive operating system ready for use. The OS handles all aspects of system initialization during boot.

At boot time, the operating system kickstarts all the essential background services, daemons, and processes the system depends on. For example, it launches networking services to enable Internet connectivity, print spooling to manage print jobs, security services for access control and authentication, and more. These background processes continue running after boot, providing crucial functionality without user intervention. The OS manages dependencies and ordering - for instance, networking must initialize before web services start. Proper initialization by the OS sets up a fully functional environment for users and other processes to operate in. The OS remains responsible for launching, monitoring, and managing these vital background services.

The intricate dance between computer hardware and operating systems shapes the computing experience, enabling the seamless execution of tasks, efficient resource management, and user-friendly interactions. Through abstraction layers, resource management mechanisms, and user interface components, operating systems bridge the gap between hardware complexity and software simplicity. As technology continues to evolve, the synergy between hardware and operating systems will remain a foundational pillar of the digital world, driving innovation and enabling us to explore the vast horizons of computing possibilities.

Review Question 1.80
During the bootstrapping process of a computer, what is the role of the bootloader?
A) To initialize the CPU and memory
B) To locate and execute the kernel
C) To launch background services
D) To provide user authentication

Review Question 1.81
What is the purpose of the firmware built into a computer's motherboard during the boot process?
A) To load the operating system code into memory
B) To initialize device drivers for hardware access
C) To execute core OS functions
D) To handle the bootstrapping sequence

Review Question 1.82
What is the final step in the boot process that brings a computer from inert hardware to an interactive operating system?
A) Initializing device drivers
B) Mounting filesystems
C) Presenting the login prompt
D) Launching networking services

Review Question 1.83
What ensures the proper ordering and initialization of background services during boot time?
A) User intervention
B) Firmware on the motherboard
C) CPU execution
D) Operating system management

Review Question 1.84
How do operating systems bridge the gap between hardware complexity and software simplicity?
A) By increasing hardware complexity
B) By reducing the need for hardware devices
C) Through abstraction layers and user interface components
D) By eliminating the need for background services

1.6 Chapter Summary

This chapter introduces fundamental operating system concepts. Operating systems manage hardware and software resources, acting as intermediaries. They synchronize components for a cohesive computing environment, handling tasks like memory management, CPU coordination, device interfacing, networking, and user interfaces. The chapter covers OS history, from early batch systems to modern GUI-based ones, driven by advances in computing power, hardware, and interfaces. Operating systems continue to manage resources, coordinate components, and provide abstraction for simplified usage. This overview forms a foundation for exploring specific OS architectures, functions, and designs in later chapters.

1.7 Exercise

Application software serves to automate various tasks in our work, including functions like accounting and inventory management. These applications rely on hardware components to function effectively. Operating systems play a pivotal role in bridging the gap between application software and hardware. Consider several real-world examples that fulfill a similar role as operating systems—these are elements that people don't interact with directly, yet significantly contribute to enhancing our daily lives, making tasks more efficient.

1.8 Solutions to Review Questions

1.1 B; 1.2 C; 1.3 C; 1.4 D; 1.5 C; 1.6 B; 1.7 B; 1.8 C; 1.9 C; 1.10 D; 1.11 A; 1.12 C; 1.13 B; 1.14 B; 1.15 A; 1.16 B; 1.17 D; 1.18 B; 1.19 B; 1.20 D; 1.21 A; 1.22 C; 1.23 C; 1.24 D; 1.25 D; 1.26 D; 1.27 B; 1.28 C; 1.29 B; 1.30 A; 1.31 B; 1.32 C; 1.33 C; 1.34 B; 1.35 D; 1.36 B; 1.37 D; 1.38 C; 1.39 B; 1.40 C; 1.41 C; 1.42 C; 1.43 C; 1.44 B; 1.45 C; 1.46 B; 1.47 C; 1.48 A; 1.49 A; 1.50 D; 1.51 C; 1.52 D; 1.53 C; 1.54 D; 1.55 D; 1.56 B; 1.57 A; 1.58 C; 1.59 D; 1.60 B; 1.61 C; 1.62 D; 1.63 B; 1.64 B; 1.65 C; 1.66 C; 1.67 C; 1.68 C; 1.69 C; 1.70 C; 1.71 C; 1.72 C; 1.73 D; 1.74 C; 1.75 C; 1.76 D; 1.77 B; 1.78 B; 1.79 C; 1.80 B; 1.81 D; 1.82 C; 1.83 D; 1.84 C

Chapter 2: Process Management

Chapter Learning Outcomes

2.1 Define and describe the concept of a process in the context of computing.
2.2 Analyze and predict the execution order of processes based on given scenarios.
2.3 Explain the various mechanisms of inter-process communication and synchronization.
2.4 Explain the advantages and challenges of using threads for parallelism and concurrency,

2.1 Introduction to Processes

In operating systems, a process represents a program in active execution. It embodies the essence of work being performed within the system. A process encompasses a range of essential attributes, including its unique process ID (PID), current state, priority level, and the valuable resources it's currently utilizing. Orchestrating these elements seamlessly is the process control block (PCB), a critical data structure that acts as the repository for all these attributes. The PCB effectively encapsulates the intricate details of a process, enabling the operating system to manage and coordinate processes efficiently. This process management allows the operating system to ensure fair resource allocation, prioritize tasks, and facilitate multitasking, all of which contribute to the smooth and optimal operation of a computer system.

2.1.1 Definition of a Process

A process is a program in execution. It is an instance of a running program, containing code, data, and system resources. A process is the basic unit scheduled and managed by the operating system.
A process can be compared to a house that is under construction. Consider a house building project as analogous to a program being executed.

The architectural plans for the house are like the program code, containing the blueprint for construction. This is the static program on disk. The physical building site where construction is happening corresponds to a process. It is where the program plans are being executed and the house is being built. The construction materials, workers, and equipment at the site are the system resources needed to build the house. These are allocated by the OS to a process. The construction foreman overseeing the project is like the OS, managing the process and directing how resources are utilized. So, in this analogy, a process is the active "site" where code execution and construction occur. Just as a foreman can manage multiple house construction projects, the OS can handle multiple processes executing programs concurrently.

A process brings a program to life by providing all the necessary resources for its code to run. It is a vital abstraction managed by the OS to enable concurrency. For example, a Firefox browser process renders and displays a web page while utilizing memory, CPU time, network connectivity and other resources.

2.1.2 Attributes of a Process

Every process has certain attributes associated with it including a unique process ID (PID), current state, priority, resources allocated, and other details stored in a process control block (PCB). The PID identifies the process. The state can be running, waiting, ready, terminated, etc. Priority determines scheduling and access to resources.

Here is an explanation of process attributes using the house construction analogy and examples:
Each house construction site has unique attributes that identify it and determine how construction proceeds. A site ID is the unique plot number that identifies each house construction site, like a process ID. The construction state indicates a site can be actively under construction, paused waiting for materials, completed and ready for handoff, etc. This is like the state of a process - running, waiting, ready, terminated. The priority level is marked on some sites by the foreman for accelerated construction, similar to process priority. The resources allocated indicates the building materials, equipment, and workers assigned to a site by the foreman based on the construction needs, just as the OS allocates resource to a process. Finally, there is project records. The foreman maintains a file for each site tracking all the above details, like the process control block.

The following are two examples of process with attributes, a Python process executing a machine learning program has attributes like:
- PID: 12345, uniquely identifying this process
- State: Running, as it is actively processing data
- Priority: Low, so the OS focuses on higher priority processes first
- Resources: 2 CPU cores, 5MB of RAM, access to the training dataset file
- PCB: Stores the above details along with others like open sockets, signals, scheduling info

Similarly, a browser process may have attributes like:

- PID: 45678
- State: Waiting, as some website content is still loading
- Priority: Normal
- Resources: 1 CPU core, 2GB RAM, network bandwidth
- PCB: Tracks everything needed to manage the browser process

The OS leverages these process attributes to schedule, control, isolate and synchronize processes effectively. The PCB contains important information about a process including its state, PID, scheduling details, pointers to resources in use, and accounting information. The PCB allows the OS to control and track each process as an independent unit. It is created when a process is created and managed by the OS.

As explained above, a process is different from a program. A key distinction is that a program is passive code on disk, while a process is the active execution of that code. One program can spawn multiple concurrent processes. Processes are created through methods like forking, where an existing process creates a child process. The OS initializes a new PCB to represent the child process. Processes terminate when the code completes execution or on certain events. The OS reclaims resources allocated to the process. Processes allow multiple programs to run concurrently on limited resources. The OS allocates resources to processes and provides isolation between them.

Review Question 2.1
What is a process in an operating system?
A) A program in storage on the disk.
B) A set of system resources.
C) A static blueprint for construction.
D) A program in active execution.

Review Question 2.2
Which of the following is NOT an attribute of a process?
A) Process ID (PID)
B) Current state
C) Static program on disk
D) Priority level

Review Question 2.3
What is the purpose of a Process Control Block (PCB)?
A) It contains the program's code and data.
B) It represents a static blueprint for a process.
C) It manages system resources.
D) It holds essential attributes of a process.

Review Question 2.4
What does the analogy of a house under construction represent in the context of processes?
A) A program's code on disk.
B) The construction materials.
C) The running instance of a program.
D) The physical site of program execution.

Review Question 2.5
How does a process relate to system resources?
A) A process manages system resources.
B) A process contains the blueprint for resources.
C) System resources are static program code.
D) A process utilizes system resources.

Review Question 2.6
What does the OS do in relation to processes?
A) Manages construction materials.
B) Allocates system resources to processes.
C) Provides architectural plans.
D) Constructs physical buildings.

Review Question 2.7
What is the primary purpose of a process in an operating system?
A) To allocate system resources.
B) To provide architectural plans.
C) To manage construction sites.
D) To execute program code using resources.

Review Question 2.8
What does a process ID (PID) uniquely identify?
A) The priority level of a process.
B) The system resources used by a process.
C) The running instance of a program.
D) The architectural plans of a program.

Review Question 2.9
What enables the operating system to manage and coordinate processes efficiently?
A) Process Control Block (PCB)
B) Static program code
C) Blueprint for construction
D) Construction materials

Review Question 2.10
What is the primary purpose of a Process Control Block (PCB)?
A) Storing program code for execution.
B) Identifying unique construction sites.
C) Allocating system resources.
D) Holding essential attributes of a process.

Review Question 2.11
What is the purpose of a process's priority attribute?
A) To determine the number of resources allocated.
B) To identify the process uniquely.
C) To accelerate the construction process.
D) To affect scheduling and resource access.

Review Question 2.12
What role does the Process Control Block (PCB) play in managing processes?
A) It stores construction materials for sites.
B) It maintains project records for houses.
C) It provides architectural plans for construction.
D) It allows the OS to control and track processes.

Review Question 2.13
How does a process differ from a program?
A) A process is passive code on disk.
B) A program is code in execution.
C) A process is a child of a program.
D) A program spawns concurrent processes.

2.2 Process Scheduling

Process scheduling is a function of the operating system that determines which process runs at any given time. The OS maintains various scheduling queues such as ready and waiting that contain processes eligible to run. It uses algorithms like first-come-first-served, shortest job first, round robin, and priority scheduling to decide which process to execute next. Context switching allows the OS to pause one process and resume another. Preemptive scheduling involuntarily switches processes while non-preemptive scheduling runs processes to completion.

2.2.1 Scheduling Queues

In order to manage processes awaiting access to the CPU, the operating system maintains various scheduling queues. These queues hold processes in different states and enable orderly allocation of the CPU.

Ready Queue: The Gateway to Execution
The ready queue stands as the initial gateway for processes that are ready and eligible to run on the CPU. Processes residing in the ready queue have already been loaded into main memory and have all required resources available and can run immediately if CPU time is allocated to them. The operating system employs scheduling algorithms to determine the order in which processes will be selected from the ready queue and allocated CPU time. The short-term CPU scheduler is responsible for selecting a process from the ready

queue to run on the CPU. The ready queue is given the highest priority, which means that the short-term CPU scheduler will always select a process from the ready queue before selecting a process from any other queue that are used in operating systems, such as the job queue (a queue of processes that are waiting to be loaded into memory).

Waiting Queue: The Path to Resource Acquisition
The waiting queue, often referred to as the blocked or sleeping queue, accommodates processes that are temporarily unable to proceed due to their dependence on external events or resources. These resources could include I/O operations, signals, or synchronization points. Processes waiting for a resource to become available are added to the waiting queue until their requested event finishes. Processes in the waiting queue are essentially in a state of suspension, holding their execution until the necessary resource becomes available. Once the resource is acquired, the process transitions from the waiting queue to the ready queue, poised for execution.

Running State: The Process Owns the CPU at the Moment
The running state refers to the process that is currently executing on the CPU. At any given time, there can only be one running process on a single processor system. When the scheduler selects a process from the ready queue to execute, it assigns the CPU to that process, which transitions to the running state. The process retains control of the CPU and remains running until one of the following occurs:
- It initiates an I/O request or other waiting operation, causing it to transition from running to blocked, upon which it is added to the appropriate waiting queue.
- It is preempted by a higher priority process becoming ready, forcing it to go from running to ready, and adding it back to the ready queue.
- Its time slice expires, moving it from running to ready and into the ready line again via time slice expiration algorithms.
- It terminates, transitioning from running to terminated state, exiting the queues.

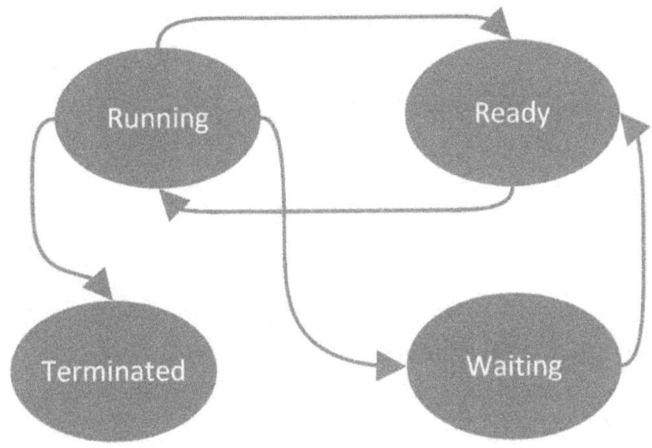

Review Question 2.14
What is the role of process scheduling in an operating system?
A) To prioritize I/O operations
B) To enable resource sharing between processes
C) To manage virtual memory
D) To determine which process runs on the CPU at a given time

Review Question 2.15
What data structure does the OS use to build processes waiting for events or resources?
A) Job queue
B) Ready queue
C) Running queue
D) Waiting queue

Review Question 2.16
Which queue has the highest priority for the CPU scheduler?
A) Job queue
B) Ready queue
C) Waiting queue
D) Owner queue

Review Question 2.17
What must a process have before it can be added to the ready queue?
A) CPU time
B) Main memory
C) I/O completion
D) Synchronization

Review Question 2.18
When does a process move from the running state to the waiting queue?
A) On termination
B) After its time slice expires
C) When it makes an I/O request
D) When it is preempted

Review Question 2.19
What occurs when a process's time slice expires?
A) It terminates
B) It waits for I/O
C) It moves to the waiting queue
D) It is preempted

Review Question 2.20
Which state can only have one process at a time on a single processor system?
A) Terminated
B) Ready
C) Waiting
D) Running

Review Question 2.21
What does the short-term scheduler control?
A) Admission to the ready queue
B) Transition from waiting to ready
C) Selection from the ready queue
D) Preemption of processes

2.2.2 Scheduling Algorithms

The operating system employs scheduling algorithms to determine which process gains access to the CPU when it becomes available. There are several common algorithms with different approaches.

First-Come, First-Served (FCFS): FCFS is the simplest scheduling algorithm. As the name suggests, it allocates the CPU to processes based on their arrival order in the ready queue. The process that enters the ready queue first is dispatched first.

For example, consider processes P1, P2, P3 arrive in the ready queue in that order. The FCFS algorithm would schedule them for CPU execution in P1, P2, P3 order. The main advantage of FCFS is its simplicity. The scheduler does not have to apply any complex logic to decide which process runs next. This makes FCFS straightforward to implement. However, a major disadvantage is that short jobs can get stuck waiting behind long ones. For instance, if P3 has a short CPU burst (the amount of time that a process uses the CPU before it is interrupted or preempted by another process) but P1 and P2 have long bursts, P3 will have to wait idly until P1 and P2 finish executing. This increases the response time and turnaround time of short processes. It works well when process CPU bursts are relatively similar in length, but performance suffers when short and long jobs are mixed unpredictably.

Shortest Job First (SJF): SJF scheduling prioritizes processes with the shortest expected processing time or CPU burst. The scheduler arranges jobs in order of shortest burst time first and allocates the CPU accordingly. For example, consider there are 3 processes in the ready queue with the following expected burst times: P1-9ms, P2-3ms, P3-7ms. SJF would schedule them in the order P2, P3, P1, since P2 has the shortest burst, followed by P3, and P1 has the longest estimated duration.

The advantage of SJF is improved response and turnaround times for short processes, since they are prioritized. However, SJF requires accurate estimations of upcoming CPU burst lengths to arrange processes effectively. Incorrect predictions can diminish its benefits. It also risks starvation of longer processes if short jobs keep arriving. SJF delivers optimized performance for short jobs by minimizing their waiting time. But it relies heavily on accurate burst time forecasts and may starve longer processes.

Round Robin (RR): RR algorithm assigns a fixed time slice or quantum to each process. It then cycles through all processes by switching between them in a circular fashion.

Using the previous example in SJF, with a 5 ms quantum, processes P1, P2, P3 would execute for at most 5ms in the order P1, P2, P3, P1, P3 and so on. If a process does not complete within the quantum, it is preempted and added back to the ready queue.

The main advantage of RR is that it equally shares the CPU among processes. Each process is guaranteed regular access to the CPU multiple times in the cycling order. This prevents starvation. However, frequently switch processes after small quanta causes significant overhead. There is extra context switching cost as the system has to suspend and resume processes at every quantum. This can diminish overall throughput.

RR provides fair scheduling via equal CPU shares but has high switching overhead. Tuning the quantum duration involves tradeoffs between fairness and performance. Short quanta increase context switches while long quanta resemble FCFS.

Priority Scheduling. In priority scheduling, each process is assigned a priority level. The scheduler then allocates CPU access based on priority, with higher priority processes getting preference.

For example, a system has three processes P1, P2, P3 with priorities 1, 2, 3 respectively, with 1 being highest priority. The scheduler would allocate the CPU to P1 first. Only when P1 is not eligible to run would P2 execute, and so on.

The advantage of priority scheduling is that it allows important processes to execute faster by prioritizing them. Critical real-time systems can minimize latency for high priority event handling. However, lower priority processes may experience indefinite starvation if high priority processes dominate CPU usage. Priorities must be judiciously assigned to prevent this. Dynamic priority adjustment based on factors like burst time can help overcome starvation.

In priority scheduling, lower priority processes can be perpetually denied CPU access by higher priority processes, leading to indefinite starvation. To prevent such starvation, priorities cannot remain static. Instead, dynamic adjustment of priorities is necessary. As processes wait longer in the ready queue, the scheduler can increment their priority level periodically.

For example, after waiting for a certain time threshold, P2's priority could be boosted from 2 to 1. Now, it will preempt P1 and free P2 from starvation. After P2 finishes, P3's priority can be upgraded to execute next.

Priorities can also be dynamically adjusted based on estimated burst times. A short process arriving after long processes can be given a priority boost to avoid waiting indefinitely. Once executed, its priority is reset.

By dynamically altering priorities based on wait times or other criteria, the scheduler can allow fair access to all processes and prevent extended starvation. Tuning priority changes requires balancing responsiveness and overload. But overall, dynamic priorities provide significant flexibility to overcome rigid static priority issues.

Selecting an appropriate scheduling algorithm requires understanding the needs of the system. There are tradeoffs between fairness, throughput, response times, overhead, and other factors when evaluating scheduling options. The best scheduling algorithm for a particular operating system will depend on the specific requirements of the system. For example, a system that needs to be responsive to user requests may use a scheduling algorithm that favors short processes, such as RR or SJF. A system that needs to maximize throughput may use a scheduling algorithm that favors long processes, such as FCFS or priority scheduling.

Review Question 2.22
What is the primary advantage of the First-Come, First-Served (FCFS) scheduling algorithm?
A) Improved response time for short processes
B) Equal CPU sharing among processes
C) Simple implementation
D) Dynamic priority adjustment

Review Question 2.23
In FCFS scheduling, what can be a major disadvantage?
A) High context switching overhead
B) Starvation of shorter processes
C) Unpredictable burst time
D) Shortest expected processing time prioritization

Review Question 2.24
Which scheduling algorithm prioritizes processes with the shortest expected processing time?
A) Round Robin (RR)
B) Priority Scheduling
C) First-Come, First-Served (FCFS)
D) Shortest Job First (SJF)

Review Question 2.25
What is the primary advantage of Shortest Job First (SJF) scheduling?
A) Improved response time for short processes
B) Equal CPU sharing among processes
C) Simple implementation
D) Guaranteed regular access to the CPU

Review Question 2.26
What does the Round Robin (RR) scheduling algorithm ensure for each process?
A) Equal CPU sharing
B) Shortest burst time
C) Highest priority access
D) First-come, first-served order

Review Question 2.27
What is a notable drawback of Round Robin (RR) scheduling?
A) High context switching overhead
B) Starvation of longer processes
C) Unpredictable burst times
D) Complex implementation

Review Question 2.28
Which scheduling algorithm allocates CPU access based on process priorities?
A) First-Come, First-Served (FCFS)
B) Shortest Job First (SJF)
C) Round Robin (RR)
D) Priority Scheduling

Review Question 2.29
What is the risk associated with Priority Scheduling if priorities remain static?
A) Starvation of longer processes
B) Starvation of lower priority processes
C) Unpredictable burst times
D) Complex implementation

Review Question 2.30
What does dynamic priority adjustment in Priority Scheduling help overcome?
A) High context switching overhead
B) Unpredictable burst times
C) Starvation of longer processes
D) Starvation of lower priority processes

Review Question 2.31
What tradeoff is associated with using dynamic priorities in Priority Scheduling?
A) Fairness and overhead
B) Short burst times and long burst times
C) Predictable burst times and unpredictable burst times
D) High context switching overhead and low overhead

Review Question 2.32
What factor should be considered when selecting an appropriate scheduling algorithm for an operating system?
A) The number of CPU cores
B) The amount of RAM
C) The clock speed of the CPU
D) The specific requirements of the system

2.2.3 Context Switching

Context switching refers to the process of saving and restoring the state of a process so that it can be resumed from where it left off. When the operating system decides to switch from executing one process to another, it performs a context switch to save the sate of the currently running process, including its program counter, registers, and other relevant data. The context switch then restores the saved state of the next process that is to be executed, allowing it to continue its execution seamlessly. Context switching lies at the heart of multitasking, where multiple processes share the CPU, and is a cornerstone of modern operating system design.

In a multitasking environment, multiple processes share the CPU's execution time. Since only one process can execute on the CPU at a given moment, the operating system must switch between processes to ensure fair allocation of CPU time to all running processes. Context switching is also critical in preemptive multitasking, where higher-priority processes can interrupt lower-priority ones, maintaining responsiveness and timely execution of critical tasks.

Rapid context switching creates the illusion of concurrent execution as the CPU seamlessly alternates between processes. However, excessive context switching introduces performance overhead. The system spends significant time saving and restoring process states rather than productive execution. Optimizing the frequency and cost of context switches is necessary. Operating system designers implement various techniques, such as utilizing hardware support and efficient data structures, to reduce context switch overhead and enhance overall system responsiveness.

When an interrupt occurs signaling a process switch, the following context switch steps occur:

1. The operating system saves the state of the currently running process. This includes values in the process control block like program counter, registers, open files etc.
2. The OS performs the actual switch to the scheduled process, upgrading the memory management unit with the new process page table.

3. The OS loads the saved state of the incoming process, restoring its program counter, memory allocations, and other resources.
4. Execution resumes for the new process from where it left off previously.

Context switching introduces challenges, such as ensuring data integrity during the transition and minimizing the impact on system performance. Careful design and optimization are required to strike a balance between efficient process switching and resource overhead.

Review Question 2.33
What is context switching in the context of operating systems?
A) The process of allocating CPU time to running processes.
B) The process of saving and restoring the state of a process.
C) The process of optimizing system performance.
D) The process of allocating memory to processes.

Review Question 2.34
What components of a process's state are typically saved during a context switch?
A) Disk storage information
B) Output devices configuration
C) Program counter, registers, and relevant data
D) Power management settings

Review Question 2.35
In a multitasking environment, why does the operating system perform context switches?
A) To allocate more memory to running processes
B) To ensure that only one process runs at a time
C) To save energy by halting inactive processes
D) To allocate CPU time to multiple running processes fairly

Review Question 2.36
Which type of multitasking involves higher-priority processes interrupting lower-priority ones?
A) Cooperative multitasking
B) Preemptive multitasking
C) Concurrent multitasking
D) Serial multitasking

Review Question 2.37
What is a potential drawback of excessive context switching?
A) Improved system responsiveness.
B) Reduced resource contention
C) Increased System throughput
D) Performance overhead

Review Question 2.38
What is one reason for optimizing the frequency and cost of context switches?

A) To reduce memory usage
B) To increase process contention
C) To enhance system responsiveness
D) To allocate more CPU time to each process

Review Question 2.39
What are the main steps involved in a context switch when an interrupt occurs?
A) Load incoming process, perform memory cleanup, update disk storage.
B) Save incoming process, load currently running process, update memory management unit.
C) Save currently running process, update page table, load incoming process.
D) Update open files, save incoming process, load currently running process.

Review Question 2.40
What is a challenge associated with context switching?
A) Maximizing context switch frequency.
B) Minimizing data integrity.
C) Reducing system responsiveness.
D) Balancing resource overhead and efficiency.

Review Question 2.41
What do operating systems utilize to determine when to perform context switches and prioritize processes effectively?
A) Random selection.
B) First-in, first-out (FIFO) queue.
C) Scheduling algorithms and heuristics
D) Interrupt-driven execution

2.2.4 Preemptive vs. Non-preemptive Scheduling

Scheduling algorithms can be categorized based on how they handle clock interrupts, which are hardware interrupts generated by a computer's real-time clock circuitry. Non-preemptive scheduling algorithms select a process to run and allow it to continue running until it either gets blocked due to I/O operations or waiting for another process, or it willingly gives up the CPU. This means that even if a process runs for an extended period, it won't be forcefully paused. Essentially, no scheduling decisions are made during clock interrupts. Once the clock interrupt processing is completed, the process that was running prior to the interrupt is resumed, unless a higher-priority process was waiting for a timeout that has now been met.

On the other hand, preemptive scheduling algorithms choose a process and permit it to run for a predefined maximum time interval. If the process is still running when the interval ends, it is suspended, and the scheduler selects another available process to run. Preemptive scheduling relies on having a clock interrupt trigger at the end of the time interval to hand control of the CPU back to the scheduler. If the system lacks a clock interrupt mechanism, non-preemptive scheduling becomes the sole option.

Preemptive is not solely pertinent to user applications; it also extends to operating system kernels, particularly monolithic ones. Nowadays, many of these kernels are designed to be preemptive. Without preemptive behavior, a poorly designed driver or a sluggish system call could monopolize the CPU resources. In a preemptive kernel, the scheduler can compel a long-running driver or system call to undergo a context switch, ensuring that other processes also get a chance to execute.

Review Question 2.42
What is the main difference between non-preemptive and preemptive scheduling algorithms?
A) Non-preemptive algorithms use clock interrupts, while preemptive algorithms do not.
B) Non-preemptive algorithms forcefully pause processes after a predefined time interval.
C) Preemptive algorithms allow processes to run indefinitely without interruption.
D) Preemptive algorithms use clock interrupts to suspend running processes.

Review Question 2.43
What happens when a process is chosen by a preemptive scheduling algorithm and its predefined time interval expires?
A) The process continues running.
B) The process is blocked
C) The process is suspended, and another process is selected to run.
D) The process is terminated.

Review Question 2.44
How do non-preemptive scheduling algorithms handle processes during clock interrupts?
A) They pause the currently running process.
B) They allow the process to continue running.
C) They terminate the currently running process.
D) They randomly select a new process to run.

Review Question 2.45
In preemptive scheduling, what triggers the suspension of a running process?
A) The process blocking for I/O.
B) The process reaching the end of its execution.
C) Clock interrupts at the end of a predefined time interval.
D) A lower-priority process becoming available.

Review Question 2.46
Why is preemptive behavior important in operating system kernels?
A) It eliminates the need for clock interrupts.
B) It ensures all processes run without interruption.
C) It prevents the need for system calls.
D) It prevents monopolization of CPU resources by long-running processes.

Review Question 2.47
When might non-preemptive scheduling become the sole option in a system?
A) When clock interrupts are unavailable.
B) When processes are well-behaved and never block.
C) When the system lacks hardware support for scheduling.
D) When all processes have the same priority.

2.3 Inter-process Communication and Process Synchronization

Inter-process communication (IPC) refers to mechanisms that allow processes to exchange data and synchronize actions. IPC mechanisms facilitate the exchange of data, synchronization of activities, and resource sharing among processes, promoting seamless coordination and interaction within a computing environment.

2.3.1 Shared Memory

Shared memory allows multiple processes to access the same region of memory, often referred to as a shared memory segment. This shared segment is created and managed by the operating system, serving as a bridge between the processes. Unlike other IPC methods that involve data copying, shared memory offers a direct, efficient means for processes to share information. By sharing a common memory area, processes can read and write data to the same memory location, allowing for real-time communication and interaction.

One of the primary advantages of shared memory is its speed and efficiency. Since processes can access the shared data directly without the need for copying, the data exchange process is swift and minimizes overhead. Additionally, shared memory is well-suited for scenarios where large volumes of data need to be exchanged rapidly between processes, as it avoids the latency associated with copying data between buffers.

Operating systems implement shared memory through a combination of hardware support and software management. The operating system sets up the shared memory segment, assigns it an identifier, and maintains control over access rights to ensure proper synchronization and protection. Processes that wish to utilize shared memory attach to the segment by associating their memory space with the shared segment, enabling them to read and write data to the same memory locations.

While shared memory provides a powerful means of data exchange, it introduces challenges related to synchronization and data consistency. Processes must coordinate their access to shared memory to prevent conflicts and ensure that data remains coherent. Techniques such as semaphores, locks, and mutual exclusion mechanisms are commonly used to safeguard against issues like race conditions and data corruption.

Shared memory finds applications in a wide range of scenarios. It is often employed in situations where multiple processes need to collaborate closely, such as in multimedia applications (for video and audio synchronization), parallel processing environments (for data sharing among concurrent tasks), and database system (for efficient data sharing between database clients and the server).

Review Question 2.48
What is one of the primary advantages of using shared memory for IPC?
A) Elimination of the need for synchronization.
B) Low-speed data exchange process.
C) Efficient and direct access to shared data.
D) Simplified management of access rights.

Review Question 2.49
What role does the operating system play in shared memory communication?
A) It manages individual process memory spaces.
B) It prevents processes from accessing shared memory.
C) It creates, controls, and maintains the shared memory segment.
D) It copies data between processes using shared memory.

Review Question 2.50
In which scenarios is shared memory particularly beneficial?
A) When processes need to work independently.
B) When minimal data exchange is required.
C) When latency in data copying is acceptable.
D) When large volumes of data need to be exchanged rapidly.

Review Question 2.51
How do processes coordinate access to shared memory in order to prevent conflicts?
A) By using hardware-based access control.
B) By minimizing data exchange.
C) By copying data to local buffers.
D) By employing synchronization techniques.

Review Question 2.52
In which application scenarios is shared memory commonly used?
A) Standalone text processing applications.
B) Low-performance data exchange scenarios.
C) Parallel processing environments.
D) Isolated single-task applications.

2.3.2 Message Passing

In IPC, message passing facilitates communication and synchronization between processes within an operating system environment. Unlike shared memory, which involves processes sharing a common memory region, message passing relies on structured messages to exchange data and coordinate activities.

Message passing involves the exchange of data and control information between processes through well-defined communication channels. Processes interact by sending and receiving messages, allowing them to share information, request actions, and synchronize their activities. This communication method is especially useful in scenarios where processes are distributed across different machines or need to operate independently with minimal shared memory.

Message passing can occur in various modes, each catering to different communication needs.

Synchronous Message Passing. In this mode, the sender blocks until the receiver acknowledges receipt of the message. This ensures that the communication is successful and that both processes are synchronized.
Asynchronous Message Passing. Here, the sender continues execution after sending the message without waiting for the receiver's acknowledgment. Asynchronous message passing enhances concurrency by allowing processes to operate independently.

The operating system provides communication mechanisms and channels through which processes can exchange messages. These mechanisms can be implemented using various techniques, such as sockets, pipes, and message queues. Sockets are particularly useful for communication between processes on different machines across a network, while pipes and message queues are suitable for local communication.

One challenge in message passing is maintaining data consistency and proper buffering. The operating system must manage message queues, ensuring that messages are delivered in the intended order and that data integrity is maintained.

Message passing finds applications in diverse scenarios. It is often used in distributed systems, where processes on different machines need to communicate, as well as in parallel processing environments, where multiple tasks collaborate on a shared goal. Message passing is also essential for implementing communication between different components of a larger application, such as microservices in a service-oriented architecture.

Review Question 2.53

How does message passing differ from shared memory in inter-process communication (IPC)?
A) Message passing uses well-defined communication channels, while shared memory involves direct memory access.
B) Message passing requires processes to share a common memory region, while shared memory uses structured messages.
C) Message passing is only suitable for local communication, while shared memory is used for distributed systems.
D) Message passing uses asynchronous communication exclusively, while shared memory uses synchronous communication.

Review Question 2.54

In IPC using message passing, what role do messages play?
A) Messages enable direct memory access.
B) Messages facilitate data copying between processes.
C) Messages allow processes to share memory segments.
D) Messages exchange data and control information between processes.

Review Question 2.55

Which communication mode in message passing involves the sender blocking until the receiver acknowledges receipt of the message?
A) Asynchronous Message Passing.
B) Synchronous Message Passing.
C) Parallel Message Passing.
D) Direct Message Passing.

Review Question 2.56

Which communication mechanism is particularly useful for communication between processes on different machines across a network?
A) Pipes.
B) Message queues.
C) Sockets.
D) Shared memory.

Review Question 2.57

What challenge is associated with message passing in maintaining data consistency?
A) Ensuring proper buffering in shared memory
B) Managing direct memory access between processes.
C) Delivering messages in intended order and maintaining data integrity.
D) Enforcing synchronization using synchronous communication.

2.3.3 Race Conditions

A race condition arises when multiple processes or threads access shared resources or variables simultaneously. Leading to unpredictable behavior. Such conditions can manifest when processes execute in parallel and attempt to modify a shared resource without proper synchronization. In these situations, the final outcome becomes dependent on the exact timing of individual process executions, introducing an element of uncertainty.

Consider two processes concurrently updating the same shared variable. Without proper synchronization mechanisms, the final value of the shared variable becomes unpredictable. The interleaving of read and write operations from these processes can lead to different outcomes depending on the timing, resulting in inconsistent or erroneous results.

Race conditions pose several challenges and potential consequences:

Data corruption: Unintended modification of shared resources can lead to data corruption or incorrect computation results.
Deadlocks: Poor synchronization can result in deadlocks, where processes are stuck waiting for resources indefinitely.
Data Integrity: Inconsistent data states can compromise data integrity and lead to erroneous program behavior.
Performance Issues: Excessive locking to prevent race conditions can lead to performance bottlenecks, reducing the benefits of parallel execution.

Mitigating race conditions requires careful synchronization of processes to ensure that shared resources are accessed in a controlled manner. Various synchronization mechanisms are employed, such as mutexes, semaphores, critical regions, and locks. These topics will be discussed later.

Review Question 2.58
What is a race condition in the context of inter-process communication (IPC)?
A) A condition where multiple processes execute sequentially.
B) A situation where multiple processes access shared resources simultaneously without proper synchronization.
C) A condition where processes deadlock due to poor synchronization.
D) A situation where processes operate independently without sharing resources.

Review Question 2.59
When do race conditions typically manifest in IPC?
A) When processes operate independently with no resource sharing.
B) When processes execute sequentially without any interaction.
C) When processes attempt to modify shared resources simultaneously.
D) When processes perform synchronization operations.

Review Question 2.60
What is a potential consequence of race conditions in IPC?
A) Predictable behavior of processes.
B) Improved data integrity.

C) Winners take all.
D) Unintended data corruption or incorrect computation results.

Review Question 2.61
What potential issue can arise from excessive locking to prevent race conditions?
A) Improved data integrity.
B) Predictable program behavior.
C) Deadlocks.
D) Reduced performance due to bottlenecks.

Review Question 2.62
How can race conditions in IPC be mitigated?
A) By executing processes sequentially.
B) By avoiding shared resources altogether.
C) By using proper synchronization mechanisms.
D) By minimizing the number of processes.

2.3.4 Critical Regions

A critical region refers to a segment of code or a region within a process where shared resources are accessed and modified. When multiple processes concurrently access shared resources, the potential for data corruption and unpredictable behavior arises. Critical regions aim to mitigate these issues by allowing only one process at a time to access the shared resources, ensuring data consistency and coherent execution.

Critical regions are introduced to eliminate race conditions by serializing the access to shared resources. By allowing only one process to enter the critical region at a time, conflicts and inconsistencies are avoided. The key objective of implementing critical regions is to achieve mutual exclusion, meaning that only one process is allowed to execute within the critical region while others are temporarily blocked. This is typically accomplished through synchronization mechanisms such as semaphores, locks, and monitors, which enforce a disciplined access protocol to shared resources.

While critical regions solve many synchronization challenges, they also pose potential issues:

Deadlocks: Inappropriate handling of locks and synchronization mechanisms can lead to deadlocks, where processes are indefinitely blocked due to circular waiting.
Starvation: Poorly designed critical region management may result in some processes being perpetually blocked, leading to resource starvation.

Review Question 2.63
What is the main purpose of critical regions in inter-process communication (IPC)?

A) To introduce race conditions.
B) To maximize data corruption.
C) To enable multiple processes to access shared resources simultaneously.
D) To ensure orderly and synchronized access to shared resources.

Review Question 2.64
How does a critical region help prevent race conditions?
A) It allows all processes to access shared resources simultaneously.
B) It eliminates the need for synchronization mechanisms.
C) It serializes the access to shared resources, allowing only one process at a time.
D) It completely isolates processes from each other.

Review Question 2.65
What is the primary objective of implementing critical regions in IPC?
A) To achieve resource starvation.
B) To encourage circular waiting.
C) To enable all processes to execute within the region.
D) To achieve mutual exclusion and prevent concurrent access.

Review Question 2.66
What potential issues can arise directly from poorly designed critical region management?
A) Data corruption.
B) Starvation and deadlocks.
C) Enhanced synchronization.
D) Parallel execution of processes.

Review Question 2.67
How do synchronization mechanisms like semaphores, locks, and monitors contribute to critical region implementation?
A) They allow all processes to enter the critical region simultaneously.
B) They eliminate the need for critical regions.
C) They enforce disciplined access to shared resources, ensuring mutual exclusion.
D) They encourage circular waiting among processes.

Review Question 2.68
What is the purpose of achieving mutual exclusion within critical regions?
A) To allow all processes to execute concurrently.
B) To maximize resource sharing.
C) To prevent all processes from accessing shared resources.
D) To prevent conflicts and ensure consistent execution by allowing only one process to access shared resources at a time.

2.3.5 Semaphores

A semaphore is a variable that serves as a signaling mechanism to control the access and synchronization of processes to shared resources. First introduced by Edsger W. Dijkstra in the 1960s, semaphores provide a means for processes to communicate and coordinate their activities through signaling and waiting operations. Several types of semaphores are commonly used, we will focus on binary semaphore for the purpose of easy understanding. The binary semaphore is also known as a mutex (short for mutual exclusion), a binary semaphore can have only two values: 0 and 1. It is often used to manage access to a critical region or protect shared resources from simultaneous access.

Semaphores offer two fundamental operations on the semaphore variable s:

1. Wait (P) Operation: When a process wishes to access a shared resource, it performs a "wait" operation on the semaphore. If the semaphore value is greater than zero, the process decrements the value and proceeds. If the value is zero, indicating that the resource is currently in use, the process is blocked until the semaphore becomes available. P(s): if s > 0 then s: s = s − 1.
2. Signal (V) Operation: Once a process has finished using a shared resource, it performs a "signal" operation on the semaphore. This operation increments the semaphore value, indicating that the resource is now available. If any processes were waiting for the semaphore, one of them is unblocked and granted access. V(s): s: = s + 1.

Let's walk through an example to understand how semaphores work in managing critical regions. Imagine there are four processes, each requesting access to a critical region. The initial value of semaphore 's' is set to 1.

1. Process P1 arrives:
- It performs a WAIT operation, decrementing the semaphore 's' to 0.
- P1 accesses the critical region.
- P1 completes its access and performs a SIGNAL operation, incrementing 's' to 1.
2. Process P2 arrives:
- It performs a WAIT operation and decrements 's' to 0.
3. Process P3 arrives (while P2 is still in progress):
- P3 performs a WAIT operation, but 's' is already 0, so P3 is blocked.
4. Process P4 arrives (while P2 is still in progress):
- P4 performs a WAIT operation, but 's' is still 0, so P4 is also blocked.
5. P2 completes its access:
- P2 performs a SIGNAL operation, incrementing 's' to 1.
6. Awakening a blocked process (depending on policy, let's assume FCFS):
- As P3 arrived before P4, P3 is unblocked and performs a WAIT operation, setting 's' to 0.
- P3 accesses the critical region, completes its task, and performs a SIGNAL operation to set 's' back to 1.
7. P4 is unblocked:
- P4 performs a WAIT operation and sets 's' to 0.
- P4 accesses the critical region, completes its task, and performs a SIGNAL operation, restoring 's' to 1.

In this example, we've demonstrated how processes interact with a semaphore 's' to access a critical region. The semaphore ensures that only one process can access the critical region at a time, while the WAIT and SIGNAL operations control the availability of the resource. Different policies for awakening blocked processes, such as First-Come-First-Served (FCFS), can determine the order in which blocked processes are unblocked when the resource becomes available again.

Solving Producer-Consumer Problem Using Semaphores:

As illustrative example of semaphore usage is the classic producer-consumer problem. In this scenario, multiple producer processes create items, and multiple consumer processes consume these items. Semaphores can be employed to ensure that the producers and consumers do not interfere with each other, preventing issues such as overproduction or underconsumption.

The solution to the producer-consumer problem using semaphore step by step:

1. Initialize Semaphores:
Create two semaphores: empty_slots and filled_slots. The empty_slots keeps track of the available empty slots (buffer space) for producers to place their items. The filled_slots keeps track of the number of filled slots (items) available for consumers to consume.
2. Producer Process:
The producer process generates items and wants to place them in the buffer. The producer first acquires the empty_slots semaphore to check if there is space available in the buffer. If the buffer is not full, the producer places the item in the buffer and releases the filled_slots semaphore to indicate that there is an item available for consumption.
3. Consumer Process:
The consumer process wants to consume items from the buffer. The consumer first acquires the filled_slots semaphore to check if there are items available for consumption. If there are items in the buffer, the consumer consumes an item, releases the empty_slots semaphore to free up a slot, and repeats the process.

Review Question 2.69
What does a semaphore manage in an operating system?
A) CPU time allocation.
B) Access to shared resources.
C) Process priority.
D) Memory allocation.

Review Question 2.70
What are the two fundamental operations performed on a semaphore S?
A) Lock(S) and Release(S).
B) Wait(S) and Signal(S).
C) Acquire(S) and Free(S).
D) Get(S) and Set(S).

Review Question 2.71
What happens when a process performs a Wait operation on a binary semaphore that is 0?
A) The process is terminated.
B) The semaphore value runs negative.

C) The process proceeds with access.
D) The process is blocked until semaphore is non-zero.

2.3.6 Mutexes

While semaphores provide a flexible mechanism for controlling access to a shared resource using a counting mechanism, mutexes offer a more specialized approach. In situations where the semaphore's counting capability isn't necessary, a simpler form called a "mutex" can be utilized. Mutexes server the specific purpose of managing mutual exclusion to shared resources or sections of code.

A mutex is essentially a shared variable with two states: unlocked or locked. Typically, only a single bit is required to represent this, although in practice, an integer is often used, with 0 representing unlocked and any other value indicating locked. Mutexes involve two key procedures. When a thread or process requires access to a critical region, it involves mutex_lock. If the mutex is currently unlocked, grating access to the critical region, the call is successful and the thread enters the critical region.

However, if the mutex is already locked, the invoking thread becomes blocked until the thread within the critical region finishes its task and subsequently calls mutex_unlock. In scenarios where multiple threads are waiting on the mutex, one of them is randomly chosen and granted access to the lock. This mechanism ensures exclusive access to critical sections and helps prevent race conditions in concurrent environments.

Review Question 2.72
How does a mutex differ from a semaphore?
A) A mutex is a simple lock while a semaphore uses counter.
B) A mutex allows concurrent access while a semaphore enforces mutual exclusion.
C) A mutex is system-level while a semaphore is user-level.
D) A mutex blocks threads while a semaphore terminates threads.

Review Question 2.73
What are the two states of a mutex?
A) Locked and unlocked.
B) Available and unavailable.
C) 0 and 1.
D) Waiting and signaled.

Review Question 2.74
What happens if mutex_lock is called while mutex is already locked?
A) The thread waits for mutex to unlock.
B) An exception is thrown.

C) The thread terminates.
D) The mutex value is incremented.

2.3.7 Monitors

While semaphores and mutexes are valuable tools for managing concurrent access to shared resources in inter-process communication (IPC), monitors offer additional benefits and higher-level abstractions that can simplify synchronization in certain scenarios. Monitor combine data and procedures into a single construct, ensuring that only one thread can access the monitor at a time, thus avoiding race conditions.

A monitor is a specialized module or package that encompasses a set of procedures, variables, and data structures. Within a monitor, processes can invoke its procedures as needed. However, the monitor's internal data structures cannot be directly accessed by procedures declared outside the monitor's scope. This encapsulation ensures controlled access to the monitor's components while allowing processes to interact with its functionality.

Here are a few reasons why monitors are used alongside semaphores and mutexes:

Simplicity and Abstraction: Monitors provide a higher-level abstraction than semaphores and mutexes. They encapsulate both the data and the synchronization operations within a single construct. This can lead to cleaner and more modular code, reducing the chances of errors due to incorrect usage of synchronization primitives.
Encapsulation: Monitors encapsulate the critical regions and data structures they protect. This encapsulation helps prevent accidental access to shared resource without proper synchronization, as all access is routed through the monitor's methods.
Deadlock Prevention: Monitors can offer deadlock prevention mechanisms. When a thread enters a monitor, it may specify which other monitors it intends to access. The monitor can then prevent a thread from entering if doing so would potentially lead to a circular waiting condition.

If you are familiar with Java programming language, the synchronized keyword is used to define synchronized methods, effectively creating monitors. For instance, a bank account class can use synchronized methods to ensure that only one thread accesses the account balance at a time.

Review Question 2.75
What benefit does a monitor offer over semaphores and mutexes in IPC?
A) Monitors prevent all processes from accessing shared resources.
B) Monitors encapsulate data and synchronization operations in a single construct.
C) Monitors eliminate the need for critical regions.

D) Monitors introduce race conditions among processes.

Review Question 2.76
How does a monitor prevent race conditions among processes?
A) By allowing all processes to access the monitor simultaneously.
B) By encapsulating critical regions and data structures, allowing only one thread to access the monitor at a time.
C) By using semaphores and mutexes internally.
D) By allowing processes to directly access shared data.

Review Question 2.77
What is a key feature of monitors that contributes to cleaner and more modular code in IPC?
A) Encapsulation of shared resources.
B) Use of semaphores and mutexes.
C) Direct access to internal data structures.
D) Integration with low-level synchronization primitives.

Review Question 2.78
How does a monitor help prevent accidental access to shared resources without proper synchronization?
A) By allowing all processes to access the monitor simultaneously.
B) By routing all access to shared resources through the monitor's methods.
C) By using semaphores and mutexes internally.
D) By requiring processes to use direct access to shared data.

Review Question 2.79
In what way can a monitor contribute to deadlock prevention?
A) By allowing all threads to enter a monitor simultaneously.
B) By avoiding the use of synchronization primitives.
C) By encapsulating only data structures, not procedures.
D) By specifying which other monitors a thread intends to access and preventing circular waiting conditions.

Review Question 2.80
What programming construct in Java can be used to create monitors?
A) Threads.
B) Synchronized methods.
C) Critical regions.
D) Semaphores.

2.3.8 Deadlock

Deadlock refers to a state where multiple processes or threads are unable to proceed because each is waiting for a resource held by another, resulting in a standstill. Understanding the causes, conditions, prevention strategies, and handling techniques of deadlock is crucial for developing reliable and efficient concurrent systems.

Deadlock arises from four primary conditions, often referred to as the "Four Coffin Conditions".

1. *Mutual Exclusion*: Resources, such as mutexes, can only be accessed by one process or thread at a time, leading to resource contention.
2. *Hold and Wait*: Processes hold resources while waiting for additional ones, preventing other processes from utilizing them.
3. *No preemption*: Resources cannot be forcibly taken away from a process; they can only be released voluntarily.
4. *Circular Wait*: A circular chain of processes exists, where each process holds a resource needed by the next process in the chain.

For a deadlock to occur, all four conditions must be met simultaneously. This scenario is infrequent but not impossible, making deadlock a constant concern in concurrent programming.

Preventing deadlock involves tackling one or more of the four Coffin Conditions:

1. *Mutual Exclusion Relaxation*: Some resources, like read-only files, may not require exclusive access and can be shared by multiple processes.
2. *Hold and Wait Avoidance*: Processes can be required to request all necessary resources at once before execution begins.
3. *Preemption*: Resources can be forcefully taken away from processes, albeit cautiously to avoid resource corruption.
4. *Circular Wait Avoidance*: Resources can be assigned unique numerical values, and processes can be required to request resources in increasing order.

When prevention is not feasible, handling deadlock involves four strategies:

1. *Process Termination*: Termination one or more processes to break the deadlock. This is often a last resort and must be performed carefully to avoid data corruption.
2. *Resource Preemption*: Temporarily take resources away from one process and allocate them to another, with proper mechanisms for resource state saving and restoration.
3. *Process Rollback*: Roll back the state of one or more processes to a safe state, allowing them to re-execute without conflicting with other processes.
4. *Wait Die and Wound-Wait Schemes*: These schemes determine which processes can wait and which must be aborted or delayed, based on their age and priority.

Deadlock prevention strategies aim to eliminate the conditions that could lead to deadlocks in the first place. However, prevention mechanisms can be complex, may impose constraints on resource allocation, and might not always be feasible to implement in all scenarios. Additionally, some prevention techniques can result in resource underutilization or decreased system performance. Due to these reasons, prevention alone might not always be sufficient to completely eliminate the possibility of deadlocks. This is where deadlock detection becomes significant, even when prevention measures are in place. Detecting deadlock involves regularly inspecting the allocation of resources and the state of processes.

One common method for deadlock detection is to use a resource allocation graph (RAG). Let's consider a simple example to illustrate a RAG and how it can be used for deadlock detection. Imagine a system with three processes (P1, P2, P3) and three types of resources (R1, R2, R3). Each process may request and hold multiple instances of these resources.

In a RAG, there are two types of directed edges. The first type represents resource allocation, where the edge is directed from a process to a resource, indicating that the process is requesting the resource. The second type represents resource release, where the edge is directed from a resource to a process, signifying that the resource is currently held by the process.

Here's the initial state of the RAG, with resource allocation represented by edges labeled with the corresponding resource type (R1 is allocated to P1; R2 is allocated to P2; R3 is allocated to P3):

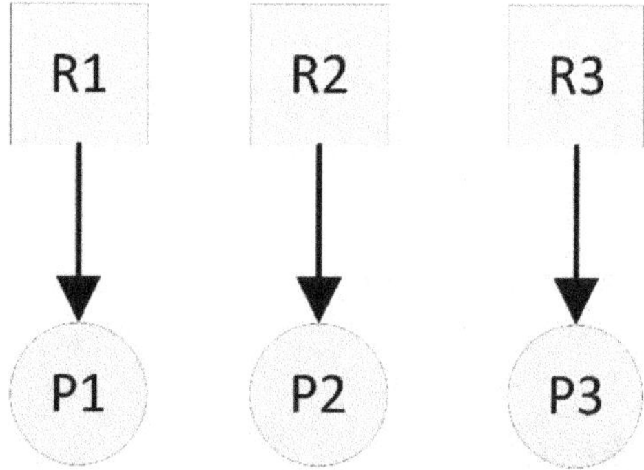

Now, let's say that Process P1 also requests another instance of resource R2, and Process P3 requests resource R1. This would lead to the following state:

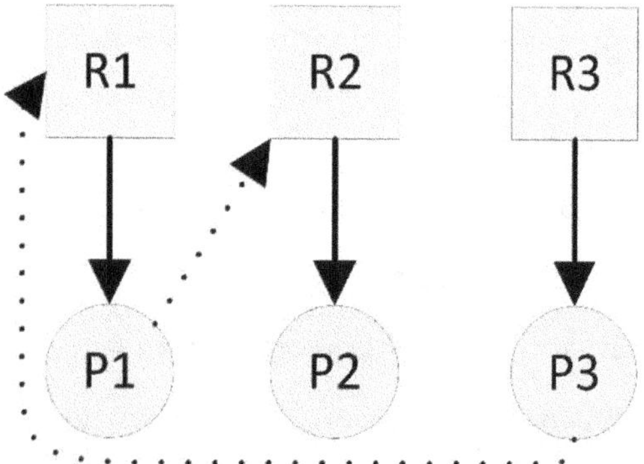

At this point, there is no deadlock yet. When P2 is done with R2, P1 can hold R2 and complete the P1. Finally, P3 can hold R1 and complete the process.

However, if before P2 is done, it also requires R3 for the process, a deadlock is formed.

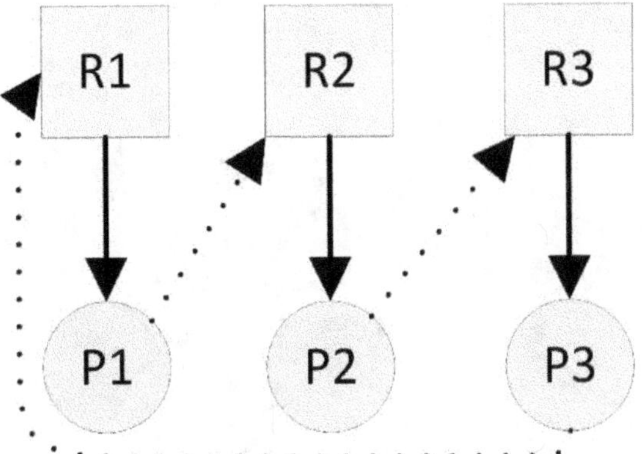

The resolution strategies could involve terminating one or more processes in the cycle or preempting resources from processes. For example, if process P3 is terminated, the state of the RAG might look like this:

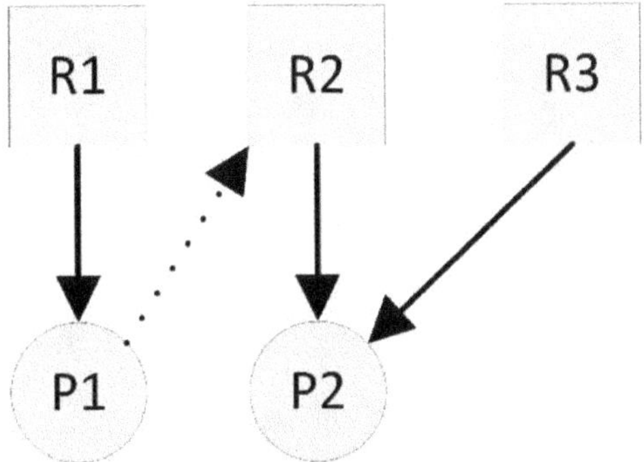

The system has now resolved the deadlock by terminating Process P3. The resources held by Process P3 are released, and the other processes can continue without being deadlocked.

Review Question 2.81
What are the four necessary conditions for deadlock to occur?
A) Starvation, Preemption, Circular wait, Concurrency.
B) Mutual exclusion, Hold and wait, No preemption, Circular wait.
C) Race conditions, Resource contention, Process blocking, Live lock.
D) Priority inversion, Resource exhaustion, Thread starvation, Deadly embrace.

Review Question 2.82
Which deadlock prevention strategy involves processes requesting all needed resources at once?
A) Mutual exclusion.
B) Hold and wait avoidance.
C) Preemption.

D) Circular wait avoidance.

Review Question 2.83
What method can help prevent circular wait in resource allocation?
A) Assigning priorities to resources.
B) Using a resource allocation graph.
C) Requesting resources randomly.
D) Assigning unique numbers to resources.

Review Question 2.84
Which is NOT a deadlock handling strategy?
A) Process termination.
B) Resource augmentation.
C) Process rollback.
D) Resource preemption.

Review Question 2.85
In a resource allocation graph, what do the nodes represent?
A) Processes and resources.
B) Threads and semaphores.
C) Resources only.
D) Processes only.

Review Question 2.86
What do the directed edges from a process to a resource in a resource allocation graph denote?
A) Resource requests.
B) Process termination.
C) Resource release.
D) Thread blocking.

Review Question 2.87
When does a cycle in a resource allocation graph indicate deadlock?
A) When it involves 3 or more nodes.
B) When it involves 2 or more processes.
C) When it involves a single resource.
D) When it involves interdependent resource requests.

Review Question 2.88
What is process termination in deadlock resolution?
A) Suspending a process temporarily.
B) Rolling back a process to a saved state.
C) Forcibly releasing resources held by a process.
D) Aborting or killing a process.

Review Question 2.89
What strategy assigns priority to processes and selectively aborts lower priority ones?
A) Resource preemption.
B) Process rollback.
C) Wait-die scheme.

D) Circular wait prevention.

Review Question 2.90
What complex issue may arise when using process termination for deadlock resolution?
A) Increased overhead.
B) Live lock.
C) Priority inversion.
D) Data corruption.

2.4 Threads

The concept of threads has revolutionized the way software harnesses the power of multicore processors. Threads are lightweight units of execution within a process, enabling concurrent operations and efficient resource utilization. Distinguished from processes threads share the same memory space, allowing them to communicate and cooperate seamlessly.

2.4.1 Distinguishing Processes and Threads

A process is an independent unit of execution with its own memory space, resources, and program counter. Processes are heavyweight entities that encapsulate the complete execution environment, including code, data, and system resources. They operate in isolation from other processes, ensuring a high degree of protection and stability. For instance, web browsers, word processors, and media players are classic examples of processes. Each instance runs as a separate process, safeguarding against one crashing and affecting others.

Threads, on the other hand, are lightweight units of execution within a process. Threads share the same memory space as their parent process, making communication and data sharing more efficient. Threads are suitable for scenarios where multiple tasks within a program need to be executed concurrently. For instance, a word processing might use multiple threads to simultaneously handle text formatting, spell checking, and user interface responsiveness. Threads can communicate and collaborate more easily, as they can directly access shared memory.

To illustrate the difference, consider a web server. A web server software running as a process can handle incoming client requests individually. However, each request could be handled by a separate thread within the server process. This allows the server to process multiple client requests concurrently, improving responsiveness.

Another example is a video editing application. The application itself runs as a process, but within it, different threads can handle tasks like video playback, rendering effects, and user interaction. This division of labor among threads enhances user experience and utilizes available CPU cores effectively.

Review Question 2.91
What is a key characteristic that distinguishes threads from processes?
A) Threads have their own memory space.
B) Threads are heavyweight entities.
C) Threads share memory with their parent process.
D) Threads cannot execute concurrently.

Review Question 2.92
In which scenario are threads more suitable compared to processes?
A) When independent execution is required.
B) When isolation and stability are essential.
C) When multiple tasks need concurrent execution.
D) When separate memory spaces are necessary.

Review Question 2.93
Which of the following accurately describes a process?
A) Processes share memory space with their parent process.
B) Processes are lightweight units of execution.
C) Processes encapsulate code, data, and resources.
D) Processes directly access shared memory.

2.4.2 Implementing Threads in User Space

User space threads, also known as lightweight threads or green threads, are managed entirely by user-level libraries or runtime environments. Unlike kernel-level threads managed by the operating system, user space threads enable application-level control over thread creation, scheduling, and management.

User space threads offer several advantages, including:

1. Fast Context Switching: Since thread management occurs in user space, context switching between threads is often faster compared to kernel-level threads.
2. Custom Scheduling: Developers can implement application-specific thread scheduling algorithms tailored to their needs.
3. Portability: User space thread libraries are typically platform-independent, enhancing application portability.

User space threads are managed by thread libraries that handle thread creation, scheduling, and synchronization. These libraries provide APIs for developers to create and manage threads seamlessly. For example, in C#, the Thread class provides methods to create and control threads, set their priority, manage thread-local storage, and handle synchronization. You can create threads by instantiating the Thread class and passing a delegate that specifies the method the thread will execute.

While user space threads offer benefits, they come with certain limitations. For instance, when a user space thread initiates a blocking system call, it can lead to the blocking of all threads within the process, causing a decrease in responsiveness. Moreover, the level of parallelism achievable with user space threads is constrained by the availability of kernel-level threads, potentially affecting the system's overall parallel processing capabilities.

Review Question 2.94
What manages user space threads entirely?
A) The operating system kernel.
B) The C standard library.
C) User-level libraries/runtimes.
D) The threading API.

Review Question 2.95
Which is an advantage of user space thread context switching?
A) Better portability.
B) Lower memory overhead.
C) Faster switching speed.
D) Improved scalability.

Review Question 2.96
What makes user space threads potable across operating systems?
A) Standard POSIX libraries.
B) Underlying kernel independence.
C) Language-level thread support.
D) Hardware abstraction layer.

Review Question 2.97
How does blocking a user space thread decrease responsiveness?
A) By increasing context switching time.
B) By blocking the entire process.
C) By exhausting kernel threads.
D) By causing race conditions.

2.4.3 Implementing Threads in Kernel

Kernel-level threads are managed by the operating system itself. Each kernel-level thread corresponds to an individual execution context and is scheduled independently by the operating system's thread scheduler.

Enabling threads within the kernel brings forth numerous benefits. Notably, kernel-level threads capitalize on multi-core processors, facilitating genuine parallel execution that optimizes CPU utilization. Unlike user space threads, individual threads in the kernel can encounter blocking calls without impeding the advancement of other threads, thus maintaining smooth progress. Additionally, the scalability of kernel-level threads extends effectively to multiple processors, delivering heightened performance advantages in multiprocessor systems.

Kernel-level threads are under the direct management of the operating system, offering developers the ability to harness their potential through system calls or threading APIs provided by the operating system itself. For instance, in the Windows operating system, developers can leverage the Windows API functions to not only initiate but also adeptly manage kernel-level threads. One of the striking advantages of these threads lies in their ability to leverage true parallel execution on multi-core systems, enabling efficient utilization of multiple processors. This means that tasks split across kernel-level threads can be simultaneously processed on different cores, resulting in optimized performance and responsiveness.

Kernel-level threads offer advantages, but they also come with considerations. Creating and managing these threads can incur more resource overhead compared to user space threads. Additionally, kernel-level threads require coordination with the operating system's thread scheduler, which can introduce complexity into thread management.

Review Question 2.98
Who is responsible for managing kernel-level threads?
A) The C standard library.
B) User-level libraries.
C) The operating system kernel.
D) Thread pooling APIs.

Review Question 2.99
How do kernel-level threads help utilize multi-core systems?
A) By enabling true parallelism.
B) By increasing thread portability.

C) By reducing context switching time.
D) By improving load balancing.

Review Question 2.100
How do kernel threads overcome limitations of blocking calls in user space threading?
A) By avoiding system calls.
B) By blocking only the individual thread.
C) By using non-blocking APIs.
D) By spinning instead of blocking.

Review Question 2.101
What is a key advantage of kernel threads over user threads?
A) Finer grained concurrency.
B) Lower resource overhead.
C) Faster context switching.
D) More customizable APIs.

Review Question 2.102
What is a potential downside of kernel-level threads?
A) Increased data corruption.
B) Lack of portability.
C) Higher overhead.
D) Worse cache performance.

2.5 Chapter Summary

This chapter explains process management. A process, as the fundamental entity under the operating systems purview, embodies an executing program with its associated code, data, and system resources. We navigated through a comprehensive exploration of various prominent scheduling algorithms, unraveling the mechanisms by which the CPU is allocated to processes awaiting execution. Substantive portions of the chapter were dedicated to shedding light on inter-process communication and process synchronization. These concepts facilitate the seamless exchange of data, synchronization of activities, and resource sharing among processes, fostering harmonious coordination and interaction in the computing environment. To cap off this chapter, we demystified threads – those nimble units of execution residing within a process, adding a layer of sophistication to the execution landscape.

2.6 Exercises

Exercise 2.1
Turnaround Time: A process arrives at time 0 and requires 5 bursts, each of 3 milliseconds, with an I/O operation of 2 milliseconds after each burst. The process completes its execution after the fifth burst. If the process is not interrupted until it finishes, calculate the turnaround time.

Exercise 2.2
Average Waiting Time: Consider three processes (P1, P2, P3) with arrival times (0, 2, 4) and burst times (5, 3, 1). If the processes are executed in the order of their arrival, calculate the average waiting time.

Exercise 2.3
Consider a system with three processes (P1, P2, P3) with arrival times (0, 2, 4) and burst times (6, 8, 5). If the processes are executed in the order of their arrival, 1) calculate the response time for each process. 2) Assuming the three processes (P1, P2, P3) with priorities (3, 1, 2). If the processes are executed according to their priorities (with 1 being the highest priority), calculate the waiting time for each process. 3) Consider three processes (P1, P2, P3) with arrival times (0, 1, 2) and burst times (20, 25, 30). If the time quantum for round robin scheduling is 10 milliseconds, calculate the turnaround time for each process.

Exercise 2.4
Consider four processes (P1, P2, P3, P4) with arrival times (0, 2, 4, 6) and burst times (8, 4, 6, 5). Calculate the average waiting time and average turnaround time for these processes using the FCFS scheduling algorithm.

Exercise 2.5
Given three processes (P1, P2, P3) with burst times (6, 8, 5). Calculate the average waiting time and average turnaround time for these processes using the SJF scheduling algorithm.
Consider three processes (P1, P2, P3) with arrival times (0, 1, 2) and burst times (20, 25, 30). If the time quantum for round robin scheduling is 10 milliseconds, calculate the average waiting time and average turnaround time for these processes.

Exercise 2.6
Given four processes (P1, P2, P3, P4) with priorities (1, 2, 3, 4) (1 being the highest priority) and burst times (10, 5, 8, 15). Calculate the average waiting time and average turnaround time for these processes using the priority scheduling algorithm.

Exercise 2.7
Scheduling Algorithm Comparison: Consider three processes (P1, P2, P3) with arrival times (0, 2, 4) and burst times (10, 5, 8). Calculate the average waiting time and average turnaround time for these processes using FCFS, SJF, Round Robin (with a quantum of 5ms), and Priority (priorities are 1, 2, 3 respectively with 1 being the highest priority) scheduling algorithms. Compare the results and discuss the advantages and disadvantages of each algorithm.

2.7 Solutions to Review Questions

2.1 D; 2.2 C; 2.3 D; 2.4 C; 2.5 D; 2.6 B; 2.7 D; 2.8 C; 2.9 A; 2.10 D; 2.11 D; 2.12 D; 2.13 D; 2.14 D; 2.15 D; 2.16 B; 2.17 B; 2.18 C; 2.19 D; 2.20 D; 2.21 C; 2.22 C; 2.23 B; 2.24 D; 2.25A; 2.26 A; 2.27 A; 2.28 D; 2.29 B; 2.30 D; 2.31 A; 2.32 D; 2.33 B; 2.34 C; 2.35 D; 2.36 B; 2.37 D; 2.38 C; 2.39 C; 2.40 D; 2.41 C; 2.42 D; 2.43 C; 2.44 B; 2.45 C; 2.46 D; 2.47 A; 2.48 C; 2.49 C; 2.50 D; 2.51 D; 2.52 C; 2.53 A; 2.54 D; 2.55 B; 2.56 C; 2.57 C; 2.58 B; 2.59 C; 2.60 D; 2.61 D; 2.62 C; 2.63 D; 2.64 C; 2.65 D; 2.66 B; 2.67 C; 2.68 D; 2.69 B; 2.70 B; 2.71 D; 2.72 A; 2.73 A; 2.74 A; 2.75 B; 2.76 B; 2.77 A; 2.78 B; 2.79 D; 2.80 B; 2.81 B; 2.82 B; 2.83 D; 2.84 B; 2.85 A; 2.86 A; 2.87 D; 2.88 D; 2.89 A; 2.90 D; 2.91 C; 2.92 C; 2.93 C; 2.94 C; 2.95 C; 2.96 B; 2.97 B; 2.98 C; 2.99 A; 2.100 B; 2.101 A; 2.102 C;

Chapter 3 Memory Management

Chapter Learning Outcomes

3.1 Define and describe the concept of memory management.
3.2 Compare and contrast different memory allocation methods.
3.3 Assess the effectiveness of segmentation.
3.4 Demonstrate the application of virtual memory concepts.

3.1 Introduction to Memory Management

Memory serves as a vital resource that facilitates the execution of programs and the efficient management of data. Understanding memory and its management is crucial for achieving optimal performance, resource allocation, and overall system stability. Memory in a computer system is organized into a hierarchy of storage devices, each with varying speed, capacity, and access times.

The primary memory types include:

Registers: These are the smallest and fastest storage units directly accessible by the CPU. Registers store temporary data and control information needed for executing instructions.
Cache Memory: Cache memory sits between the CPU and main memory and is designed to provide fast access to frequently used data. It helps reduce the latency associated with fetching data from main memory.
Main Memory (RAM): Main memory, often referred to as Random Access Memory (RAM), is a volatile memory that stores both program instructions and data. It serves as the primary working area for the operating system and running applications.
Secondary Storage: Secondary storage devices, such as hard drives and solid-state drives (SSDs), provide non-volatile storage for long-term data retention. Unlike main memory, secondary storage has larger capacity but slower access times.

Memory organization efficiently caters to OS and user app needs by segmenting memory into purpose-specific regions. The *kernel space*, housing core OS components, remains shielded from user processes for system robustness. In contrast, the *user space* hosts apps, code, data, and user stacks in isolation, ensuring stability, security, and efficient system operation. Efficient memory management prevents conflicts, optimizing resource utilization, and establishing as table operational environment for applications.

Operating systems employ a range of memory management techniques to accomplish these objectives. One such technique is *address translation*. Here, the operating system facilitates the conversion of logical addresses, generated by individual processes, into corresponding physical addresses. This seamless translation mechanism expedites access to memory locations, contributing to overall system efficiency.

Memory allocation, another fundamental aspect, entails the allocation of memory blocks to processes upon their creation. To achieve this allocation effectively, techniques like paging and segmentation are harnessed. These methods streamline memory distribution and utilization across processes.

Incorporating memory protection, the system deploys safeguards to prevent processes from accessing memory areas attributed to other processes or the core operating system. This proactive measure fortifies system security and stability, curtailing unauthorized data access and interference. An ingenious strategy known as *virtual memory* extends the memory management repertoire. By enabling processes to employ more memory than physically available, virtual memory orchestrates a dynamic data exchange between main memory and secondary storage. This innovative technique accommodates diverse memory needs while optimizing system performance and responsiveness.

Review Question 3.1
What is the primary purpose of memory organization in a computer system?
A) Enhancing power efficiency.
B) Reducing the number of CPU cores.
C) Catering to user app needs.
D) Managing network connections.

Review Question 3.2
Which memory type is directly accessible by the CPU and stores temporary data and control information?
A) Cache Memory
B) Secondary Storage
C) Main Memory (RAM)
D) Registers

Review Question 3.3
What is the primary function of cache memory in a computer system?
A) Storing long-term data.
B) Providing non-volatile storage.
C) Shielding user processes.
D) Providing fast access to frequently used data.

Review Question 3.4
Which type of memory serves as the primary working area for the operating system and running applications?

A) Secondary Storage
B) Cache Memory
C) Registers
D) Main Memory (RAM)

Review Question 3.5
What does the term "volatile memory" refer to?
A) Memory with fast access times.
B) Memory that stores long-term data.
C) Memory that is directly accessible by the CPU.
D) Memory that loses data when power is lost.

Review Question 3.6
Which memory management technique allows processes to use more memory than physically available?
A) Address Translation
B) Memory Allocation
C) Virtual Memory
D) Memory Protection

Review Question 3.7
What does memory protection ensure in a computer system?
A) Preventing conflicts between processes.
B) Increasing CPU speed.
C) Reducing power consumption.
D) Enhancing graphics performance.

Review Question 3.8
Which memory type is shielded from user processes to ensure system stability?
A) Cache Memory
B) Main Memory (RAM)
C) Secondary Storage
D) Kernel Space

Review Question 3.9
What does "non-volatile storage" mean in the context of memory?
A) Memory that loses data when power is lost.
B) Memory that is directly accessible by the CPU.
C) Memory that retains data even when power is lost.
D) Memory with fast access times.

Review Question 3.10
Which memory management technique involves converting logical addresses into corresponding physical addresses?
A) Memory Allocation
B) Virtual Memory
C) Memory Protection
D) Address Translation

3.2 Memory Allocation Methods

Memory allocation refers to how the memory manager assigns portions of main memory to various running processes in a multi-programmed operating system. Efficient allocation of memory among competing processes is crucial for optimal system performance and usage of available memory space. Each method has its own advantages and disadvantages in fragmentation, allocation efficiency, and ease of programming. Choosing the right allocation method is an important aspect of building an operating system capable of effectively sharing memory resources among concurrent processes.

3.2.1 Fixed Partitioning

Fixed partitioning is one of the earliest and simplest methods used for memory allocation in multi programmed operating systems. In this method, the main memory is divided into several fixed-sized regions or partitions. At least one partition must be large enough to accommodate the largest process that will be loaded into memory. The memory layout is predefined, with each partition having a fixed capacity. This approach aims to simplify memory management by providing a clear structure for process allocation.

To illustrate fixed partitioning, imagine a theater with a certain number of rooms, each room representing a memory partition. In this analogy, different performances (processes) require different numbers of seats (memory). The theater management decides to allocate which room foreach performance. For instance, they might allocate a 20-seat room for a small play, a 50-seat room for a concert, and a 100-seat room for a movie screening.

A fixed partitioning can be equal-size partitions. In the simplest approach, memory is divided into equal-sized partitions. If a process cannot fit into a partition, it is not loaded into main memory. This approach can lead to wastage if the process size is much smaller than the partition size.

A fixed partitioning can also be variable-size partitions. Having partitions of varying sizes is an improvement over equal partition. This allows more flexibility in allocating larger or smaller partitions as per process size. Smaller processes can fit into the smaller partitions leaving more space for larger processes. However, determining the optimal partition sizes is complex. The number of partitions determines the degree of multiprogramming supported by the system. A system with more partitions can have a higher degree of multiprogramming, i.e. more processes loaded into memory at the same time. However, if processes do not fit perfectly into available partitions, it leads to wasted memory known as *internal fragmentation*.

The main advantage of fixed partitioning is its simplicity. Partition sizes are fixed, so allocation just involves finding a partition that can accommodate the process. However, the major limitation is that partitions are static leading to low memory utilization due to internal fragmentation. The internal fragmentation occurs when a process is allocated a partition larger than its size, leading to wasted memory. For instance, if a small process occupies a larger partition, the remaining space is left unused. Additionally, processes must fit within allocated partitions, which can restrict the execution of larger processes. Dynamic partitioning methods were developed to overcome these inefficiencies.

Review Question 3.11
What is the primary concept behind fixed partitioning in memory allocation?
A) Allocating varying-sized memory regions.
B) Dynamically adjusting memory partitions.
C) Dividing memory into a fixed number of rooms.
D) Allowing unlimited memory for each process.

Review Question 3.12
In the analogy of a theater for computer memory, what do the different rooms represent?
A) Sizes of memory partitions.
B) Sizes of processes.
C) Types of processes.
D) Number of partitions.

Review Question 3.13
What is the advantage of variable-size partitions over equal-size partitions in fixed partitioning?
A) Reduced internal fragmentation.
B) Simplicity in allocation.
C) Fixed process allocation.
D) Better memory and resources utilization.

Review Question 3.14
What does the number of partitions in fixed partitioning determine?
A) The number of available processes.
B) The degree of multiprogramming.
C) The size of each process.
D) The speed of memory access.

Review Question 3.15
What is a major limitation of fixed partitioning in memory allocation?
A) Dynamic partitioning efficiency.
B) High memory utilization.
C) Low memory utilization due to internal fragmentation.
D) Increased complexity in process allocation.

Review Question 3.16
Why were dynamic partitioning methods developed?
A) To reduce memory capacity.
B) To increase internal fragmentation.
C) To overcome inefficiencies of fixed partitioning.
D) To limit the degree of multiprogramming.

3.2.2 Dynamic Partitioning

Memory management in operating systems necessitates strategies that can accommodate processes of varying sizes efficiently. Dynamic partitioning is a memory allocation technique designed to handle such variability. Dynamic partitioning involves dividing the available memory into variable sized partitions to allocate processes. Unlike fixed partitioning, where partitions are of fixed size, dynamic partitioning adapts to the sizes of incoming processes. When a process arrives, the system allocates an appropriately sized partition to it, minimizing wasted memory.

There are several common algorithms for dynamic partitioning. The *First Fit* algorithm for dynamic partitioning works as follows:

When a process arrives, it requests memory of a particular size based on its requirements.

The memory manager looks through the free memory chunks in the list/map of free space and finds the first chunk that can fulfill that request.

It allocates that chunk to the process. The remaining free space in that chunk, if any, is kept track of for future requests.

So, the partition size is determined on demand by the process, and First Fit simply allocates the first suitable free chunk to the process. The first fit algorithm is quick and easy to implement but can lead to larger leftover spaces and fragmentation (external fragmentation).

Best Fit Algorithm: The Best Fit algorithm assigns the smallest partition that can hold the process, aiming to minimize wastage. However, it requires more searching and can result in external fragmentation.

Worst Fit Algorithm: The Worst Fit algorithm assigns the largest available partition to a process. This approach attempts to leave larger contiguous free spaces, but it can lead to inefficient memory utilization. Dynamic partitioning addresses the issue of internal fragmentation found in fixed partitioning. However, it introduces a different form of fragmentation known as *external fragmentation*. External fragmentation occurs when unoccupied memory blocks are dispersed across the memory space, creating obstacles in allocating larger continuous blocks for processes. This phenomenon arises due to the allocation and deallocation of processes, which results in gaps that are insufficient in size to accommodate new processes.

Review Question 3.17
What is the primary purpose of dynamic partitioning in memory management?
A) Handling processes of varying sizes efficiently.
B) Allocating fixed-sized partitions to processes.
C) Reducing the number of available processes.
D) Maximizing internal fragmentation.

Review Question 3.18How does the First Fit algorithm for dynamic partitioning allocate memory?
A) It allocates the smallest free partition.
B) It allocates the largest free partition.
C) It allocates the first suitable free partition.
D) It allocates all available partitions equally.

Review Question 3.19What is a drawback of the First Fit algorithm in dynamic partitioning?
A) It leads to larger leftover spaces.
B) It requires more searching.
C) It results in internal fragmentation.
D) It increases memory utilization.

Review Question 3.20
What does the Best Fit algorithm aim to minimize in dynamic partitioning?
A) Process sizes.
B) External fragmentation.
C) Wasted memory.
D) Number of processes.

Review Question 3.21
What does the Worst Fit algorithm aim to achieve in dynamic partitioning?
A) Smallest available partitions.
B) Maximum internal fragmentation.
C) Efficient memory utilization.
D) Largest available partitions.

Review Question 3.22
What is a consequence of dynamic partitioning in memory management?
A) Reduced process variability.
B) Elimination of internal fragmentation.
C) Introduction of external fragmentation.
D) Decreased memory allocation efficiency.

3.2.3 Paging

Paging is a dynamic memory allocation technique employed by modern operating systems to efficiently manage memory and address the limitations posed by fixed and dynamic partitioning. In the paging approach, memory (an abstract concept representing all storage available to processes) is divided into fixed-size blocks called pages. Similarly, the physical memory (RAM) is divided into blocks called frames. Pages and frames have uniform sizes, and the goal is to map pages to frames to facilitate memory allocation. Each page or frame has a unique identifier, enabling seamless referencing.

A *page table* is a critical component in paging. It holds the mapping information, associating each page with the corresponding frame in physical memory. To quickly access the page table, a *page table base register (PTBR)* is utilized. This register points to the base address of the page table, expediting the translation of logical addresses to physical addresses. While the page table keeps track of where each page of memory is stored, the PTBR points to the location of the page table itself. This allows the system to quickly switch between processes by changing the value of the PTBR

Let's use the library as an analogy. Imagine a library as the physical memory and books as pages. The shelves represent frames in memory. A librarian's catalog functions as the page table, guiding readers(processes) to the precise shelf (frame) containing the desired book (data). The page table base register is comparable to the librarian's quick access to the catalog. *Page faults* occur when a process references a page that isn't currently in memory. This necessitates fetching the required page from secondary storage into a free frame. The page table is updated to reflect the new mapping, and the process resumes execution. Page faults are managed by the operating system, which optimizes the movement of pages between memory and secondary storage. In scenarios where memory becomes saturated, page replacement algorithms come into play. These algorithms determine which page to evict from memory to make room for incoming pages.

Common algorithms include:

FIFO (First-In-First-Out): Evicts the oldest page, akin to a queue.
LRU (Least Recently Used): Evicts the least recently accessed page, preserving recently used pages.
Optimal: Evicts the page with the longest future access delay, theoretically minimizing page faults.

An analogy example of restaurant seating may explain the concept better. Imagine a restaurant with a limited number of tables (frames) and a waiting area (secondary storage). As guests (pages) arrive, they are seated at available tables. When a new guest arrives and all tables are occupied, the restaurant staff must decide which guest to ask to leave (evict) to make room. Different strategies (page replacement algorithms) guide this decision, such as asking the longest-seated guest to leave (LRU).

Review Question 3.23
What is the primary purpose of paging in modern operating systems?
A) To divide memory into fixed-size blocks.
B) To divide memory into variable-size blocks.
C) To manage the library catalog.
D) To map logical addresses to physical addresses.

Review Question 3.24
Which component holds the mapping information between pages and frames in paging?
A) Page table base register (PTBR).
B) Page fault handler.
C) Secondary storage.
D) Page replacement algorithm.

Review Question 3.25
In the analogy of a library as physical memory provided in the book, what does the librarian's catalog represent?
A) Physical memory.
B) Secondary storage.
C) Page table.
D) Page table base register.

Review Question 3.26
What happens when a process references a page that isn't in memory?
A) The process is terminated.
B) The operating system fetches the page from the CPU cache.
C) A page fault occurs, and the required page is fetched from secondary storage.
D) The process resumes execution without any interruption.

3.3 Segmentation

Segmentation is a memory management technique that divides the logical memory into variable-sized segments tailored to program needs. Segments have characteristics like length, privileges, etc. tracked in a segment table.

3.3.1 Characteristics of Segmentation

Paging offers advantages like virtual memory and efficient memory utilization by retaining frequently used pages in the main memory. However, it comes with a significant drawback in the form of increased overhead due to tables and page interrupts.

Segmentation is a memory management concept inspired by the way programmers structure their programs into modules, logically grouping pieces of code. In segmented memory allocation, each module corresponds to a segment, resulting in variable segment sizes. Before segmentation, virtual memory addresses were one-dimensional, with address numbers ranging from 0 to a certain limit.

This one-dimensional addressing posed issues, such as the stack of one program potentially affecting the addresses of other programs. Segmentation addresses this problem by introducing a separate address space for each segment, creating a two-dimensional addressing system. A logical address now consists of two numbers (n, m), where the first number indicates the segment, and the second number represents the logical address within that segment. This isolation ensures that one segment's need for additional space doesn't impact other segments.

Another advantage of segmentation is shared memory. Code libraries can be placed in a segment and shared among multiple processes. While pure paging can achieve the same result, segment management is simpler since you only deal with one segment instead of multiple pages.

Segmentation also offers enhanced protection levels. Each segment can have a unique protection level; for example, one segment can be set as "execute only," preventing any attempts to read from or write into it.

Segmentation divides memory into logical segments, each corresponding to a specific type of data or program component. Unlike paging, which uses fixed-size blocks, segmentation allows segments to have varying sizes, aligning better with program and data structures. Segments can represent code, data, stack, heap, and other components.

Key characteristics of segmentation include variable segment sizes, logical grouping, simplified protection and sharing, and flexibility. Variable segment sizes enable efficient memory usage by matching each segment's size to its actual memory requirements, reducing wasted memory. Logical grouping keeps related information together, such as keeping code and data together. Protection and sharing are simplified, with segments individually protected and easily shared among processes.

Lastly, the two-part addressing scheme, using a segment number and an offset (a relative address within a segment), enables efficient segment access while allowing dynamic relocation of segments in memory.

An analogy to city blocks can help illustrate segmentation. Imagine a city divided into distinct blocks, each representing a segment. Within each block, you find various establishments serving specific purposes, such as houses, shops, parks, and offices. Just as a city accommodates diverse activities in different blocks, segmentation caters to varied memory needs by allocating memory in logical segments.

Review Question 3.27
What is one disadvantage of paging in memory management?
A) overhead
B) virtual memory
C) memory utilization
D) shared memory

Review Question 3.28
Which memory management concept is inspired by the way programmers structure their programs into modules?
A) Paging
B) Variable segment sizes
C) Segmentation
D) Shared memory

Review Question 3.29
Before the introduction of segmentation, what issue did one-dimensional addressing in virtual memory cause?
A) Decreased virtual memory size
B) Variable segment sizes
C) Physical grouping problems
D) Address conflicts between programs

Review Question 3.30
How does segmentation address the problem of address conflicts between segments?
A) By introducing two-dimensional addressing
B) By reducing overhead
C) By simplifying protection levels
D) By eliminating shared memory

Review Question 3.31
What is one benefit of placing code libraries in a segment in memory management?
A) Simplified address space
B) Enhanced protection levels
C) Reduced overhead
D) Improved shared memory

Review Question 3.32
In segmentation, how can protection levels be customized for each segment?
A) By using variable segment sizes
B) By introducing two-dimensional addressing
C) By simplifying logical grouping
D) By assigning unique protection levels to each segment

Review Question 3.33
What distinguishes segmentation from paging in memory management?
A) Variable segment sizes
B) Logical grouping of code
C) Fixed-size segments
D) Efficient memory utilization

Review Question 3.34
What is a key characteristic of segmentation that reduces wasted memory?
A) Logical grouping
B) Efficient memory utilization
C) Variable segment sizes
D) Simplified protection levels

Review Question 3.35
What does the two-part addressing scheme in segmentation consist of?
A) Code and data
B) A segment number and an offset
C) Fixed-size blocks
D) Virtual memory addresses

Review Question 3.36
Which analogy in the book is used to help illustrate the concept of segmentation?
A) A library
B) A shopping mall
C) A city divided into blocks
D) A puzzle

Review Question 3.37
How does segmentation cater to varied memory needs in memory management?
A) By using fixed-size blocks
B) By eliminating shared memory
C) By reducing protection levels
D) By allocating memory in logical segments

Review Question 3.38
What is the key difference between segmentation and paging?
A) Segmentation uses fixed-size blocks, while paging uses variable-size segments.
B) Segmentation divides memory into logical segments, while paging divides memory into fixed-size blocks.
C) Segmentation and paging are identical memory allocation techniques.
D) Segmentation does not support protection and sharing of memory.

Review Question 3.39
How does segmentation reduce internal fragmentation compared to fixed block sizes?
A) By allowing each segment to have a size that matches its memory requirements.
B) By preventing unauthorized access to segments.
C) By using a two-part addressing scheme.
D) By grouping related information together.

3.3.2 Paging vs Segmentation

Paging and segmentation are two prominent techniques in memory management. They serve as cornerstones for efficiently allocating and organizing memory within an operating system. Each technique offers distinct advantages and addresses specific challenges.

Paging divides memory into uniform fixed-size blocks called pages in both physical and logical address spaces. The primary goal is to eliminate the limitations of fixed and dynamic partitioning. Paging separates the logical view of memory used by processes from its physical allocation. Page numbers in logical addresses serve as indices in the page table, which contains entries mapping these logical page numbers to their corresponding frames in physical memory. The separation of logical and physical addresses enables efficient memory management, reducing internal fragmentation and offering protection against address space conflicts.

Paging offers several advantages in memory management. The uniformity of pages, all of the same size, streamlines memory administration. Additionally, the isolation of processes is achieved by maintaining separate logical and physical addresses, ensuring each process remains independent. Moreover, the flexibility afforded by paging eliminates the requirement for contiguous memory allocation, enhancing the versatility of memory allocation strategies.

However, paging comes with certain drawbacks. Paging can lead to internal fragmentation due to the presence of unused memory within allocated pages, potentially impacting memory efficiency. Moreover, the management of large address spaces might necessitate extensive page tables, introducing an additional layer of overhead to the system's memory management process.

Different from paging, segmentation divides memory into variable-sized segments, accommodating the diverse requirements of processes. Each segment corresponds to a distinct data type or component, such as code, data, or stack. The segment table maintains the mapping between logical segment numbers and their physical base addresses. Segmentation aligns memory allocation with the structure of programs, offering protection, sharing, and efficient addressing.

Segmentation provides several advantages over other memory management methods. Firstly, it allows for flexible allocation of memory, since segment sizes can match the actual memory needs of program components rather than forcing fixed allocations. This optimization helps reduce wasted memory. Additionally, segmentation logically groups related code and data together into coherent program components or modules within segments. This logical organization and modularity make programs easier to understand, modify, and debug. Finally, segments support controlled protection and sharing of programs and data across processes. Specific access privileges can be applied to each segment, enhancing security, access control, and collaboration between processes.

While segmentation provides benefits, it also comes with some drawbacks. One disadvantage is the potential for internal fragmentation within segments. Since segment sizes are tailored to program modules, a segment may end up being larger than strictly needed, resulting in unused memory wasted within that segment. This internal fragmentation means memory utilization is not maximized.

There are several possible reasons why a segment might exceed the actual requirements of the module it contains. One significant factor is the consideration of future expansion in the module's memory needs. By allocating additional space upfront, the segment size can accommodate anticipated growth, eliminating the need for resizing in the future. Another factor is the potential performance advantages associated with allowing certain data structures to expand in place without requiring relocation. This approach helps reduce fragmentation and can lead to more efficient memory utilization. Lastly, there is the aspect of simplicity. It can be easier to overestimate memory requirements and create a static segment initially, rather than dealing with the complexities of dynamic resizing at a later stage. This approach simplifies memory management and can streamline the overall system designs.

Another issue of segmentation is that the variable-sized segments can result in uneven memory allocation over time as programs request and free segments of differing sizes. This uneven allocation can lead to external fragmentation, as holes of free memory are scattered throughout the address space.

The choice between paging and segmentation depends on the specific needs of the system and its processes.

In practice, modern operating systems often combine these techniques, implementing paged segmentation. This approach combines the advantages of both methods by dividing memory into segments and further dividing segments into pages. We will explain the combination in the next.

Review Question 3.40
Which of the following is a key advantage of paging?
A) Logical grouping of memory
B) Flexible segment sizes
C) Protection through access privileges
D) Isolation of process address spaces

Review Question 3.41
What is one drawback of paging mentioned in the book?
A) External fragmentation
B) Fixed partition sizes
C) Lack of modularity
D) Internal fragmentation

Review Question 3.42
What does the segment table maintain in a segmentation system?
A) Page to frame mapping
B) Page access rights
C) Logical to physical mapping
D) Free frame tracking

Review Question 3.43
How does segmentation cater to program memory needs compared to paging?
A) Larger page sizes
B) Fixed partition sizes
C) Lazy components allocation
D) Variable segment sizes

Review Question 3.44
Which characteristic of segmentation helps reduce wasted memory?
A) External fragmentation
B) Logical organization
C) Access privileges
D) Flexible allocation

Review Question 3.45
What is a potential downside of estimating segment sizes to accommodate future expansion?
A) Complex paging
B) Frequent resizing
C) External fragmentation
D) Internal fragmentation

Review Question 3.46

What memory management approach do modern systems often combine?
A) Paging and encryption
B) Segmentation and swapping
C) Page and segmentation
D) Virtual and segmentation

Review Question 3.47
What causes external fragmentation in segmentation systems?
A) Fixed partition sizes
B) Scattered free memory blocks
C) Excess unused memory
D) Separate logical addresses

3.3.3 Segmentation with Paging

Segmentation with paging integrates the segmentation and paging techniques to optimize memory allocation in modern operating systems. This hybrid approach divides memory into segments, similar to segmentation, and then divides each segment into pages, akin to paging. Each segment maintains its specific attributes, while pages within a segment share the same size across all segments.

In this approach, the memory space is divided into segments, each of which contains multiple pages. Each segment has a dedicated segment table entry, much like the standard segmentation approach. Within each segment, pages are individually managed using a page table. This two-level hierarchy provides the flexibility of segmentation and the efficient management of paging simultaneously. Segmentation with paging combines the benefits of both methods to provide an optimal memory management solution. This hybrid approach offers flexible memory allocation, as segmentation allows segments of variable sizes to be tailored to process needs. At the same time, paging within each segment minimizes wasted memory from internal fragmentation. The logical isolation of address spaces also ensures process separation and protection. Finally, the two-tier translation from segment to page to physical address streamlines address translation and memory access. Overall, segmentation with paging provides the flexibility of variable-sized segments mapped to contiguous logical addresses, while avoiding external fragmentation between pages within those segments. This optimal utilization of physical memory along with efficient address translation and protection makes segmentation with paging a highly effective memory management technique for modern operating systems.

The synergistic combination draws on the strengths of both methods, while minimizing their individual disadvantages. Segmentation with paging mitigates the limitations present in both segmentation and paging techniques. It resolves the external fragmentation problem associated with segmentation while addressing the issues of internal fragmentation and large page tables in paging.

Review Question 3.48
What is the primary advantage of segmentation with paging in memory management?
A) Elimination of all fragmentation
B) Enhanced memory allocation flexibility
C) Simplicity in page table management
D) Reduction of external fragmentation

Review Question 3.49
How does segmentation with paging manage memory within each segment?
A) Using a single page table for all segments
B) Employing a two-level hierarchy with segment tables and page tables
C) Dynamically resizing segments as needed
D) Assigning a dedicated page table for each segment

Review Question 3.50
What is the main advantage of using segmentation with paging in modern operating systems?
A) Efficient memory access
B) Elimination of process separation
C) Optimal memory utilization
D) Reduction of page table complexity

Review Question 3.51
How does segmentation with paging address the limitations of both segmentation and paging techniques?
A) By eliminating segmentation and using only paging
B) By using fixed-sized segments with variable-sized pages
C) By minimizing their individual disadvantages while preserving their strengths
D) By using only external fragmentation reduction techniques

Review Question 3.52
What problem does segmentation with paging help resolve regarding paging?
A) Internal fragmentation
B) External fragmentation
C) Internal fragmentation and Large page table sizes
D) Memory access complexity

3.4 Virtual Memory

Virtual memory uses disk storage to provide programs an address space larger than the physically available main memory. With virtual memory, addresses used by programs are virtual addresses that are abstracted from physical memory addresses. Pages of memory are swapped between main memory and disk storage as needed using demand paging. When a program accesses a virtual address not currently mapped to main memory, the operating system fetches the required page from disk. This page swapping allows virtual address spaces to span both main memory and disk capacity.

3.4.1 Concept of Virtual Memory

Virtual memory expands address space beyond physical limits. Virtual memory is an abstraction that allows processes to access a larger address space than the available physical memory. Virtual memory addresses the challenge of limited physical memory by creating an illusion of a larger memory space. It achieves this by utilizing a portion of the secondary storage (usually the hard disk) as an extension of physical memory. Processes interact with this virtual memory space, unaware of whether data resides in physical memory or on the secondary storage.

The primary component facilitating virtual memory is the page table. It translates virtual addresses generated by processes into corresponding physical addresses. When a process references a virtual address, the page table directs the system to the appropriate physical location, ensuring seamless data access.

Virtual memory relies on a mechanism known as *paging* to manage data between physical memory and secondary storage. When a process accesses a page that is not in physical memory, a page fault occurs. The operating system then retrieves the required page from secondary storage and loads it into a free frame in physical memory. This process is transparent to the process and enables on demand data loading.

Virtual memory brings about a host of advantages that significantly impact the efficiency and functionality of modern operating systems. Address Space Expansion: One of the most profound benefits of virtual memory is its ability to provide processes with an apparent expansive address space. This means that processes can execute larger and more complex programs without being constrained by the actual physical memory available.

Memory Isolation: Each process in the system perceives its very own dedicated memory space. This not only ensures that processes remain isolated from each other but also prevents them from directly interfering with one another's memory. Such isolation is essential for maintaining the stability and integrity of the operating system and its running processes.

Efficient Use of Physical Memory: Virtual memory introduces a clever mechanism wherein only the necessary pages of a process are loaded into the limited physical memory at any given time. This approach optimizes the utilization of physical memory resources. As a result, processes can collectively use more memory than the system's physical memory capacity without causing undue strain on the hardware.

Memory Protection: The isolation ensures that one process cannot accidentally or deliberately manipulate memory being used by another process. Processes are confined to their own virtual address spaces. Any attempt to access unauthorized memory is blocked by the virtual memory system. In this way, virtual memory provides a layer of security by allowing only approved access to memory areas allotted to each process. Effective memory protection is vital for safeguarding overall system integrity and stability.

Let's see an analogy of a library overflow room. Imagine a library with limited shelf space (physical memory) but a vast collection of books (virtual memory). When the shelves are full, rarely used books are moved to an overflow room (secondary storage). Readers (processes) can request books from the overflow room, and librarians (operating system) fetch them as needed.

Review Question 3.53
What does the page table contain in a virtual memory system?
A) Page fault records
B) Free frame pointers
C) Virtual to physical mapping
D) Secondary storage addresses

Review Question 3.54
What mechanism brings pages into physical memory from disk on demand?
A) Dynamic allocation
B) Demand paging
C) Dynamic partitioning
D) External fragmentation

Review Question 3.55
How does virtual memory create the illusion of a larger address space?
A) Page fault handling
B) Secondary storage paging
C) Abstraction of physical memory
D) Virtual address spaces

Review Question 3.56
What is the benefit of isolating process address spaces in virtual memory?
A) Paging
B) Protection

C) Dynamic linking
D) Expanded capacity

Review Question 3.57
What is the overflow room analogous to in the library analogy of the book in virtual memory?
A) Page table
B) Physical memory
C) Secondary storage
D) Virtual address space

Review Question 3.58
When does a page fault occur in virtual memory?
A) On program exit
B) On illegal access
C) On address translation
D) On non-resident page access

Review Question 3.59
How does virtual memory efficiently utilize physical memory?
A) Caching
B) Segmentation
C) On demand paging
D) Dynamic allocation

Review Question 3.60
How does virtual memory benefit large programs?
A) Secondary storage
B) Expanded capacity
C) Dynamic linking
D) Page faults

3.4.2 Demand Paging

In memory management, demand paging stands as a dynamic technique that optimizes memory utilization by loading only the required pages into physical memory when they are actually needed. Demand paging operates on the premise of "bring only what you need." Instead of loading an entire program into memory at once, only the pages that are immediately required for execution are loaded. This approach conserves valuable physical memory and ensures that processes are efficient in terms of memory usage.

Central to demand paging is the concept of *page faults*. When a process references a page that is not currently in physical memory, a page fault occurs. This signals the need to fetch the page from secondary storage into an available frame in physical memory. However, demand paging leverages a critical principle called the locality of references to minimize the impact of page faults. The locality of references suggests that during program execution, processes tend to access a specific set of pages repeatedly within a short time frame. This behavior creates two types of locality:

1. *Temporal Locality*: This refers to the tendency of a process to access the same pages multiple times in quick succession. For example, a loop in a program repeatedly accesses the same set of instructions.

2. *Spatial Locality*: Spatial locality arises when a process accesses neighboring pages in memory shortly after accessing the current page. For instance, accessing elements of an array sequentially.

When a page fault occurs, the operating system responds systematically to ensure smooth process execution. The steps involved in handling a page fault typically include:

1. *Locate Free Frame*: The operating system searches for a free frame in physical memory to accommodate the incoming page.

2. *Swap Out Victim Page*: If no free frames are available, the operating system selects a "victim" page currently residing in a frame. This victim page is swapped out to make room for the incoming page.

3. *Swap In Required Page*: The page causing the page fault is brought in from secondary storage to the selected frame, completing the process of page fault handling.

Demand paging epitomizes efficiency by loading pages into physical memory only when they are needed, optimizing memory usage while taking advantage of the principles of locality of references. The handling of page faults involves a systematic process that ensures smooth execution of processes even when required pages are not immediately available in memory. By leveraging demand paging's resource-conscious approach, operating systems manage memory in a manner that aligns with the dynamic demands of modern computing environments.

Review Question 3.61
What is the primary principle behind demand paging in memory management?
A) Load the entire program into memory at once.
B) Load only the pages that are immediately required for execution.
C) Load all pages from secondary storage into physical memory.
D) Load pages randomly into physical memory.

Review Question 3.62
When does a page fault occur in demand paging?
A) When a process is terminated.
B) When a process references a page that is not currently in physical memory.
C) When a process accesses neighboring pages in memory.
D) When a process accesses the same set of instructions multiple times.

Review Question 3.63
What is the concept of "locality of references" in demand paging?
A) Loading all pages into physical memory simultaneously.
B) The tendency of a process to access different pages randomly.
C) The tendency of a process to access the same set of pages repeatedly within a short time frame.
D) The tendency of a process to access pages sequentially in memory.

Review Question 3.64
Which type of locality arises when a process accesses neighboring pages in memory shortly after accessing the current page?
A) Temporal Locality
B) Spatial Locality
C) Sequential Locality
D) Random Locality

Review Question 3.65
What are the steps involved in handling a page fault in demand paging?
A) Locate Free Frame, Load All Pages, Swap Out Victim Page
B) Locate Free Frame, Swap Out Victim Page, Swap In Required Page
C) Locate Free Frame, Terminate the Process, Reload the Program
D) Randomly Allocate Memory, Swap In Victim Page, Swap Out Required Page

Review Question 3.66
How does demand paging optimize memory usage?
A) By loading all pages from secondary storage into physical memory.
B) By swapping out all pages in physical memory to create more space.
C) By loading pages into physical memory only when they are needed.
D) By allocating a fixed amount of memory for each process.

3.4.3 Page Replacement Algorithms

Within virtual memory, page replacement algorithms emerge as fundamental strategies to optimize memory utilization when space is limited. Page replacement algorithms come into play when the operating system must decide which page to evict from memory to accommodate incoming pages. These algorithms strive to minimize page faults and enhance overall system performance by strategically choosing which pages to retain and which to replace.

FIFO (First-In-First-Out) operates on the principle of treating memory as a queue. The algorithm evicts the oldest page first, mirroring the behavior of a queue where the first item to arrive is the first to leave. While easy to implement, FIFO is prone to the Belady's Anomaly, where increasing the number of frames may paradoxically lead to more page faults. Let's see an example, suppose you have a process that needs the following pages in that sequence: P1, P2, P3, P4, P1, P2, P5, P1, P2, P3, P4, P5. With a 3-frame memory, you will see the following page faults:

P1	P1	P1	P2	P3	P4	P1	P1	P1	P2	P5	P5
	P2	P2	P3	P4	P1	P2	P2	P2	P5	P3	P3
		P3	P4	P1	P2	P5	P5	P5	P3	P4	P4
Fault	Fault	Fault	Fault	Fault	Fault	Fault			Fault	Fault	

Next, with a 4-frame memory, you will see the following page faults:

P1	P1	P1	P1	P1	P1	P2	P3	P4	P5	P1	P2
	P2	P2	P2	P2	P2	P3	P4	P5	P1	P2	P3
		P3	P3	P3	P3	P4	P5	P2	P2	P3	P4
			P4	P4	P4	P5	P1	P2	P3	P4	P5
Fault	Fault	Fault	Fault			Fault	Fault	Fault	Fault	Fault	Fault

A simple comparison reveals that the 4-frame memory has one more page fault.

LRU (Least Recently Used) targets the page that has not been accessed for the longest time. This algorithm is based on the assumption of locality of references, wherein recently accessed pages are more likely to be accessed again. However, LRU can be computationally intensive and requires careful bookkeeping of page access history.

LFU (Least Frequently Used) replaces the page that has been accessed the least number of times. It accounts for scenarios where short bursts of high-frequency page references occur. Yet, it struggles to predict future usage patterns accurately, and its effectiveness can diminish over time.

OPT (Optimal) algorithm serves as a benchmark for page replacement strategies. It selects the page that will not be used for the longest period in the future. While OPT theoretically offers the lowest possible number of page faults, implementing it practically is often infeasible due to the need for future usage prediction.

NUR (Not Used Recently) simplifies the LRU algorithm by categorizing pages based on recent usage. It divides pages into classes and replaces pages from the lowest class, reducing computational overhead compared to full LRU implementations.

Review Question 3.67
What is the primary objective of page replacement algorithms in virtual memory?

A) To maximize the number of page faults.
B) To minimize page faults and enhance system performance.
C) To prioritize the most recently accessed pages.
D) To replace pages randomly.

Review Question 3.68
Which page replacement algorithm operates on the principle of treating memory as a queue?
A) LRU (Least Recently Used)
B) LFU (Least Frequently Used)
C) FIFO (First-In-First-Out)
D) OPT (Optimal)

Review Question 3.69
What is one major drawback of the FIFO page replacement algorithm?
A) It is computationally intensive.
B) It requires careful bookkeeping of page access history.
C) It is prone to Belady's Anomaly.
D) It always provides the optimal solution.

Review Question 3.70
Which page replacement algorithm targets the page that has not been accessed for the longest time?
A) LRU (Least Recently Used)
B) LFU (Least Frequently Used)
C) FIFO (First-In-First-Out)
D) NUR (Not Used Recently)

Review Question 3.71
Which page replacement algorithm accounts for scenarios where short bursts of high-frequency page references occur?
A) LRU (Least Recently Used)
B) LFU (Least Frequently Used)
C) FIFO (First-In-First-Out)
D) NUR (Not Used Recently)

Review Question 3.72
Which page replacement algorithm serves as a benchmark for page replacement strategies but is often impractical to implement?
A) LRU (Least Recently Used)
B) OPT (Optimal)
C) FIFO (First-In-FIFO-Out)
D) LFU (Least Frequently Used)

Review Question 3.73
What does NUR (Not Used Recently) do to simplify the LRU algorithm?
A) It replaces pages based whether it is used.
B) It replaces pages based on their frequency of access.
C) It divides pages into classes based on the recently used and replaces from the lowest class.
D) It predicts future usage patterns accurately.

Review Question 3.74
Which page replacement algorithm is based on the assumption of locality of references?
A) LRU (Least Recently Used)
B) LFU (Least Frequently Used)
C) FIFO (First-In-FIFO-Out)
D) NUR (Not Used Recently)

Review Question 3.75
Which page replacement algorithm is suitable for scenarios with high-frequency page references?
A) OPT (Optimal)
B) LFU (Least Frequently Used)
C) NUR (Not Used Recently)
D) FIFO (First-In-First-Out)

Review Question 3.76
What is the primary drawback of the OPT (Optimal) page replacement algorithm?
A) It is computationally intensive and hard to predict the future usage.
B) It always provides the optimal solution.
C) It is too simple.
D) It requires careful bookkeeping of page access history.

3.4.4 Thrashing and Methods for Its Prevention

In virtual memory, an undesirable phenomenon known as thrashing can emerge, severely hampering system performance. Thrashing occurs when the system is overwhelmed by excessive paging activity, leading to a continuous cycle of page faults and page replacements that consumes more time than actual computation.

Thrashing arises from a delicate balance between the number of processes in memory and the available physical memory space. When the demand for physical memory exceeds its supply, the system is forced to swap pages in and out at an alarming rate. Consequently, the majority of the time is spent in handling page faults and performing page replacements, leaving minimal resources for actual computation. This results in a performance bottleneck and a steep decline in overall system efficiency.

There are several factors that can contribute to thrashing, including:
1. Insufficient physical memory: This is the most common cause of thrashing. When the system does not have enough physical memory to store all of the active processes' code and data, it is forced to swap pages out to disk. This can significantly slow down the system, as disk access is much slower than memory access. Consider a loop that is loaded across two pages, but the physical memory only has one free frame. The first page containing the start of the loop will load first. As execution continues, it will reach the second part of

the loop contained in the second page. Since there is only one free frame, the first page will need to be swapped out to load this second page. When the loop finishes its first iteration and starts again, the second page will now need to be swapped out to reload the first page for the top of the loop. This pattern of swapping the two loop pages in and out will repeat each time the loop iterates, assuming no additional free frames become available during execution. This can lead to thrashing.

2. Over-allocation: Over-allocation occurs when the operating system allocates more memory to a process than it actually needs. This can also lead to thrashing, as the process will be forced to swap out pages that it is not currently using.

3. Uneven allocation: Uneven allocation occurs when the operating system allocates memory unevenly among processes. This can cause some processes to frequently access disk-stored pages, while other processes do not. This can also lead to thrashing, as the system will be constantly swapping pages between memory and disk. The consequences of thrashing are severe, encompassing a range of detrimental effects on system performance, such as severe performance degradation, increased response, and resource waster.

The occurrence of thrashing jeopardizes the efficiency and effectiveness of virtual memory systems, ushering in a cascade of negative effects that hinder both process execution and the optimal utilization of system resources. Given the detrimental impact of thrashing, operating systems implement various methods to prevent its occurrence.

One such method is the working set model. The working set of a process refers to the set of pages actively used by the process during a specific time interval. By monitoring and ensuring that the working set of each process is present in memory, the system can mitigate thrashing.

Another method is the global replacement algorithms. Algorithms like WSClock(Working Set Clock) monitor the working set of all processes collectively, aiming to ensure that the combined working sets fit within the available physical memory.

A third method is the priority based allocation. In this approach, processes are assigned priorities based on their memory requirements and past behavior. Lower-priority processes are swapped out before higher-priority ones to prevent thrashing.

Review Question 3.77
What is thrashing in virtual memory systems?
A) A phenomenon where processes execute too quickly, causing system overload.
B) A situation where the system is overwhelmed by excessive paging activity.
C) The process of defragmenting the hard drive to improve system performance.
D) A mechanism that prevents excessive memory usage in the system.

Review Question 3.78
What is one of the most common causes of thrashing?
A) Over-allocation of memory.
B) Insufficient physical memory.
C) Uneven allocation of memory.
D) Rapid execution of processes.

Review Question 3.79
How can over-allocation of memory contribute to thrashing?
A) It slows down the execution of processes.
B) It causes the system to allocate more physical memory.
C) It forces processes to use less memory than needed.
D) It results in processes swapping out pages they are not using.

Review Question 3.80
What does the working set model aim to achieve in preventing thrashing?
A) Allocating a fixed amount of memory to each process.
B) Reducing the working set of each process to a minimum.
C) Ensuring that the working set of each process is present in memory.
D) Eliminating page faults entirely.

Review Question 3.81
What are the consequences of thrashing on system performance?
A) Improved response time and resource utilization.
B) Severe performance degradation and increased response time.
C) Reduced page faults and optimal resource usage.
D) Faster execution of processes and enhanced system efficiency.

Review Question 3.82
Which factor can lead to thrashing by causing some processes to frequently access disk-stored pages while others do not?
A) Over-allocation of memory.
B) Insufficient physical memory.
C) Rapid execution of processes.
D) Uneven allocation of memory.

3.5 Memory Leaks

A memory leak occurs when a program dynamically allocates memory, but fails to release it when no longer needed. As a result, the allocated memory remains inaccessible to the program, leading to gradual memory consumption that can degrade system performance, eventually leading to crashes or slowdowns.

The consequences of memory leaks are far-reaching and can severely impact software and system performance. It can reduce memory availability. As memory leaks accumulate, available memory gradually diminishes, ultimately leading to resource scarcity and a higher likelihood of application crashes or system slowdowns.

Additionally, it degrades performance. As memory usage becomes inefficient, applications experience performance degradation due to excessive memory consumption, leading to slower response times and overall sluggishness.

Finally, there is stability Issues. Uncontrolled memory leaks can destabilize applications and the entire system. A sudden shortage of available memory can cause applications to crash, jeopardizing user experience and data integrity.

Detecting and addressing memory leaks requires a systematic approach and the adoption of best practices. The first approach is to use memory management tools. Utilize specialized memory management tools and profilers to identify memory leaks and track memory usage patterns. The second approach is to adopt good coding practices. Follow best practices in memory allocation and deallocation. Allocate memory only when necessary and ensure that memory is properly released using the appropriate functions. The third approach is to profile and test. Regularly profile your application to monitor memory usage and detect any upward trends that might indicate memory leaks.

Extensive testing, including stress testing and boundary testing, can help identify memory leak scenarios. Stress testing is a software testing technique that evaluates how a system or application performs under extreme and beyond-normal conditions. The goal of stress testing is to identify the system's breaking points, bottlenecks, and behavior when subjected to an unusually high load or demand.

Boundary testing, on the other hand, focuses on testing the boundaries or limits of input values for a particular function or feature within a software application. The goal of boundary testing is to identify potential issues, errors, or vulnerabilities that may occur when input values approach or reach the boundaries or edge cases of the acceptable range.

Finally, you can implement garbage collection. In languages with garbage collection mechanisms(e.g., Java, C#), use these features to automatically manage memory and identify unreachable objects for cleanup.

Review Question 3.83
What is a memory leak in programming?
A) When a program fails to allocate memory properly.
B) When a program releases memory too early.
C) When a program dynamically allocates memory but fails to release it.
D) When a program uses too much memory intentionally.

Review Question 3.84
What is one consequence of memory leaks?
A) Make it difficult for developers to update code.
B) It can damage the RAM.
C) System performance sometimes improved.
D) Higher likelihood of application crashes.

Review Question 3.85
What is the primary goal of stress testing?
A) To identify memory leaks.
B) To evaluate system performance under extreme conditions.
C) To optimize memory allocation.
D) To test boundary values.

Review Question 3.86
What is the primary goal of boundary testing?
A) To evaluate system performance.
B) To identify memory leaks.
C) To test the boundaries of input values.
D) To optimize memory allocation.

Review Question 3.87
How can garbage collection help manage memory in programming languages like Java and C#?
A) By manually releasing memory.
B) By allocating memory only when necessary.
C) By identifying memory leaks.
D) By automatically managing memory and identifying unreachable objects.

3.6 Garbage Collection and Memory Cleanup

Within the domain of memory management, the concept of garbage collection emerges as a fundamental strategy to automatically manage memory resources, relieving developers from the burden of manual memory deallocation. Garbage collection is a systematic process that identifies and reclaims memory occupied by objects that are no longer reachable or in use by the program. By automatically detecting and cleaning up unreferenced objects, garbage collection prevents memory leaks and helps maintain an optimal balance between memory usage and system performance.

Garbage collection employs various mechanisms to identify and manage unreferenced memory. One such technique is reference counting, which keeps track of the number of references pointing to each object. When an object's reference count drops to zero, it is deemed unreachable and can be safely deallocated.

Another approach is the mark-and-sweep algorithm, which involves traversing through all reachable objects, marking them as active, and then sweeping through the memory to deallocate objects that were not marked as active.

Additionally, generational garbage collection is utilized to enhance the efficiency of the collection process. This method divides objects into multiple generations based on their age. Younger objects typically have shorter lifespans, making them more likely to become unreachable sooner. By collecting objects in generations, this algorithm optimizes the overall efficiency of the garbage collection process.

Garbage collection brings forth several significant advantages in the realm of software development. Firstly, it plays a crucial role in preventing memory leaks by automating the memory deallocation process. This automation minimizes the risk of memory leaks, which, if left unchecked, can result in performance degradation and system instability.

Secondly, garbage collection simplifies memory management for developers. By removing the burden of manual memory tracking and release, it lessens the likelihood of programming errors stemming from memory-related issues. This simplification not only improves the reliability of software but also reduces the debugging effort required during development.

Moreover, the adoption of garbage collection leads to enhanced developer productivity. It lightens the cognitive load on programmers by eliminating the need for meticulous manual memory management. Consequently, developers can redirect their focus towards crafting and refining application logic and functionality, thereby accelerating the development process and fostering more efficient software creation.

Despite its numerous advantages, garbage collection comes with its fair share of challenges that developers must contend with. One such challenge is the performance overhead associated with garbage collection. As the garbage collection algorithm identifies and reclaims memory, it introduces computational overhead that can, at times, have a noticeable impact on application performance, potentially leading to slower execution.

Another challenge arises in the form of "stop-the-world" pauses, particularly prevalent in certain garbage collection algorithms like the mark-and-sweep technique. During these pauses, the application is temporarily halted while memory cleanup operations take place. These pauses, though often brief, can disrupt the real-time responsiveness of an application and are a consideration that developers must carefully address to maintain smooth user experiences.

Review Question 3.92
What is the primary purpose of garbage collection in memory management?
A) To increase the complexity of memory deallocation
B) To manually manage memory resources
C) To automatically identify and reclaim unreferenced memory
D) To create more memory leaks

Review Question 3.93
Which technique keeps track of the number of references pointing to each object and deallocates objects with a reference count of zero?
A) Reference Counting
B) Mark-and-Sweep
C) Generational Garbage Collection
D) Stop-the-World Pauses

Review Question 3.94
What is the main advantage of generational garbage collection?
A) It makes all objects equal in terms of memory management.
B) It speeds up the collection process for older objects.
C) It ensures that older objects have shorter lifespans.
D) It eliminates the need for memory management entirely.

Review Question 3.95
What is the consequence of memory leaks in software development?
A) Applications won't run
B) Developers have to stop the leaks before any applications can run
C) Performance degradation and system instability
D) Reduced memory usage

Review Question 3.96

How does garbage collection impact developer productivity?
A) It increases the need for manual memory management.
B) It complicates memory tracking for developers.
C) It reduces cognitive load by automating memory management.
D) It adds debugging effort to the development process.

Review Question 3.97
What is a notable challenge associated with garbage collection in terms of application performance?
A) Elimination of memory leaks
B) Reduced computational overhead
C) Slower execution due to performance overhead
D) Elimination of stop-the-world pauses

Review Question 3.98
In which garbage collection technique are "stop-the-world" pauses a potential issue?
A) Reference Counting
B) Generational Garbage Collection
C) Mark-and-Sweep
D) Memory Leak Prevention

3.7 Chapter Summary

This chapter introduces memory management concepts. Computer memory stores the data and instructions currently in use by the computer. For this reason, it is often called the computer's "workspace." Efficiently allocating memory across running processes is vital for optimal system performance and full utilization of available memory. This chapter covered several different memory allocation methods. Fixed partitioning pre-divides memory into set partitions. Dynamic partitioning allocates partitions flexibly based on process needs. Paging divides memory into fixed-size frames that can hold pages of processes. Segmentation allocates memory in variable-sized segments mapped to processes. Virtual memory uses disk storage to simulate additional main memory space.

3.8 Exercises

Exercise 3.1 A program dynamically allocates memory for an array of floating-point numbers. The array size can change during the runtime of the program. Initially, the program allocates memory for 50 floating-point numbers. Each floating-point number requires 8 bytes of memory. Later, the program needs to store additional 20 floating-point numbers and reallocates the memory accordingly.
Question 1: How much memory is initially allocated for the array in bytes?
Question 2: How much memory is allocated after the reallocation in bytes?

Exercise 3.2 A system uses paging for memory management. The system has a page size of 4 KB (1 KB =

1024 bytes). A program running on this system requires 50000 bytes of memory.

Question 1: How many pages does the program need?

Question 2: What is the total memory allocated for this program in bytes (considering full pages are allocated)?

Exercise 3.3 Consider a system with a virtual address space of 16 MB, physical memory of 4 MB, and a page size of 4 KB.

Question 1: How many entries are there in the page table?

Question 2: If a virtual address is represented as (page number, offset), what is the maximum value for the offset?

Exercise 3.4 A system uses demand paging. It has a page size of 8 KB, and the average page-fault service time is 10 milliseconds.

Question: If a program generates a page fault once every 1000 memory references, what is the effective memory access time? Assume that the time to service a page fault is 100 times the time to access memory.

3.9 Solutions to Review Questions

3.1 C; 3.2 D; 3.3 D; 3.4 D; 3.5 D; 3.6 C; 3.7 A; 3.8 D; 3.9 C; 3.10 D; 3.11 C; 3.12 A; 3.13 A; 3.14 B;3.15 C; 3.16 C; 3.17 A; 3.18 C; 3.19 A; 3.20 B; 3.21 D; 3.22 C; 3.23 D; 3.24 A; 3.25 C; 3.26 C; 3.27 A; 3.28 C; 3.29 D; 3.30 A; 3.31 D; 3.32 D; 3.33 A; 3.34 C; 3.35 B; 3.36 C; 3.37 D; 3.38 B; 3.39A; 3.40 D; 3.41 D; 3.42 C; 3.43 D; 3.44 D; 3.45 D; 3.46 C; 3.47 B; 3.48 B; 3.49 B; 3.50 C; 3.51 C; 3.52 C; 3.53 C; 3.54 B; 3.55 D; 3.56 B; 3.57 C; 3.58 D; 3.59 C; 3.60 B; 3.61 B;3.62 B; 3.63 C; 3.64 B; 3.65 B; 3.66 C; 3.67 B; 3.68 C; 3.69 C; 3.70 A; 3.71 B; 3.72 B; 3.73 C; 3.74 A;3.75 B; 3.76 A; 3.77 B; 3.78 B; 3.79 D; 3.80 C; 3.81 B; 3.82 D; 3.83 C; 3.84 D; 3.85 B; 3.86 C; 3.87 D; 3.88 C; 3.89 A; 3.90 B; 3.91 C; 3.92 C; 3.93 C; 3.94 C

Chapter 4 Device Management

Chapter Learning Outcomes

4.1 List the key objectives of device management in computing.
4.2 Describe how device drivers mediate between hardware and software layers.
4.3 Describe various types of mass storage devices
4.4 Describe the concept of I/O hardware in the context of operating system device management

4.1 Introduction

Device management is the process of controlling and coordinating the use of hardware devices by the operating system and other software. It is responsible for tasks such as detecting and configuring devices, allocating resources to devices, and managing device drivers.

4.1.1 Role of Device Management

Device management orchestrates the interaction between hardware devices and software applications. Device management facilitates a crucial abstraction layer that shields software applications from the complexities of hardware interactions. It presents a standardized interface for software to communicate with devices, effectively decoupling application code from hardware specifics. This abstraction fosters portability, allowing applications to function on different hardware configurations without extensive modifications.

Operating systems often manage a multitude of devices with varying capabilities and resource requirements. Device management plays a role in allocating resources such as memory, bandwidth, and processing time among competing devices and processes. It prevents resource conflicts that could otherwise result in system instability or performance degradation.

Device management monitors device health, status, and performance. It detects anomalies and errors, such as hardware failures or communication glitches, and takes appropriate actions. These actions might include alerting system administrators, initiating automatic recovery procedures, or attempting to restart the malfunctioning device.

For end-users, device management enables interaction with hardware peripherals. Whether it's printing a document, connecting a USB drive, or adjusting display settings, the operating system relies on device management to facilitate these interactions and provide a user-friendly experience.

Review Question 4.1
What is the primary purpose of device management in the context of software and hardware interactions?
A) To optimize performance by directly accessing hardware functions
B) To standardize hardware interfaces for software
C) To provide an additional layer for security mechanisms
D) To make applications dependent on hardware specifics

Review Question 4.2
How does device management contribute to the portability of software applications?
A) By increasing the system calls required for I/O operations
B) By simplifying hardware interactions for applications
C) By requiring proprietary libraries for each hardware platform
D) By limiting applications to certified hardware configurations

Review Question 4.3
What role does device management play in resource allocation within an operating system?
A) It isolates hardware resources to designated processes.
B) It prevents resource conflicts among devices and processes.
C) It bypasses the operating system's access mediation.
D) It minimizes the resource requirements of devices.

Review Question 4.4
How does device management respond to anomalies and errors related to hardware devices?
A) It takes no action and ignores errors.
B) It alerts system administrators and initiates automatic recovery procedures.
C) It deallocates hardware resources to isolate points of failure.
D) It reroutes requests to backup devices through redundant channels.

Review Question 4.5
What is one of the benefits of device management for end-users?
A) It isolates end-users from direct hardware management.
B) It reduces the need for user-friendly experiences.
C) It facilitates interactions with hardware peripherals for a user-friendly experience.
D) It makes hardware peripherals independent of the operating system.

Review Question 4.6
How does device management contribute to system stability?

A) By allowing applications to directly access hardware functions
B) By ignoring hardware anomalies and errors
C) By standardizing hardware interfaces
D) By making applications dependent on hardware specifics

4.1.2 Characteristics of Devices and Device Controllers

Devices in a computing system encompass a wide array of hardware peripherals, each tailored to specific tasks and functions. These devices can be broadly categorized based on their functionalities:

1. Input Devices: Input devices, such as keyboards, mice, and touchscreens, enable users to input data into the system. They are responsible for converting user interactions into digital signals that can be processed by the operating system and applications.
2. Output Devices: Output devices, including monitors, printers, and speakers, display or render processed information to users. They convert digital data into human-readable or perceivable forms.
3. Storage Devices: Storage devices, like hard drives, solid-state drives (SSDs), and optical drives, enable data storage and retrieval. They provide persistent storage for applications, files, and system data. Non-volatile memory technologies like magnetic disks and flash memory retain data in the absence of power.
4. Communication Devices: Communication devices, such as network adapters and modems, facilitate data exchange between systems over networks. They enable connectivity and data transmission in both local and wide area networks.

Device controllers act as intermediaries between devices and the operating system. They are specialized hardware components responsible for managing device-specific operations and interactions. The characteristics of device controllers include:

1. Interface Compatibility: Device controllers are tailored to the specific interface standards and protocols of the devices they manage. For example, a USB device controller handles USB communication, while a SATA controller manages data transfers for storage devices using the SATA protocol.
2. Data Translation: Device controllers translate data formats between the device's internal representation and the format understood by the operating system and applications. They handle data encoding, decoding, and protocol conversion.
3. Resource Management: Device controllers manage device-specific resources, such as buffers and registers, required for data transmission and control. They ensure efficient utilization of these resources to optimize device performance.
4. Interrupt Handling: Device controllers generate and handle interrupts to notify the operating system of important events, such as data arrival or completion of a task. Interrupt handling allows timely responses and ensures smooth interaction with devices.
5. Error Detection and Recovery: Device controllers monitor device operations for errors and anomalies. They implement error detection mechanisms, such as parity checks or checksums, and initiaterecovery procedures when errors are detected.

Review Question 4.7
Which of the following is a key responsibility of input devices in a computing system?
A) Translating digital data into human-readable form
B) Enabling persistent storage of data
C) Facilitating network connectivity
D) Converting user interactions into digital signals

Review Question 4.8
What aspect of storage devices enables the persistent retention of data even when the system power is off?
A) High transmission speeds
B) Large data buffers
C) Non-volatile memory
D) Standardized interfaces

Review Question 4.9
Which characteristic of device controllers enables them to communicate properly with associated devices?
A) Interrupt handling
B) Resource optimization
C) Interface compatibility
D) Error recovery mechanisms

Review Question 4.10
How does interrupt handling by device controllers facilitate timely system response to external events?
A) By decreasing power consumption of devices
B) By minimizing errors in data transfers
C) By allowing preemptive multitasking
D) By notifying the OS of events needing attention

Review Question 4.11
What mechanism do device controllers use to detect errors in device operations?
A) Parity and checksums
B) Priority scheduling
C) Mutual exclusion
D) Overprovisioning

4.2 Drivers

A device driver is a software program that allows the operating system to communicate with a specific hardware device. It provides a layer of abstraction between the operating system and the hardware, so that the operating system does not need to know the details of how the hardware works. Device drivers are typically written in C or C++ and are loaded into the operating system kernel when the device is first attached to the system.

4.2.1 Role of Device Drivers

Device drivers facilitate the interaction between hardware devices and the software layers of an operating system. It serves as a bridge between the operating system and hardware devices. It provides a standardized interface that allows the operating system and applications to communicate with and control hardware peripherals effectively. Device drivers act as translators, enabling higher level software to issue commands and receive data from devices without needing to understand the intricacies of device-specific communication protocols.

Device drivers perform a range of essential functions that enable efficient communication and interaction with hardware devices:

1. Device Initialization: Device drivers initialize hardware devices upon system boot or device connection. This includes setting up device registers, configuring communication parameters, and ensuring the device is ready for operation.
2. Data Translation: Device drivers translate higher-level software requests and data formats into instructions that the hardware device understands. They ensure that data is formatted correctly for device-specific communication protocols.
3. Interrupt Handling: Device drivers manage interrupts generated by hardware devices to signal important events. They handle interrupt requests and ensure that the operating system is promptly notified of events like data arrival or device errors.
4. Resource Allocation: Device drivers allocate and manage resources required for devicecommunication. This includes managing memory buffers, device registers, and other resources needed for data transfer and control.
5. Error Handling: Device drivers monitor device operations for errors and anomalies. They implement error detection mechanisms and recovery procedures to maintain the reliability and stability of the system.
6. Power Management: Device drivers are involved in managing power states of devices to optimize energy consumption. They may put devices in low-power modes when they are not actively used and bring them back to full power when needed.

Device drivers exhibit various models and interfaces, contingent upon the specific operating systemand underlying hardware architecture. These distinctions are paramount in comprehending how these drivers facilitate hardware-software interaction. The different models include monolithic drivers, microkernel drivers, and user-space drivers.

The monolithic drivers are ingrained within the operating system's kernel and hold direct access to hardware components. This setup ensures efficient performance, allowing for swift communication between software and hardware. However, a caveat is that encountering errors within these drivers could potentially impinge on the overall system stability.

In contrast, microkernel-based operating systems opt for an architecture where drivers operate outside the kernel. While this approach bolsters system stability by keeping drivers separate from the kernel, there might be a trade-off involving a slight reduction in performance efficiency.

Another model involves user-space drivers, which function within a distinct domain from the kernel. These drivers prioritize system stability by isolating them from the kernel's sensitive functions. However, this arrangement could introduce additional overhead due to the necessity for frequent user-kernel transitions. As such, the choice of driver model often hinges on a balancing act between performance optimization and system stability, all while considering the unique requirements of the operating system and hardware configuration.

Here's an analogy from real-world. Think of a device driver as an interpreter facilitating communication between international delegates. The delegates (applications) speak different languages (communication protocols), and the interpreter (device driver) translates messages (data)between them, ensuring smooth communication despite language barriers.

Review Question 4.12
What is the primary role of device drivers in computing?
A) To optimize performance by bypassing software abstraction layers
B) To provide a standardized interface for hardware and software interaction
C) To directly control hardware components without software intervention
D) To minimize the need for communication protocols

Review Question 4.13
What function do device drivers perform during device initialization?
A) Translating communication protocols
B) Configuring communication parameters
C) Handling interrupts
D) Managing power states

Review Question 4.14
How do device drivers contribute to efficient communication with hardware devices?
A) By directly controlling hardware components
B) By minimizing the need for communication protocols
C) By translating higher-level software requests
D) By handling system boot processes

Review Question 4.15

What is the role of device drivers in managing interrupts generated by hardware devices?
A) Handling power management
B) Configuring communication parameters
C) Managing interrupt requests
D) Translating communication protocols

Review Question 4.16
In which device driver model are drivers integrated within the operating system's kernel?
A) Microkernel drivers
B) User-space drivers
C) Monolithic drivers
D) Kernelless drivers

Review Question 4.17
What is a potential advantage of microkernel-based operating systems in terms of device drivers?
A) Improved performance efficiency
B) Enhanced system stability
C) Direct access to hardware components
D) Simplified communication protocols

Review Question 4.18
What is the primary concern with user-space drivers?
A) Slower device initialization
B) Frequent user-kernel transitions
C) Reduced system stability
D) Limited access to hardware components

Review Question 4.19
How can you describe the choice of device driver model in terms of system performance and stability?
A) Performance optimization always outweighs system stability.
B) There is no impact on system performance or stability.
C) It involves a balancing act between performance and stability.
D) System stability is not a consideration in driver model selection.

Review Question 4.20
What real-world analogy can help understand the role of a device driver?
A) A chef preparing a meal
B) A tour guide leading a group
C) An interpreter facilitating communication between international delegates
D) A traffic controller directing vehicles

4.2.2 Driver Interfaces

Device drivers provide interfaces that allow applications to interact with hardware devices in a standardized manner. These interfaces ensure that application developers can utilize device capabilities without needing to understand the intricate details of device communication.

Driver interfaces typically consist of four part. The first part is application programming interface (API). The API defines the functions and methods that applications can use to communicate with the device. This abstracts away the complexity of device-specific communication protocols and operations.

The second part is device file system. Many operating systems represent devices as files in the filesystem. The device file system provides a uniform way for applications to access devices using file operations like reading and writing.

The third part is control and configuration interfaces. Drivers often expose interfaces for configuring device settings and parameters. This allows applications to tailor device behavior to their specific needs.

The final part is interrupt handlers. Drivers provide mechanisms for applications to register interrupt handlers that respond to specific device events. This enables applications to be notified of events like data arrival without continuously polling the device.

Review Question 4.21
What is the primary purpose of the application programming interface (API) in device drivers?
A) To directly control hardware devices
B) To represent devices as files in the file system
C) To define functions for application-device communication
D) To manage interrupt handlers for device events

Review Question 4.22
How does the device file system facilitate application-device interaction?
A) By providing control and configuration interfaces
B) By exposing interrupt handlers
C) By representing devices as files in the file system
D) By directly accessing hardware registers

Review Question 4.23
What purpose do control and configuration interfaces serve in device drivers?
A) They manage interrupt handlers.
B) They provide a standardized API.
C) They tailor device behavior to specific application needs.
D) They define functions for device communication.

Review Question 4.24
What is the role of interrupt handlers in device drivers?
A) They define functions for application-device communication.

B) They provide mechanisms for accessing device files.
C) They abstract device-specific communication protocols.
D) They allow applications to respond to specific device events.

Review Question 4.25
Which part of the device driver interface abstracts the complexity of device-specific communication
protocols and operations?
A) Control and configuration interfaces
B) Device file system
C) Interrupt handlers
D) Application programming interface (API)

4.2.3 Character vs Block Device Drivers

In device management, the distinction between character device drivers and block device drivers constitutes
a crucial underpinning that governs how data is accessed, manipulated, and communicated between
hardware devices and software layers of an operating system.

Character device drivers are tailored for devices that interact with data on a character-by-characterbasis,
without concern for data block structures. These drivers facilitate stream-oriented communication, where
data is accessed sequentially and treated as a continuous stream. In the context of character-oriented
communication, these drivers facilitate the seamless flow of data in an unbroken stream, akin to the process
of reading from or writing to a file. Notable instances ofcharacter devices encompass input peripherals like
keyboards, mice, terminals, and serial ports.

The role of character device drivers lies in managing input-output (I/O) operations on an individual
character basis. With each character that is read or written, these drivers meticulously oversee the process,
making them particularly well-suited for devices where data is handled without adherence to a
predetermined block structure. An additional notable aspect is that character devices typically do not adopt
block buffering mechanisms. The rationale behind this choice lies in the fact that these devices do not
operate with fixed data blocks. Consequently, each individual character is processed promptly as it is read
orwritten, ensuring the continuity and integrity of the data flow.

In contrast, block device drivers are tailored to devices that operate by processing fixed-size data blocks,
such as sectors found in storage devices. These drivers are adept at overseeing block-based data
management, where the manipulation and retrieval of data occur in predefined block units. Devices

managed by block device drivers interact with data in unvarying block sizes. This design renders them particularly suitable for hardware like hard drives, solid-state drives (SSDs), and optical drives. Each block is standardized to contain a specific quantity of data, such as 512 bytes or 4 KB. Block device drivers are responsible for orchestrating input-output (I/O) operations on a per-block basis. The process of reading or writing data involves accessing entire blocks of information, and the operating system assumes the management of these data block-level read and write activities.

Block devices often incorporate block buffering mechanisms as part of their operational strategy to optimize I/O operations. This mechanism involves storing data in buffers, thus reducing the frequency of physical read and write interactions with the device. By minimizing these interactions, block buffering aims to enhance overall efficiency in data handling.

Selecting the appropriate driver type depends on the characteristics and functionalities of the device. The character device drivers are suitable for devices that process data as a continuous stream, without a fixed block structure. They are commonly used for devices where data arrives in asequence, such as input devices like keyboards or serial ports. The block device drivers are ideal fordevices that operate on fixed-size data blocks, such as storage devices. They provide efficient data management for storage-related operations, ensuring that data is accessed and manipulated in predefined block units.

Review Question 4.26
What distinguishes character device drivers from block device drivers in device management?
A) Character drivers handle block-based data management.
B) Block drivers facilitate stream-oriented communication.
C) Character drivers process data character by character.
D) Block drivers manage input-output (I/O) operations on a per-character basis.

Review Question 4.27
Which type of devices are character device drivers particularly suitable for?
A) Storage drives
B) Input peripherals like keyboards
C) Optical drives
D) Solid-state drives (SSDs)

Review Question 4.28
What role do character device drivers play in data management?
A) They manage data in fixed-size blocks.
B) They process data as a continuous stream.
C) They optimize input-output (I/O) operations for storage devices.

D) They enforce data block-level read and write activities.

Review Question 4.29
Why do character devices typically not adopt block buffering mechanisms?
A) Because they process data in fixed-size blocks
B) Because they use standardized block sizes
C) Because they operate with variable block sizes
D) Because they focus on data continuity and integrity

Review Question 4.30
What type of devices are block device drivers designed for?
A) Keyboards and mice
B) Devices with variable block sizes
C) Devices that operate with continuous data streams
D) Storage devices with fixed-size data blocks

Review Question 4.31
How do block device drivers manage input-output (I/O) operations?
A) On a per-character basis
B) On a per-block basis
C) On a per-stream basis
D) On a per-protocol basis

Review Question 4.32
What is the primary advantage of block buffering mechanisms in block device drivers?
A) Reducing the frequency of physical read and write interactions
B) Enabling continuous data stream processing
C) Eliminating the need for standardized block sizes
D) Simplifying data continuity and integrity

Review Question 4.33
When should character device drivers be chosen over block device drivers for a specific device?
A) When the device operates with fixed-size data blocks
B) When data arrives in a continuous stream without a fixed block structure
C) When block buffering mechanisms are required
D) When the device handles data in variable block sizes

4.3 Buffering

Buffering is a technique used in device management to compensate for mismatches in speed between the CPU and I/O devices. CPUs can process data much faster than mechanical devices like disks can read/write it. Without buffering, the CPU would stall waiting on I/O, leading to inefficient utilization. Buffering uses memory buffers to hold data during transfers between fast and slow components.

Common buffering methods include double buffering which uses two alternating buffers, and circular buffers with read/write pointers. Device drivers and controllers implement buffering to optimize flows. Benefits include absorbing data rate mismatches, smoothing data flow, allowing parallelism between CPU and I/O, minimizing costly context switches, and increasing overall efficiency. Buffering is an essential technique to maximize performance of computer systems.

In device management, buffering is a strategy to navigate the inherent discrepancies in data processing speeds between hardware devices and software layers of an operating system. Device speed mismatch arises due to the disparate processing speeds between hardware devices and software applications. Devices often operate at varying speeds, influenced by factors such as device latency, data transmission rates, and internal processing capabilities. Conversely, software applications execute tasks at their own pace, potentially leading to a mismatch in data supply and demand.

Buffering is a fundamental technique that serves as a bridge to synchronize the pace of data exchange between devices and software layers. It involves the creation of intermediate storage areas, known as buffers, where data is temporarily stored before being transferred between the device and the software. This buffering mechanism plays a role in overcoming speed discrepancies by providing many benefits. Buffers act as intermediaries that absorb bursts of data from fast devices and gradually release it to slower software layers. This smoothing effect ensures that data is supplied at a rate that the software can handle, preventing data loss or overload. Buffers enable devices to continue operating even when the software layer experiences delays. This decoupling allows the device to operate at its full speed while the software retrieves and processes data from the buffer at its own pace. Buffers reduce the latency experienced by devices waiting for the software to process data. The device can continue providing data into the buffer, allowing the software to retrieve and process it without causing delays in the device's operation.

Different buffering strategies can be employed to manage device speed mismatch effectively. A single buffer is used to temporarily store data. This is suitable when the device speed mismatch is occasional and the buffer size is sufficient to handle bursts of data. In the double buffer strategy, two buffers are used alternately. While one buffer is being filled by the device, the other buffer is being emptied by the software. This approach ensures continuous data flow without interruptions. The circular buffer,also known as a ring buffer, this strategy involves a fixed-size buffer that wraps around itself. New data overwrites the oldest data when the buffer is full, ensuring a constant flow of data.

Review Question 4.34
What is the primary purpose of buffering in device management?
A) To synchronize the processing speed of hardware devices and software layers
B) To eliminate the need for intermediate storage areas
C) To maximize data transmission rates between devices
D) To prevent the CPU from stalling during I/O operations

Review Question 4.35
Why does buffering play a crucial role in device management?
A) To eliminate the need for device drivers
B) To increase data transmission rates
C) To minimize data supply and demand mismatches
D) To maximize device processing speeds

Review Question 4.36
How do buffers help in device management?
A) By speeding up device operations
B) By increasing data transmission rates
C) By temporarily storing data during transfers
D) By eliminating the need for device drivers

Review Question 4.37
Which buffering strategy uses two alternating buffers to ensure continuous data flow?
A) Single buffer
B) Circular buffer
C) Double buffering
D) Triple buffering

Review Question 4.38
What is the purpose of a circular buffer in device management?
A) To maximize device processing speeds
B) To ensure continuous data flow without interruptions
C) To eliminate the need for intermediate storage areas
D) To prevent data transmission between devices

Review Question 4.39
How does buffering contribute to minimizing device latency in device management?
A) By maximizing data transmission rates
B) By allowing the slower devices to operate at their own pace
C) By reducing the need for device drivers
D) By absorbing bursts of data from fast devices

4.4 Power Management

Power management aims at optimizing energy consumption and enhancing the efficiency of hardware devices within an operating system. Energy consumption is a crucial consideration in modern computing environments. As the number and variety of devices increase, efficient power management becomes paramount. The objectives of power management are multi-faceted.At its core, power management strives to minimize energy consumption exhibited by devices,whether they are in active operation or idle states. By accomplishing this, not only are operational costs reduced, but an equally significant contribution is made to the overarching goal of environmental sustainability.

Particularly relevant in the realm of portable devices such as laptops, smartphones, and tablets, power management strategies ensure that battery life is prolonged to its maximum potential. This extension in battery endurance permits users to engage in work or interaction for extended durations without necessitating frequent recharging.

The efficient implementation of power management mechanisms directly impacts the generation of heat within hardware components. By effectively managing power consumption, the resultant reduction in heat generation has a domino effect, contributing to the enhanced reliability and longevity of these components over time.

Power management strategies vary based on the device type, usage patterns, and desired trade-offs between performance and energy conservation. Devices can enter idle or low-power states when not actively in use. These states reduce power consumption by slowing down or turning off non-essential components. Processors can dynamically adjust their clock frequency based on the workload. Lower frequencies consume less power, makingfrequency scaling an effective strategy for managing power consumption without compromising performance when it's not needed.

Devices can have multiple power states, ranging from fully active to completely powered off. Devices transition between these states based on usage patterns. For instance, hard drives can spindown when not in use. The Dynamic Voltage and Frequency Scaling (DVFS) involves adjusting both voltage and frequency to find an optimal balance between performance and power consumption. This strategy is especially effective for processors. The operating system plays a pivotal role in power management by implementing policies and mechanisms that govern device behavior.

The operating system coordinates device states, ensuringthat devices enter low-power modes when not in use and return to active states when needed. Power management necessitates efficient interrupt handling.

The operating system manages device interrupts, enabling devices to transition between power states without interrupting ongoing tasks. The operating system may provide user-configurable power settings, allowing users to customize power management behavior based on their preferences and usage patterns.

Review Question 4.40
What is the primary objective of power management in an operating system?
A) Maximizing hardware performance
B) Minimizing operational costs
C) Prioritizing energy conservation over performance
D) Ensuring reliability and business continuity

Review Question 4.41
What is one of the benefits of effectively managing power consumption in hardware components?
A) Enhanced user experience
B) Enhanced heat dissipation
C) Enhanced component longevity
D) Maximized hardware performance at all times

Review Question 4.42
Which strategy allows processors to adjust their clock frequency dynamically based on workload?
A) Frequency scaling
B) Voltage adjustment
C) Power states
D) Energy states

Review Question 4.43
Which power management strategy involves adjusting both voltage and frequency to balance performance and power consumption?
A) Frequency scaling
B) Voltage adjustment
C) Power states
D) DVFS

4.5 Mass Storage

Mass storage devices such as hard disks (magnetic disks), USB flash drives, Magnetic Tapes, and SSDs provide non-volatile, high capacity storage to computer systems and users. Managing these devices presents key challenges including performance optimization, reliability, and abstraction.

4.5.1 Magnetic Disks

The magnetic disks are pioneering solutions that have revolutionized data storage and retrieval within computing environments. Magnetic disks consist of multiple platters, each coated with a magnetic material that allows data to be recorded and retrieved through magnetic read/write heads. These platters are stacked on a spindle, forming the core structure of a disk drive. The platters are divided into concentric rings called tracks, which are further subdivided into smaller units known as sectors (512 Bytes). Each sector constitutes the smallest unit of data that can be read from or written to a disk. Magnetic disks operate on the principle of magnetization. Data is stored in the form of magnetic patterns on the platters. When data needs to be read or written, the read/write heads are precisely positioned over the relevant track, allowing the magnetic patterns to be interpreted as binary data.

The process of reading or writing data involves three key steps:

1. Seeking: The read/write heads move to the desired track. This is known as the seek operation and represents the positioning of the heads over the appropriate data location.
2. Rotational Latency: Once the heads are positioned, the platters rotate to bring the desired sector under the heads. This rotational latency represents the time taken for the desired sector to rotate under the read/write heads.
3. Data Transfer: Once the desired sector is under the heads, data is read from or written to the sector. This data transfer phase is characterized by the movement of data between the disk and the computer's memory.

The access time of a magnetic disk, a key performance metric, includes the time needed to read or write data. It is the sum of the seek time, rotational latency, and data transfer time. Seek time, typically ranging from 2-10ms, is the time required to position the heads over the correct track. Rotational latency, averaging around 4ms, is the time for the desired sector to rotate under the heads. Data transfer time depends on factors like the transfer rate between the disk and memory, and can be significant, especially when transferring large amounts of data. While advancements in technology have reduced seek times and rotational latencies, and improved data transfer rates, the dominant factor in access time can vary depending on the specific hardware and the operations being performed. Therefore, it's important to refer to the specifications of the specific hardware for the most accurate information.

Review Question 4.44
What is the smallest unit of data that can be read from or written to a magnetic disk?
A) Platter
B) Track
C) Sector
D) Concentric ring

Review Question 4.45

Which component of access time accounts for the time taken to position the read/write heads over the desired track?
A) Rotational Latency
B) Data Transfer Time
C) Seeking Time
D) Concentric Ring Time

Review Question 4.46
What is the primary principle on which magnetic disks operate for storing and retrieving data?
A) Magnetization
B) Encryption
C) Compression
D) Rotation

Review Question 4.47
Which phase of the data access process involves moving data between the disk and the computer's memory?
A) Rotational Latency
B) Seeking
C) Data Transfer
D) Concentric Ring Transfer

Review Question 4.48
What term describes the concentric rings on a magnetic disk's platters?
A) Sectors
B) Tracks
C) Spindles
D) Concentric Units

4.5.2 Solid State Drives (SSDs)

Solid State Drives (SSDs) are transformative solutions that have revolutionized data storage by prioritizing speed, reliability, and energy efficiency. Unlike traditional magnetic disks, SSDs do not have moving parts, which contributes to their durability. They are constructed using NAND flash memory technology. It refers to a type of flash memory that is named after the NAND logic gate (NOT AND) due to its similarity in operation. This memory is organized into blocks, which are further grouped into larger units called pages. Each page holds a fixed amount of data, typically ranging from 4 KB to 16 KB, although this can vary depending on the specific SSD and its underlying technology.

SSDs operate through the principles of electronic data storage. Data is stored as electrical charges within memory cells, and reading/writing involve manipulating these charges. Compared to traditional hard drives, SSDs offer several distinct advantages.

The absence of mechanical components eliminates seek and rotational latency, resulting in significantly faster access times. This speed is especially noticeable during boot-up, application launching, and data retrieval. With no moving parts, SSDs are more resilient to physical shocks and vibrations. This durability makes them ideal for portable devices and environments prone to mechanical stress.

SSDs consume less power since they don't require energy-intensive spinning of disks. This efficiency contributes to extended battery life in laptops and reduced power consumption in data centers. The lack of moving parts minimizes wear and tear, leading to improved long-term reliability and fewer failures.

However, the technology has its share of shortcomings, as NAND flash memory has a limited number of write cycles before it degrades. To extend the lifespan of SSDs, wear-leveling techniques are employed. These techniques distribute write and erase cycles across memory cells to prevent overuse of specific cells. Additionally, SSDs employ garbage collection mechanisms to reclaim space occupied by deleted data, ensuring optimal performance and preventing storage depletion. Performance metrics for SSDs include read speed, write speed, and input/output operations per second (IOPS). The endurance of an SSD is measured by its terabytes written (TBW), indicating the amount of data that can be written to the drive over its lifespan.

Review Question 4.49
What does NAND stand for in NAND flash memory technology?
A) Notable Android Data
B) New-Age NAND Technology
C) Notable NAND Device
D) NOT AND

Review Question 4.50
How are data stored in Solid State Drives (SSDs)?
A) As magnetic charges on spinning disks
B) As electrical charges within memory cells
C) As mechanical vibrations on moving parts
D) As optical signals on rotating platters

Review Question 4.51
What advantage do SSDs have over traditional hard drives regarding access times?
A) SSDs have faster access times due to enhanced mechanical components.
B) SSDs have faster access times due to enhanced rotational technology.
C) SSDs have faster access times due to the absence of mechanical components.
D) SSDs have faster access times due to their optimal moving parts.

Review Question 4.52
Why are SSDs considered more durable in terms of physical shocks and vibrations?
A) They use magnetic shielding to protect data.
B) They have shock-absorbing casing.
C) They lack moving parts.
D) They have larger memory cells.

Review Question 4.53
What technique is used to extend the lifespan of NAND flash memory in SSDs?
A) Write and erase cycles are not distributed.
B) Wear-leveling techniques are employed.
C) Garbage collection mechanisms are disabled.
D) Data is stored in larger pages.

Review Question 4.54
How is the endurance of an SSD measured?
A) In read speed and write speed
B) In input/output operations per second (IOPS)
C) In terabytes written (TBW)
D) In access times and latency

4.5.3 Redundant Array of Independent Disks (RAIDs)

RAID is a sophisticated strategy to enhance data reliability, availability, and performance by combining multiple physical drives into a single logical unit. It is characterized by its ability to distribute data across multiple disks in a manner that offers redundancy, improved performance, or a combination of both. The primary motivations behind implementing RAID include data protection against disk failures and the optimization of data read and write operations.

RAID encompasses several levels, each offering a unique combination of data protection and performance enhancement. Some prominent RAID levels include:
RAID 0: Known as striping, this level divides data into blocks and writes them to different disks. While it boosts read/write speeds, it offers no redundancy, meaning a single disk failure results in data loss.
RAID 1: Referred to as mirroring, RAID 1 duplicates data across two or more disks, ensuring redundancy. Although read performance improves, write performance may be impacted.
RAID 5: Utilizing block-level striping and parity data, RAID 5 provides redundancy and better performance. Each stripe typically consists of one data block from each of the member drives in the array, along with a parity block. If a single disk fails, data can be reconstructed using parity information of the same stripe. However, if more than one block of data in the same stripe failed, data cannot be recovered.
RAID 6: Similar to RAID 5, RAID 6 incorporates additional parity information, allowing it to withstand the failure of two disks simultaneously. The additional parity makes RAID 6 slower than RAID 5 in most cases.
RAID 10 (1+0): Combining features of RAID 1 and RAID 0, RAID 10 mirrors data and then stripes it across mirrored pairs. This level offers redundancy and high performance.

RAID brings forth a multitude of advantages that significantly contribute to the augmentation of data management. One of the key benefits is the establishment of data redundancy, which stands as a foundational principle in various RAID configurations. This redundancy ensures that data remains readily accessible even when faced with the possibility of disk failures, offering an invaluable layer of protection against potential data loss. Furthermore, RAID introduces the potential for marked improvements in system performance.

Particularly prominent in certain RAID levels, such as those centered around striping, this enhancement becomes palpable in the realm of data read and write operations. Through the distribution of data across multiple disks and the utilization of parallel processing, RAID delivers noticeable performance boosts, facilitating swifter and more efficient data handling.

An additional advantage of RAID pertains to its cost-effectiveness. By adopting an approach that involves the integration of multiple smaller disks instead of relying solely on a single, larger disk, RAID offers an economical path to achieving both redundancy and performance enhancements. Large disks often have a premium cost per TB due to higher manufacturing costs and demand. The per unit storage cost tends to decline for smaller disks. This strategic utilization of hardware resources results in a judicious allocation of resources, allowing organizations to optimize their data management capabilities without incurring excessive costs.

In essence, RAID's suite of benefits encompasses the fortification of data integrity through redundancy, the enhancement of operational speed through performance optimization, and the astute use of resources to achieve an equilibrium between functionality and cost-effectiveness.

Review Question 4.55
What is the primary motivation behind implementing RAID?
A) Enhancing system aesthetics
B) Protecting data against disk failures
C) Increasing system power consumption
D) Reducing hardware costs

Review Question 4.56
Which RAID level offers redundancy and better performance through block-level striping and parity data?
A) RAID 0
B) RAID 1
C) RAID 5

D) RAID 6

Review Question 4.57
What RAID level can withstand the failure of two disks simultaneously?
A) RAID 0
B) RAID 1
C) RAID 5
D) RAID 6

Review Question 4.58
Which RAID level combines mirroring and striping to provide redundancy and high performance?
A) RAID 0
B) RAID 1
C) RAID 5
D) RAID 10 (1+0)

Review Question 4.59
What is the key benefit of data redundancy in RAID configurations?
A) Improved system aesthetics
B) Enhanced system cooling
C) Protection against potential data loss
D) Reduced hardware complexity

Review Question 4.60
How does RAID contribute to cost-effectiveness?
A) By decreasing power consumption
B) By using a single, larger disk
C) By integrating multiple smaller disks
D) By minimizing data redundancy

Review Question 4.61
What does RAID offer through the utilization of parallel processing and the distribution of data across multiple disks?
A) Improved data security
B) Reduced data redundancy
C) Noticeable performance boosts
D) Decreased hardware flexibility

4.6 Components of the I/O Subsystem

The I/O subsystem in an operating system encompasses the supporting infrastructure needed to manage and coordinate input/output operations. It provides a software abstraction layer on top of physical devices to offer uniform I/O access across hardware. It is responsible for transferring data between the CPU and the devices, as well as for managing the devices themselves.

4.6.1 The I/O Hardware

I/O hardware serves as the bridge that connects the CPU and the peripheral devices, ranging from storage devices to input/output devices. Its primary purpose lies in facilitating the smooth exchange of data between the CPU and these peripherals, ensuring that computations are able to interact with the external world in a coherent and timely manner. I/O hardware relies on dedicated ports and addresses to establish communication with the CPU. These ports serve as endpoints for data transfer, and each device possesses a distinct I/O address through which it can be accessed by the CPU.

Control registers within I/O hardware play a crucial role in governing the behavior of devices. These registers store configuration information, status flags, and control commands that facilitate device operation and communication.

To prevent bottlenecks and ensure smooth data flow, I/O hardware often incorporates data buffers. These temporary storage areas act as intermediaries between the CPU and devices, allowing for efficient data transfer. Data paths within the I/O hardware dictate the route through which data travels between the CPU, memory, and devices.

I/O hardware employs synchronization mechanisms to ensure harmonious communication. These mechanisms coordinate data transfer between devices and the CPU, preventing data loss or corruption.

Interrupts are central to the functioning of I/O hardware. When a peripheral device requires attention or data transfer is complete, the device issues an interrupt signal to the CPU, prompting it to divertits attention to the relevant task. This asynchronous communication prevents the CPU from being continuously engaged in polling for device status.

Direct Memory Access (DMA) is a technique that allows peripheral devices to directly access main memory, bypassing the CPU. This enables faster and more efficient data transfer between devices and memory, freeing up the CPU for other tasks.

Review Question 4.62
What is the primary purpose of I/O hardware?

A) Processing data
B) Storing data
C) Facilitating data exchange between CPU and peripherals
D) Controlling the system clock

Review Question 4.63
How do dedicated ports and addresses relate to I/O hardware?
A) They serve as temporary storage areas
B) They store configuration information
C) They facilitate communication with the CPU
D) They control the system clock

Review Question 4.64
What role do control registers play in I/O hardware?
A) Storing data buffers
B) Storing control commands and status flags
C) Coordinating data transfer between devices
D) Managing memory allocation

Review Question 4.65
What purpose do data buffers in I/O hardware serve?
A) They control device operation
B) They store configuration information
C) They facilitate efficient data transfer
D) They synchronize data transfer

Review Question 4.66
What role do synchronization mechanisms play in I/O hardware?
A) They manage memory allocation
B) They store data buffers
C) They coordinate data transfer between devices and the CPU
D) They control the system clock

Review Question 4.67
What is the purpose of interrupts in I/O hardware?
A) To store configuration information
B) To control device operation
C) To continuously poll for device status
D) To prompt the CPU to divert attention to relevant tasks

Review Question 4.68
What is the role of Direct Memory Access (DMA) in I/O hardware?
A) To control the system clock
B) To store control commands
C) To directly access main memory, bypassing the CPU
D) To synchronize data transfer

Review Question 4.69
Why is Direct Memory Access (DMA) beneficial in I/O operations?

A) It controls device operation.
B) It stores configuration information.
C) It allows faster and more efficient data transfer.
D) It continuously polls for device status.

4.6.2 Principles of I/O Software

The principles of I/O software facilitate the interaction between the central processing unit (CPU) and various peripheral devices. I/O software serves as the critical intermediary that bridges the gap between the CPU and the diverse array of peripheral devices. Its primary objective is to streamline data communication, ensure data integrity, and manage the exchange of information between the CPU and external devices in a coherent and organized manner.

Before we discuss the principles of I/O software, let's take a look at the two components of I/O software. The device independence layer (DIL) is a foundational component of I/O software. It abstracts the specific details of each individual device, allowing applications to interact with devices using a standardized interface. The DIL is a layer of software that sits between the operating system and the I/O driver layer. This layer shields applications from the intricacies of various device models and enables seamless transition between different devices.

The I/O drivers constitute the heart of I/O software. These drivers are specialized programs designed to facilitate communication between the operating system and specific hardware devices. They interpret high-level I/O requests from applications and translate them into low-level commands that devices can understand. I/O drivers play a pivotal role in ensuring efficient data transfer, error handling, and device management.

One of the fundamental principles of I/O software is device independence. By providing a uniform interface for accessing devices, the software shields applications from the intricacies of various devices. This independence simplifies application development and maintenance, as applications remain unaffected by changes in underlying hardware.

I/O software employs the principles of abstraction and virtualization to present devices as logical entities with standardized behaviors. Abstraction hides the technical complexities of devices, while virtualization creates the illusion of multiple instances of a single device, enabling efficient sharing and resource allocation.

I/O software incorporates buffering and caching mechanisms to optimize data transfer. Buffers temporarily hold data during transmission, allowing for smoother communication between devices and the CPU. Caches store frequently accessed data in memory, reducing the need for repeated access to slower external devices.

Review Question 4.70
What is the primary objective of I/O software?
A) To shield the CPU from external devices
B) To manage device models
C) To streamline data communication and manage information exchange
D) To replace peripheral devices

Review Question 4.71
What is the role of the device independence layer in I/O software?
A) To manage I/O drivers
B) To shield applications from device details and provide a standardized interface
C) To translate high-level I/O requests
D) To optimize data transfer

Review Question 4.72
What are I/O drivers in I/O software?
A) High-level I/O requests from applications
B) Specialized programs that facilitate communication with specific hardware devices
C) Virtualized instances of devices
D) Cache management tools

Review Question 4.73
What fundamental principle of I/O software simplifies application development and maintenance?
A) Device complexity
B) Device independence
C) Abstraction
D) Virtualization

Review Question 4.74
How does I/O software employ the principle of virtualization?
A) By hiding technical complexities of devices
B) By creating the illusion of multiple instances of a single device
C) By optimizing data transfer
D) By translating high-level I/O requests

Review Question 4.75
What do buffering mechanisms in I/O software temporarily hold during transmission?
A) I/O drivers
B) High-level I/O requests
C) Data

D) Error messages

Review Question 4.76
What do caches in I/O software store to reduce the need for repeated access to slower external devices?
A) Error messages
B) Virtualized instances of devices
C) Frequently accessed data in memory
D) I/O drivers

Review Question 4.77
Which component of I/O software interprets high-level I/O requests from applications andtranslates them into low-level commands for devices?
A) Device independence layer
B) Abstraction layer
C) Virtualization layer
D) I/O drivers

4.6.3 I/O Software Layers

Within the domain of the I/O subsystem, the I/O software layers emerge as a hierarchical framework that orchestrates and manages the intricate process of data communication between the central processing unit (CPU) and peripheral devices. The architecture of I/O software layers is structured in a hierarchical manner, each layer building upon the foundation of the layer beneath it. This layering ensures modular and organized management of data communication, enabling efficient interaction between the CPU and a variety of peripheral devices.

The uppermost layer, often referred to as user-level I/O libraries, provides high-level interfaces that shield application programs from the complexities of underlying hardware. These libraries offer standardized functions and commands for I/O operations, enabling applications to request data transfers without needing to delve into low-level details.

The middle layer, known as the operating system I/O supervisor, acts as an intermediary between user level applications and device-specific drivers. It translates high-level I/O requests from applications into device-independent commands that can be understood by various hardware devices. The I/O supervisor manages device allocation, scheduling, and error handling.

The lowest layer comprises device drivers, which directly interface with hardware devices. These drivers translate the commands from the operating system I/O supervisor into device-specific instructions. Device drivers manage device initialization, data transfer, and error reporting, ensuring effective communication with peripheral devices.

The I/O software layers provide two major functions. First is abstraction and virtualization. Each layer of the I/O software hierarchy contributes to abstraction and virtualization. The user-level libraries abstract the complexities of hardware devices, while the I/O supervisor creates a virtualized environment that presents devices as logical entities with standardized behaviors. This abstraction simplifies application development and device management.

Second is efficient resource utilization. I/O software layers ensure efficient resource utilization by managing device allocation, scheduling, and data buffering. The operating system I/O supervisor optimizes the sharing of devices among multiple applications, preventing resource contention and ensuring fair access.

Review Question 4.78
What is the primary role of the user-level I/O libraries in the I/O software hierarchy?
A) Managing device drivers
B) Shielding applications from hardware complexities
C) Translating high-level I/O requests
D) Interfacing directly with hardware devices

Review Question 4.79
What function does the operating system I/O supervisor serve in the I/O software hierarchy?
A) Directly managing hardware devices
B) Translating high-level I/O requests into device-independent commands
C) Managing device initialization
D) Providing standardized interfaces for applications

Review Question 4.80
Which layer of the I/O software hierarchy is responsible for interfacing directly with hardware devices?
A) User-level I/O libraries
B) Operating system I/O supervisor
C) Device drivers
D) Abstraction layer

Review Question 4.81
What is the primary benefit of abstraction in the I/O software layers?
A) Device initialization
B) Simplifying application development and device management
C) Managing device allocation
D) Resource utilization

Review Question 4.82
What is the role of the I/O supervisor in managing resource utilization?
A) Managing device initialization
B) Optimizing sharing of devices among multiple applications
C) Shielding applications from hardware complexities
D) Translating high-level I/O requests

Review Question 4.83
Which layer of the I/O software hierarchy provides standardized functions and commands for I/O operations?
A) Abstraction layer
B) User-level I/O libraries
C) Operating system I/O supervisor
D) Device drivers

Review Question 4.84
Which layer directly manages device initialization, data transfer, and error reporting?
A) User-level I/O libraries
B) Abstraction layer
C) Operating system I/O supervisor
D) Device drivers

4.7 Chapter Summary

In this chapter, you learn the critical aspects of device management within an operating system (OS). It explores the fundamental concepts of device controllers and drivers, elucidating their roles in facilitating communication between the OS and hardware devices. The chapter also discusses buffering mechanisms, emphasizing their importance in optimizing data transfer efficiency. Furthermore, it delves into power management strategies, highlighting the OS's role in conserving energy. Mass storage and the intricacies of handling diverse input and output devices within the I/O subsystem are also comprehensively covered in this chapter.

4.8 Exercise

Exercise 4.1
Disk Access Time Calculation Suppose a disk has an average seek time of 5ms, an average rotational latency of 4ms, and a data transfer rate of 50MB/s. If a program needs to read a file of size 10MB from the disk, calculate the total time required to read the file from the disk.

Exercise 4.2
Disk Capacity Calculation Consider a magnetic disk with 2000 tracks per surface, 100 sectors per track, and

each sector can hold 512 Bytes of data. If the disk has 2 platters (4 surfaces), calculate the total storage capacity of the disk in GB.

Exercise 4.3

RAID Level 0 - Data Distribution Calculation Suppose a file of size 500MB needs to be stored in a RAID 0 configuration with 5 disks. Calculate how much data will be stored on each disk if the data is divided into blocks and written evenly across the disks.

Exercise 4.4

RAID Level 5 - Parity Calculation Consider a RAID 5 configuration with 4 disks. If each disk has a capacity of 1TB, calculate the total usable storage capacity considering that RAID 5 uses block-level striping with parity data. Remember, in RAID 5, one disk's worth of space is used for parity information to provide redundancy.

4.9 Solutions to Review Questions

4.1 B; 4.2 B; 4.3 B; 4.4 B; 4.5 C; 4.6 C; 4.7 D; 4.8 C; 4.9 C; 4.10 D; 4.11 A; 4.12 B; 4.13 B; 4.14 C;4.15 C; 4.16 C; 4.17 B; 4.18 B; 4.19 C; 4.20 C; 4.21 C; 4.22 C; 4.23 C; 4.24 D; 4.25 D; 4.26 C; 4.27 B;4.28 B; 4.29 D; 4.30 D; 4.31 B; 4.32 A; 4.33 B; 4.34 A; 4.35 C; 4.36 C; 4.37 C; 4.38 B; 4.39 D; 4.40 C;4.41 C; 4.42 A; 4.43 D; 4.44 C; 4.45 C; 4.46 A; 4.47 C; 4.48 B; 4.49 D; 4.50 B; 4.51 C; 4.52 C;4.53 B; 4.54 C; 4.55 B; 4.56 C; 4.57 D; 4.58 D; 4.59 C; 4.60 C; 4.61 C; 4.62 C; 4.63 C; 4.64 B;4.65 C; 4.66 C; 4.67 D; 4.68 C; 4.69 C; 4.70 C; 4.71 B; 4.72 B; 4.73 B; 4.74 B; 4.75 C; 4.76 C; 4.77 D; 4.78 B; 4.79 B; 4.80 C; 4.81 B; 4.82 B; 4.83 B; 4.84 D;

Chapter 5 File Management

Chapter Learning Outcomes

5.1 Demonstrate a good understanding of file organization
5.2 Demonstrate a clear understanding of the directory structure
5.3 Remember key characteristics and features of various file system types
5.4 Demonstrate a foundational knowledge of file management.
5.5 Explain the significance of security measures in safeguarding data against incidents.

5.1 Introduction to File Management

In operating systems, the file management component orchestrates the organization, storage, retrieval, and manipulation of data in a coherent and structured manner. File management is the bedrock upon which data organization and access are built within an operating system. It encompasses the tasks of creating, naming, storing, retrieving, and organizing digital information, ranging from text documents to multimedia files. Files serve as digital containers that hold data, enabling users and applications to interact with information in a structured manner. Let's take a look at the key components of file management.

At the heart of file management lies the file system, a complex hierarchical structure that organizes files and directories in a manner analogous to a digital filesystem. It provides the framework for data storage, retrieval, and management. Different operating systems utilize diverse file systems, each with its own characteristics and capabilities.

Files possess a multitude of attributes that provide metadata about their properties. These attributes include the file's name, size, creation date, modification date, permissions, and ownership details. These attributes facilitate effective categorization, search, and manipulation of files.

Files are organized within directories, forming a hierarchical structure. Directories act as containers for files and other directories, creating an organized framework for efficient data management. This structure mirrors the way physical files are organized in cabinets and drawers.

This organization ensures that files are logically arranged, enhancing ease of retrieval. File management systems implement mechanisms to safeguard data integrity and security. This includes access controls, permissions, encryption, and backup strategies that prevent unauthorized access, data loss, and corruption. Effective file management systems facilitate swift and efficient data retrieval. Users can locate specific files through search queries, and applications can access data without unnecessary delays.

Review Question 5.1
What is the primary function of the file management component in operating systems?
A) Data encryption
B) Data retrieval
C) Avoid data corruption
D) Minimize data loss

Review Question 5.2
What is the purpose of the file system in file management?
A) Data encryption
B) Data retrieval
C) Data storage framework
D) Data modification

Review Question 5.3
How are files organized within file management?
A) In a linear structure
B) In a random structure
C) In a hierarchical structure
D) In a circular structure

Review Question 5.4
What mechanisms are implemented by file management systems to safeguard data integrity and security?
A) File deletion
B) Data duplication
C) Access controls, permissions, encryption, and backup strategies
D) File renaming

5.2 File System Concepts

Files are a fundamental abstraction used to store and retrieve data in computer systems. A file represents a logical storage unit consisting of a related collection of bytes or records that appear as a contiguous sequence to the user. Files have metadata attributes like name, type, size, protection level, owner, timestamps, etc. that describe and manage them. The operating system provides file operations like create, open, read, write, close, and delete to manipulate files. Files are mapped by the file system to their actual physical storage organization on disk. This separation enables more flexible and reliable access. Effective file management enables naming, organization, storage, retrieval and sharing of persistent data in computer systems through file abstractions independent of physical storage details.

5.2.1 Files and Metadata Attributes

At the core of file management within an operating system lies the relationship between files and their associated metadata attributes. Files represent the fundamental units of data in a computing environment. A file can contain various types of information, ranging from text and images to multimedia content and program code. Each file is assigned a unique name that facilitates identification and access. Files encapsulate data in a format that can be easily interpreted and utilized by applications and users.

Metadata attributes provide essential context and information about files, allowing the operating system and users to understand and manage the characteristics of each file. These attributes are integral to effective file management and enhance the usability and accessibility of digital information. The following are some key metadata attributes:

File Name: The file name is a fundamental metadata attribute that serves as the primary identifier for a file. A well-chosen and descriptive file name enables users to quickly recognize the content and purpose of the file.
File Size: The file size attribute indicates the amount of storage space occupied by a file. This attribute is crucial for optimizing storage and assessing the feasibility of transferring or sharing files. In a plain text file, one character takes one byte. Therefore, 1024 characters count as 1KB (kilobyte).
Creation and Modification Timestamps: The creation timestamp records the date and time when a file was initially created, while the modification timestamp indicates the last time the file was modified. These attributes provide historical context and assist in tracking changes to files over time.
File Type and Format: The file type attribute signifies the format or content type of the file. Different file types are associated with distinct applications and behaviors. For instance, a .txt file is typically associated with plain text, while a .jpg file is associated with image data.
Access Permissions: Access permissions control who can interact with a file and the type of interactions allowed. These permissions ensure data security and restrict unauthorized access or modifications.
Ownership Information: Ownership attributes indicate the owner of the file and the associated group.

Metadata attributes enable the categorization and classification of files. This categorization simplifies data organization, making it easier to manage and navigate large volumes of information. Attributes such as creation and modification timestamps assist in version control, enabling users to track changes and restore previous versions of files if necessary.

An inode (index node) is a data structure used in many file systems, including Unix and Linux. It contains the metadata attributes of a file. In addition to the attributes mentioned above, an inode also contains pointers to the data blocks of the file. These pointers are what allow the file system to locate the actual data of the file on the disk. Pointers to data blocks store the addresses of the disk blocks that store the file's actual data. When a file is accessed, the operating system uses the inode number to quickly locate the file's metadata without having to search the entire filesystem. An important point to note is that the inode does not store the file data itself. Instead, it contains pointers to the blocks that hold the actual data.

Review Question 5.5
What uniquely identifies a file within a file system?
A) File type
B) File size
C) File name
D) Creation timestamp

Review Question 5.6
What is the primary purpose of file metadata attributes in file management within an operating system?
A) To store the content of the file
B) To provide essential context and information about files
C) To control access to the file
D) To assign unique names to files

Review Question 5.7
Which metadata attribute controls who can interact with a file and the type of interactions allowed?
A) File Name
B) File Size
C) Access Permissions
D) Ownership Information

Review Question 5.8
How do metadata attributes assist in version control?
A) They provide access permissions.
B) They indicate the owner of the file.
C) They record creation timestamps.
D) They help track changes and restore previous versions of files.

5.2.2 Operations on Files

File operations enable users and applications to interact with digital information. The creation of a file marks the inception of a digital entity that can hold various forms of data. When a file is created, it is assigned a unique name, which becomes its primary identifier. Creation can occur through user initiated actions or as a result of application-generated content.

Opening a file involves initiating access to its content for reading or writing. When a file is opened, the operating system establishes a communication channel between the file and the requesting application. This allows data to be transferred between the file and the application.

Reading from a file involves extracting data from the file's content and transferring it to an application or user. Reading enables applications to retrieve information stored within files and use it for various purposes.

Writing to a file involves adding new data or modifying existing data within the file's content. Writing enables applications to update files with new information, which can include user input, program output, or configuration changes.

Deleting a file involves removing it from the file system. When a file is deleted, its associated storage space is marked as available for reuse. However, the actual content of the file may not be immediately erased from the storage medium.

There are two major modes of execution in file systems. In sequential access, data is read from or written to a file in a linear manner, one item at a time. This mode is suitable for scenarios where data is processed in the order it appears within the file. On the contrary, random access enables data to be read from or written to any location within a file, regardless of the sequential order. This mode is ideal for situations where non-sequential data access is required, such as search.

Review Question 5.9
What does "sequential access" mode in file systems entail?
A) Reading or writing data from or to a file in any order
B) Reading or writing data from or to a file in a linear manner, one item at a time
C) Creating a new file with a unique name
D) Deleting a file from the file system

Review Question 5.10
What happens when a file is deleted in a computer file system?
A) The file's content is immediately erased from the storage medium.
B) The file's associated storage space is marked as available for reuse.
C) The file's unique name is changed.
D) The file's content is compressed to save space.

Review Question 5.11
In which mode of execution can data be read from or written to any location within a file, regardless of sequential order?
A) Sequential access
B) Reading access
C) Random access
D) Linear access

Review Question 5.12
What is the primary function of reading from a file in a computer system?
A) To create a new file
B) To initiate access to a file's content for writing
C) To extract data from the file's content and transfer it to an application or user
D) To add new data or modify existing data within the file's content

5.2.3 File Storage Organization on Disks

The organization of files on physical storage devices influences efficiency, performance, and accessibility of an operating system. File storage on disk involves the allocation of physical storage space to accommodate the content of files. Storage devices, such as hard drives or solid-state drives, serve as the repositories for files, holding the digital information in a structured manner that optimizes retrieval and manipulation.

File storage on disk revolves around the concepts of blocks and sectors. A block is the smallest unit of data that can be read from or written to a storage device. A sector, on the other hand, is the smallest physical storage unit on a disk. Files are divided into blocks, which are then mapped to sectors for actual storage.

Various disk allocation methods determine how files are stored on disk. In contiguous allocation, the blocks of a file are stored next to each other or contiguously on the disk. This enables the disk head to access the entire file without significant seeking. It provides faster sequential access compared to non-contiguous allocation methods like linked or indexed allocation where file blocks are scattered. Contiguous allocation does lead to external fragmentation over time as files cannot grow beyond their initial allocation easily.

In linked allocation, files are stored as linked lists of blocks, each file block contains a pointer to the next block in the chain. This enables files to occupy non-contiguous blocks on disk. As files grow, new blocks can be allocated from anywhere on disk and linked. If files shrink, blocks can be deallocated. This provides more flexibility compared to contiguous allocation where files are restricted to their initial set of contiguous blocks. However, linked allocation leads to slower access times as blocks are scattered.

The indexed allocation aims to provide the advantages of both contiguous and linked allocation for file storage. In indexed allocation, each file is given its own index block that stores pointers to the data blocks making up the file. The key idea is that the index block is stored in a fixed location on disk that can be directly accessed, while the data blocks can be located anywhere on the disk - they don't need to be contiguously stored. When a file is accessed in indexed allocation, the file system first retrieves the index block by its known location. The index block contains addresses pointing to each data block of the file. The filesystem can then follow the pointers in a random access fashion to fetch the desired data blocks, regardless of where they are physically located on disk. This enables indexed allocation to support fast direct access to any file block through the index without needing to traverse a linked list sequentially. It also minimizes external fragmentation, since files can grow flexibly by allocating new data blocks from anywhere on disk, then updating the index block pointers. However, indexed allocation requires space to store index blocks, adding metadata overhead. Managing dynamic index blocks also increases programming complexity and index corruption can make files inaccessible. Overall, indexed allocation trades this complexity for the combined benefits of both contiguous and linked allocation.

Efficient file storage organization enhances data accessibility by optimizing the placement of files on disk. Well-structured organization methods minimize delays in retrieving data. In addition, file storage organization affects space utilization on storage devices. Effective organization methods aim to minimize wastage and fragmentation of storage space.

Review Question 5.13
What is the smallest unit of data that can be read from or written to a storage device in file storage on disk?
A) Block
B) Sector
C) File
D) Index

Review Question 5.14
What is the primary advantage of contiguous allocation for file storage on disk?
A) Faster file retrieval
B) Flexible storage allocation
C) Minimization of fragmentation
D) Efficient space utilization

Review Question 5.15
What is the primary advantage of linked allocation for file storage on disk?
A) Efficient file access
B) Minimization of internal fragmentation

C) Secure data and information in a file
D) Flexible storage allocation

Review Question 5.16
In which allocation method are files associated with index blocks that store pointers to actual data blocks?
A) Contiguous allocation
B) Linked allocation
C) Indexed allocation
D) Flexible allocation

Review Question 5.17
How does efficient file storage organization affect data accessibility?
A) It minimizes delays in retrieving data.
B) It increases storage space wastage.
C) It introduces fragmentation.
D) It impacts the physical storage unit size.

Review Question 5.18
What is the drawback of contiguous allocation for file storage on disk?
A) Inefficient space utilization
B) Complex file access
C) High internal fragmentation
D) Slow block traversal

5.2.4 File Access Methods

The efficiency and effectiveness of data retrieval hinge upon the methods employed to access files. This section introduces three such methods: sequential, random, and indexed file access. Sequential file access involves reading or writing data from or to a file in a linear, sequential manner. Data is processed in the order it appears within the file. This method is analogous to reading a book page by page, where each page is accessed one after the other.

Sequential access offers several advantages. It is characterized by its simplicity and ease of implementation, making it well-suited for processing data that follows a natural order. However, sequential access also comes with limitations. It is not efficient for random access scenarios, where retrieving specific data or navigating to a particular location within the file can be time-consuming and inefficient. Furthermore, sequential access is not ideal for situations that require updates to the file. Modifying or updating specific portions of the file can be challenging, as it often involves shifting adjacent data to accommodate changes. These limitations highlight the trade-offs between the advantages of simplicity and storage efficiency.

On the other hand, random file access, also known as direct access, enables the retrieval of data from any location within a file, regardless of its sequential order. This method is akin to accessing individual pages of a book without reading each page in sequence.

Random access offers distinct advantages. One of its primary strengths lies in its efficiency for specific data retrieval, making it particularly well-suited for scenarios where diverse data retrieval needs exist. Additionally, random access enables seamless updates and modifications to specific segments of a file, enhancing data manipulation capabilities. However, random access does have its limitations. Unlike sequential access, where data is stored contiguously on disk, the implementation of random access necessitates the use of pointer mechanisms to locate specific data blocks within the file, adding a layer of complexity to the system.

A third method is the indexed file access, which combines the benefits of both sequential and random access methods. An index block is maintained for each file, containing pointers to the actual data blocks within the file. This index block acts as a roadmap, guiding the operating system to the desired data.

Indexed access offers notable advantages. One of its key strengths lies in its efficient random access capabilities while ensuring the contiguity of data within blocks. This means that indexed access allows for quick and direct retrieval of specific data, making it suitable for scenarios where random access is essential. However, indexed access also comes with its limitations. The maintenance of index blocks introduces additional overhead in terms of both storage and management. This overhead is due to the need to store and manage the index structure alongside the actual data.

Review Question 5.19
What is a primary advantage of sequential file access?
A) Efficient for random access scenarios
B) Suitable for diverse data retrieval needs
C) Ease of implementation and simplicity
D) Allows for seamless updates and modifications

Review Question 5.20
When is random file access, or direct access, particularly well-suited?
A) For scenarios where diverse data retrieval needs exist
B) For processing data in a linear, sequential manner
C) For scenarios where updates to the file are challenging
D) For reading a book page by page

Review Question 5.21

What is a limitation of random file access compared to sequential file access?
A) Complexity in locating specific data blocks
B) Inability to efficiently retrieve specific data
C) Challenges in updating the file
D) Lack of contiguity in data storage

Review Question 5.22
Which file access method combines the benefits of both sequential and random access?
A) Sequential file access
B) Random file access
C) Indexed file access
D) Direct file access

Review Question 5.23
What is a significant advantage of indexed file access?
A) Contiguity of data within blocks
B) Minimal storage and management overhead
C) Simplicity and ease of implementation
D) Efficient random access capabilities

Review Question 5.24
What is a drawback of indexed file access?
A) Contiguity of data within blocks
B) Minimal storage and management overhead
C) Complexity in locating specific data blocks
D) Inefficient for diverse data retrieval needs

5.3 Directories

A directory is a special type of file that contains information about other files and directories. It is used to organize files and directories into a hierarchical structure, making it easier to find and manage them. The root directory is the top-level directory in a file system, and all other directories and files are contained within it. Directories can be nested, meaning that a directory can contain other directories. This allows for a very flexible and efficient way to organize files.

5.3.1 Directory Structure and Path Traversal

A well-organized directory structure and effective path traversal are essential for efficient organization, navigation, and access to files. A directory structure, often referred to as a file system hierarchy, is akin to the organizational framework of a filing cabinet. It provides a systematic way to categorize and store files and directories (folders), ensuring efficient data management and retrieval.

Directory structures follow a hierarchical layout, where directories are organized into a tree-like structure. The top-level directory is known as the root directory, and all other directories stem from it. Path traversal is the process of navigating the directory structure to locate specific files or directories. Paths serve as addresses that guide users and applications to the desired location within the hierarchy. An absolute path specifies the complete path from the root directory to the target file or directory. It provides an unambiguous reference, allowing direct access to the desired location. On the other hand, a relative path specifies the path from the current working directory to the target file or directory. It is shorter and convenient for navigating within the same branch of the directory structure.

Each entry within a directory corresponds to either a file or a subdirectory. Entries are characterized by their names, metadata attributes, and links to the actual content or further directories. A well designed directory structure ensures organized data management, enabling users to categorize files into logical groupings. Additionally, effective path traversal simplifies navigation through the directory structure, saving time and effort in locating files. Also, Clear directory structures facilitate collaborative work, as multiple users can easily access and locate shared files.

Review Question 5.25
What is the purpose of a directory in a file system?
A) To store metadata attributes of files
B) To organize files and directories into a hierarchical structure
C) To contain the root directory
D) To serve as a top-level file

Review Question 5.26
What is the top-level directory in a file system called?
A) Root directory
B) Nested directory
C) Absolute directory
D) Relative directory

Review Question 5.27
What is the purpose of path traversal in file systems?
A) To create new directories
B) To rename files and directories
C) To navigate the directory structure and locate specific files or directories
D) To delete files and directories

Review Question 5.28
What is the key difference between an absolute path and a relative path in a file system?
A) An absolute path specifies the complete path from the root directory, while a relative path specifies the path from the current working directory.

B) An absolute path is shorter, while a relative path is longer.
C) An absolute path always starts from the root directory, while a relative path can start from any directory.
D) An absolute path is used for file names, while a relative path is used for directory names.

Review Question 5.29
What do entries within a directory correspond to in a file system?
A) File names only
B) Subdirectory names only
C) Either files or subdirectories
D) Metadata attributes of files

Review Question 5.30
How does a well-designed directory structure benefit data management?
A) It simplifies metadata attribute management.
B) It provides a shorter path for navigation.
C) It enables users to categorize files into logical groupings.
D) It eliminates the need for path traversal.

5.3.2 Single-level, Hierarchical, and Tree Directories

A single-level directory is the simplest form of directory structure, resembling a flat list of files. Each file is assigned a unique name, and retrieval is accomplished by directly specifying the file name. Single-level directories offer distinct advantages. Their simplicity in terms of implementation and management makes them particularly suitable for small-scale systems with a limited number of files. This straightforward approach simplifies the process of adding, deleting, and accessing files within the directory.

However, single-level directories come with limitations. Their scalability is limited, especially as the number of files grows. Navigating and locating specific files become progressively more challenging due to the lack of organizational structure. Without the ability to categorize or group files, the directory can become cluttered and inefficient for larger systems. This trade-off highlights the balance between simplicity and scalability that administrators must consider when choosing the appropriate directory structure for their file management needs.

Hierarchical directories introduce a layered organizational structure, providing a more systematic way to manage files. The structure resembles a family tree, with each directory potentially containing subdirectories and files. Hierarchical directories offer notable advantages. One of them is the logical organization they provide for files. By allowing files to be categorized and grouped in a hierarchical structure, these directories facilitate straightforward access and navigation. This logical arrangement enables users to locate and manage files more efficiently. Furthermore, hierarchical directories offer scalability. As the number of files grows, the nested structure of directories allows for accommodating a larger volume of files without sacrificing organization. The ability to create subdirectories within directories supports a more organized and manageable file system.

However, hierarchical directories also come with limitations. Deep nesting of subdirectories within subdirectories can lead to lengthy and complex file paths. This deep hierarchy can make path traversal challenging and increase the likelihood of errors when specifying file locations. Striking a balance between organizing files logically and avoiding excessive nesting is essential to ensure efficient file management within a hierarchical directory structure.

Review Question 5.31
In a single-level directory structure, how is retrieval of files accomplished?
A) By specifying the file's path within the directory hierarchy
B) By directly specifying the file name
C) By navigating through subdirectories
D) By using a hierarchical directory structure

Review Question 5.32
What is a significant advantage of single-level directories?
A) Logical organization of files
B) Scalability for a large number of files
C) Simplified process of adding, deleting, and accessing files
D) Deep nesting of subdirectories

Review Question 5.33
What is one limitation of single-level directories?
A) Logical organization of files
B) Complexity in managing files
C) Scalability as the number of files grows
D) Deep nesting of subdirectories

Review Question 5.34
What does a hierarchical directory structure resemble?
A) A flat list of files
B) A complex network of directories
C) A family tree
D) A single-level directory

Review Question 5.35
What advantage does a hierarchical directory structure provide for file organization?
A) Simplicity in implementation and management
B) Logical organization and categorization of files
C) Avoid nesting for efficient file access

D) Layered structure improves performance of file access

Review Question 5.36
What is one limitation associated with deep nesting of subdirectories within a hierarchical directory structure?
A) Increased file storage space
B) Reduced flexibility of file organization
C) Increased likelihood of path traversal errors
D) Can break the rule of 3-layer limit in any OS

5.4 File System Implementation

File system implementation is the process of designing, developing, and implementing the software components that manage the organization, allocation, and access to files on a storage device in an operating system. There are many different types of file systems, each with its own strengths and weaknesses. Some of the most common file systems include FAT32, NTFS, ext4, and APFS. A file system is a way of organizing data on a storage device. It creates a logical structure for the data, making it easier for the operating system to access and manage. Some key attributes that differ across file system types include performance, complexity, fault-tolerance features, capacity limits, metadata structures used, journaling capabilities, and support for specific media like SSDs.

5.4.1 File System Types: FAT

The FAT file system (File Allocation Table) is a simple file system that is used on a variety of storage devices, including floppy disks, USB flash drives, and memory cards. It is also the default file system for many mobile devices and embedded systems. The FAT file system stores data in a series of clusters, which are the smallest unit of allocation. The size of a cluster is determined by the size of the storage device. The FAT file system uses a table called the File Allocation Table (FAT) to keep track of which clusters are allocated to each file.

The FAT is located at the beginning of the storage device and is divided into two copies. This is done to protect the FAT from corruption in case of a power outage or other problem. Each file in the FAT file system has a directory entry. The directory entry contains the file name, the file size, and the starting cluster number for the file. The directory entries are stored in a directory, which is a special file that contains a list of other files. The FAT file system is a simple and efficient file system that is well-suited for small storage devices. However, it has some limitations, such as a maximum file size of 4 GB and a maximum partition size of 2 TB.

Here are some of the advantages of the FAT file system:

Simple and efficient
Widely supported by operating systems and devices
Good performance for small files

Here are some of the disadvantages of the FAT file system:

Limited file size and partition size
Not as secure as some other file systems
Susceptible to corruption

Sometimes, you may notice a number after the FAT, which indicates the number of bits in the file allocation table. Here's a simple comparison:

Feature	FAT	FAT16	FAT32
File allocation table size	12 bits	16 bits	32 bits
Maximum file size	32 MB	2 GB	4 GB
Maximum partition size	2 GB	2 TB	2 TB
Supported operating systems	DOS, Windows	DOS, Windows	DOS, Windows, macOS, Linux

Overall, the FAT file system is a good choice for small storage devices that need to be compatible with a wide range of operating systems and devices. However, for larger storage devices or devices that need more security, a different file system, such as NTFS or exFAT, may be a better choice.

Review Question 5.37
What is a file system primarily responsible for?
A) Creating logical structures
B) Managing computer hardware
C) Optimizing CPU performance
D) Formatting storage devices

Review Question 5.38
Which file system is often used as the default for mobile devices and embedded systems?
A) NTFS
B) ext4
C) FAT
D) APFS

Review Question 5.39
In the FAT file system, what is the smallest unit of allocation?
A) Cluster
B) Sector
C) Block
D) Segment

Review Question 5.40
How many copies of the File Allocation Table (FAT) are typically stored in the FAT file system?
A) One
B) Two
C) Three
D) Four

Review Question 5.41
What information does a directory entry in the FAT file system contain?
A) File size only
B) File name only
C) File name, file size, and starting cluster number
D) File name and starting sector

Review Question 5.42
What is one limitation of the FAT file system?
A) Maximum file size of 10 GB
B) Maximum partition size of 1 TB
C) Maximum file size of 4 GB
D) Maximum partition size of 5 TB

Review Question 5.43
Which of the following is NOT an advantage of the FAT file system?
A) Simplicity
B) Wide support by operating systems and devices
C) Good performance for large files
D) Efficiency

Review Question 5.44
What may the number after "FAT" (e.g. 12, 16, 32) indicate in the FAT file system?
A) The number of bytes in the FAT
B) The number of bits in the file allocation table
C) The number of clusters in use
D) The number of files in the directory

Review Question 5.45
When might a different file system like NTFS or exFAT be a better choice than FAT?
A) For small storage devices
B) For compatibility with a wide range of operating systems
C) For larger storage devices or increased security
D) For optimizing CPU performance

5.4.2 File System Types: NTFS

NTFS stands for New Technology File System. It is a proprietary file system developed by Microsoft for use in its Windows operating systems. NTFS became the default for boot drives on NT-based Windows starting with NT 3.1 (1993). But FAT16/FAT32 remained an option for data drives until Vista (2007) made NTFS the exclusive default file system. NTFS is a journaling file system, which means that it keeps a log of all changes made to the file system. This makes it easier to recover data in the event of a system crash or power outage. NTFS also supports features such as file compression, encryption, and disk quotas.

The NTFS has emerged as the most advanced file system available for Windows platforms. Introduced with Windows NT 3.1 in 1993, it offers a number of compelling advantages over older file systems like FAT32. First, NTFS supports very large partition sizes up to 256 terabytes and large file sizes up to 16 exabytes. This removes practical limits on storage capacity. Second, NTFS utilizes journaling to strengthen fault tolerance and recoverability. Third, built-in compression and encryption allow efficient use of space and enhanced security. Further, administrators can apply disk quotas to constrain usage per user. Finally, advanced features like shadow copies enable backups and remote storage functionality.

However, NTFS does have some disadvantages compared to FAT32. It is not as widely supported across devices and operating systems. The complexity of NTFS drivers makes adoption slower on non-Windows platforms. Also, for smaller files, NTFS can be slower than FAT32 in some workloads.

NTFS includes several key features that make it well-suited for use as the primary file system on Windows operating systems. One major feature of NTFS is its journaling capability. The file system keeps a log or journal of any changes made, tracking file edits, deletions, new files added, permission changes, and more. This journal can then be used to reliably recover data and return the file system to a consistent state in the event of an unexpected shutdown or crash. Journaling improves reliability and prevents file corruption.

NTFS also supports built-in file compression. By transparently compressing files, disk space utilization can be optimized. This saves storage capacity and reduces the footprint for transferring files across networks. Encryption is another feature that allows sensitive data to be securely stored and protected. For multi-user environments, NTFS implements disk quotas that constrain the storage usage per user or group. This prevents accidental or intentional overuse of disk space. Advanced features like shadow copies enable point-in-time backups and snapshots. And remote storage support allows files to be stored on network servers and accessed remotely. The robust feature set of NTFS makes it an efficient, secure, and highly functional file system well suited for most Windows platforms, especially corporate environments. The capabilities go well beyond older file systems like FAT32.

Review Question 5.46
What does NTFS stand for?
A) New Technology File System
B) Network Transfer File System
C) Non-Technical File Storage
D) New Text Formatting System

Review Question 5.47
Which operating systems primarily use NTFS as the default file system?
A) Linux-based systems
B) macOS
C) Windows-based systems
D) Android

Review Question 5.48
What advantage does journaling provide in NTFS?
A) Faster file access
B) Improved data recovery in case of system crashes or power outages
C) Enhanced encryption
D) Smaller partition sizes

Review Question 5.49
What is one advantage of NTFS over older file systems like FAT32?
A) Smaller partition sizes with agility
B) Simplicity
C) Support for very large partition sizes and file sizes
D) Faster performance with smaller files

Review Question 5.50
What does NTFS journaling primarily help with?
A) Faster file compression
B) Enhanced data encryption
C) Reliable data recovery after unexpected events
D) Improved storage capacity

Review Question 5.51
What is one major advantage of journaling in NTFS?
A) It reduces storage capacity.
B) It speeds up file access.
C) It strengthens fault tolerance and recoverability.
D) It encrypts files automatically.

Review Question 5.52

Which feature allows NTFS to optimize disk space utilization?
A) Journaling
B) Encryption
C) Built-in file compression
D) Disk quotas

Review Question 5.53
What does the implementation of disk quotas in NTFS prevent?
A) Data loss
B) Unauthorized access
C) Accidental or intentional overuse of disk space
D) File corruption

Review Question 5.54
What feature of NTFS allows point-in-time backups and snapshots?
A) Journaling
B) Encryption
C) Built-in file compression
D) Shadow copies

5.4.3 File System Types: ext4

The ext4 is a journaling file system that is the default file system for most Linux distributions. It is a successor to the ext3 file system, and it supports features such as larger file sizes, faster performance, and better reliability. The ext4 file system offers several important improvements over previous file systems like FAT32 and exFAT. One key advantage is the ability to support much larger files, with a maximum file size of 16 terabytes. Ext4 also provides faster performance through features like extents, which allow allocating multiple blocks of data in one operation, and delayed allocation, which puts off actually assigning blocks until they are needed. Reliability is enhanced as well with journaling, which logs all file system changes to prevent data loss after a crash, and checksums that verify data integrity.

The ext4 file system incorporates several key features that set it apart from earlier file systems. One crucial capability is journaling, which maintains a log of all changes made so that data can be recovered in the event of a crash. For efficient handling of large files, ext4 uses extents, or contiguous blocks of storage space allocated together, reducing the overhead of managing each block separately. Delayed allocation is another performance optimization, putting off actually assigning storage blocks until they are needed, speeding up writes for small files. Reliability features include checksums that verify data integrity to avoid corruption. Beyond the performance and reliability enhancements, ext4 retains standard file system functionality like subdirectories for hierarchical organization and symbolic links to connect files or folders.

Review Question 5.55
What is the maximum file size that the ext4 file system supports?
A) 2 gigabytes
B) 4 terabytes
C) 8 gigabytes
D) 16 terabytes

Review Question 5.56
Which feature of the ext4 file system allows it to allocate multiple blocks of data in one operation, improving performance?
A) Journaling
B) Checksums
C) Extents
D) Delayed allocation

Review Question 5.57
What is the purpose of journaling in the ext4 file system?
A) To reduce overhead when managing storage blocks
B) To allocate storage blocks only when they are needed
C) To log all changes made for data recovery after a crash
D) To verify data integrity to prevent corruption

Review Question 5.58
How does delayed allocation in the ext4 file system improve write performance for small files?
A) By reducing the overhead of managing storage blocks
B) By allocating storage blocks only when they are needed
C) By using checksums to verify data integrity
D) By organizing files hierarchically in subdirectories

Review Question 5.59
Which of the following is NOT a feature of the ext4 file system?
A) Hierarchical organization of files
B) Checksums for data integrity
C) Journaling for data recovery
D) Support for smaller file sizes

5.4.4 File System Types: APFS

APFS stands for Apple File System. It is a proprietary file system developed by Apple Inc. for use in its macOS, iOS, iPadOS, and tvOS operating systems. APFS is the default file system for all Macs released since 2017. APFS is designed to be more efficient and reliable than the previous file system used by macOS, HFS+.

APFS supports features such as snapshots, which allow users to create a point-in-time copy of a file system, and cloning, which allows users to create an exact copy of a file system. APFS introduces several key enhancements for performance, reliability, and versatility. One major addition is snapshot support, allowing point-in-time copies of the file system for backup and restoration of deleted or corrupted files. APFS also enables cloning to make exact duplicates of file systems for distribution or backup. To speed up operation, APFS utilizes copy-on write, whereby only file changes are written instead of whole copies, and deduplication, storing identical data once. Reliability is bolstered through features like checksums to verify data integrity and prevent errors, along with garbage collection to free up unused space over time. Together, these APFS capabilities deliver fast, resilient performance well-suited for modern storage on Macs. More specifically, copy-on-write reduces large file write times, while deduplication saves storage space and improves efficiency. Checksums and garbage collection enhance reliability and longevity of storage devices. And APFS retains standard hierarchical directories and symbolic links to maintain compatibility with traditional file system organization and connections.

Review Question 5.60
What key feature of APFS allows users to create point-in-time copies of a file system for backup and restoration?
A) Checksums
B) Cloning
C) Deduplication
D) Snapshots

Review Question 5.61
How does APFS optimize storage efficiency and performance when making file changes?
A) By using garbage collection
B) By employing checksums
C) By implementing copy-on-write
D) By utilizing deduplication

Review Question 5.62
What is the purpose of garbage collection in APFS?
A) To verify data integrity
B) To create point-in-time copies of the file system
C) To free up unused storage space over time
D) To make exact duplicates of file systems

5.5 File Systems Management and Optimization

File system management and optimization is the process of configuring, monitoring, and tuning a file system to improve its performance and reliability. This involves tasks such as defragmenting the disk, allocating space efficiently, and configuring file system parameters. File system management and optimization is important for ensuring that files can be accessed quickly and reliably, especially on large file systems.

5.5.1 Disk Space Management

Disk quotas are used to limit the amount of disk space a user or group of users can utilize on a filesystem. Disk quotas offer several advantages in effective disk management. One notable benefit is their role in ensuring fair resource allocation among users. By imposing quotas, the system can prevent any individual user from monopolizing excessive disk space, promoting an equitable distribution of storage resources across the user base. Additionally, disk quotas contribute to controlled disk growth. By setting specific limits on storage usage for each user, quotas help prevent unexpected depletion of disk space, ensuring that the available storage remains manageable and preventing scenarios of storage exhaustion.

However, implementing disk quotas also presents certain challenges. Administrative overhead is one such concern. The process of implementing and managing disk quotas can require continuous administrative effort, including monitoring usage, adjusting quotas as needed, and handling any potential quota violations. This administrative overhead can increase the complexity of disk management tasks. Furthermore, there can be a user impact associated with strict quotas. If quotas are set too restrictively, they may impede user productivity by limiting their ability to store and manage files effectively.

Striking a balance between resource allocation control and user flexibility is crucial in implementing disk quotas effectively within an operating system environment. Sparse file allocation is a technique where only actual data is allocated space on disk, rather than reserving space for empty or zero-filled sections. This approach optimizes disk utilization for files with significant empty sections. One significant benefit is its space efficiency. Sparse allocation means that areas of the file containing no actual data are not allocated any physical storage, resulting in optimal usage of available disk space. Additionally, by avoiding the allocation of physical storage for empty sections, the overhead associated with maintaining such space is minimized.

However, sparse file allocation also presents certain challenges. Fragmentation is one such concern. Despite its space-saving attributes, sparse allocation can still lead to fragmentation over time. As files are created, modified, and deleted, the allocated sections can become fragmented, impacting the efficiency of disk usage.

Another challenge is related to file recovery. Recovering sparse files can be complex, as the actual data of the file may be scattered across non-contiguous blocks due to the nature of sparse allocation.

Review Question 5.63
What is one notable advantage of using disk quotas in effective disk management?
A) Preventing fragmentation
B) Promoting equitable resource allocation among users
C) Optimizing disk utilization for sparse files
D) Minimizing administrative overhead

Review Question 5.64
What challenge is associated with implementing disk quotas?
A) Fragmentation of files
B) Administrative overhead
C) User impact on file recovery
D) Space efficiency concerns

Review Question 5.65
What is the primary benefit of sparse file allocation?
A) Preventing fragmentation
B) Optimizing disk utilization for files with empty sections
C) Minimizing administrative overhead
D) Enhancing file recovery efficiency

Review Question 5.66
What challenge is associated with sparse file allocation?
A) Administrative overhead
B) Preventing storage exhaustion
C) Fragmentation of allocated sections
D) Equitable resource allocation

Review Question 5.67
What to balance when implementing disk quotas?
A) To balance minimizing fragmentation and optimizing disk utilization
B) To balance optimizing disk utilization and preventing storage exhaustion
C) To balance preventing storage exhaustion and minimizing fragmentation
D) To balance resource allocation control and user flexibility

5.5.2 Defragmenting Disks

The disk defragmentation aims at optimizing storage utilization, improving data access speed, and enhancing overall file system performance. Fragmentation occurs when files are stored on a storage device in non-contiguous blocks, leading to inefficiencies in data access and storage space utilization.

Disk defragmentation is a process that reorganizes the allocation of data blocks on a storage device to minimize fragmentation and improve file system performance. It involves rearranging file data blocks to ensure that files are stored in contiguous blocks, thereby reducing the effects of fragmentation.

Disk defragmentation is the process of rearranging data on a storage device to improve performance. It involves three main steps: analysis, reorganization, and allocation. First, the filesystem analyzes the entire storage device to identify which files are fragmented across noncontiguous blocks and where there is free space scattered in small pieces. Next is reorganization, where the blocks of fragmented files are reordered and consolidated together in one place, while also combining all the little chunks of free space into a few large contiguous free blocks. Finally, with the space optimized, allocation can write new data in these large free blocks in a sequential order, minimizing fragmentation of new files.

Disk defragmentation offers a range of advantages that contribute to optimized disk performance. One significant benefit is the improved data access speed. Defragmenting files leads to contiguous data storage, enabling the drive head to read data blocks without excessive movement, which in turn results in faster data access times. Additionally, defragmentation enhances storage utilization by reducing wasted space, ensuring that the available disk space is used more efficiently. Another advantage is the potential extension of hardware lifespan. As defragmentation reduces disk activity by organizing data in a more efficient manner, it minimizes wear and tear on storage devices, contributing to their longevity.

However, disk defragmentation is not without its challenges. One notable challenge is its resource intensive nature. The process of disk defragmentation can consume significant system resources and time, potentially impacting overall system performance during the defragmentation process. Despite this challenge, modern operating systems often offer a solution by providing background execution for defragmentation. Background defragmentation allows the process to run during system idle periods, minimizing its impact on user activities and system responsiveness. Balancing the advantages of improved data access speed, enhanced storage utilization, and extended hardware lifespan with the resource and time demands of the defragmentation process is essential for effective disk management.

Review Question 5.68
What is the primary goal of disk defragmentation?
A) Minimizing wear and tear on storage devices

B) Reducing resource consumption during file access
C) Improving data access speed and storage space utilization
D) Enhancing system responsiveness during the defragmentation process

Review Question 5.69
Which of the following is NOT one of the main steps involved in the disk defragmentation process?
A) Analysis
B) Reorganization
C) Allocation
D) Compression

Review Question 5.70
How does defragmentation improve data access speed?
A) By compressing files to reduce their size
B) By minimizing the wear and tear on storage devices
C) By organizing files into contiguous data blocks
D) By reducing the time it takes to analyze the disk

Review Question 5.71
What is one advantage of disk defragmentation for storage utilization?
A) Reducing wear and tear on storage devices
B) Minimizing the impact on system responsiveness
C) Enhancing storage utilization by reducing wasted space
D) Increasing the speed of the defragmentation process

Review Question 5.72
How can modern operating systems mitigate the resource impact of disk defragmentation?
A) By disabling the defragmentation process
B) By minimizing system idle periods
C) By balancing the advantages of defragmentation
D) By providing background execution for defragmentation

Review Question 5.73
What is essential for effective disk management when considering the challenges of disk defragmentation?
A) Disabling defragmentation to conserve system resources
B) Maximizing the impact of the defragmentation process
C) Balancing the advantages of defragmentation with its resource demands
D) Prioritizing system responsiveness over storage utilization

5.5.3 Disk Partitioning and Volume Management

Disk partitioning and volume management are techniques that enable users to effectively allocate and manage storage space on their devices. Disk partitioning involves dividing a physical storage device, such as a hard drive or SSD, into multiple logical sections known as partitions. Each partition behaves as an independent unit, with its own file system and data storage.

Disk partitioning offers a variety of benefits that contribute to efficient data organization and management. One of the key advantages is isolation, where different partitions can be designated to host separate operating systems or data sets. This isolation enhances security by preventing unintended access to sensitive information. Additionally, partitioning promotes efficient data management by segregating data into distinct storage areas. This segregation makes tasks such as data backup and recovery more streamlined and organized.

However, several considerations need to be considered when implementing disk partitioning. The allocation of partition sizes is of paramount importance. Properly sizing partitions ensures that they can accommodate current data needs while also allowing for future data growth. Balancing the number of partitions is another critical factor. Striking the right balance prevents excessive complexity in managing multiple partitions and helps avoid potential fragmentation issues that can arise from an excessive number of partitions.

Incorporating thoughtful disk partitioning strategies based on the benefits and considerations can greatly enhance overall data management, security, and system efficiency. Volume management extends the concept of disk partitioning by offering advanced features such as spanning, striping, and redundancy across multiple physical devices. RAID is a technique in volume management that combines multiple physical disks into a single logical unit, providing data redundancy and improved performance. Common RAID levels include RAID 0, RAID 1, RAID 5, and RAID 10. Logical Volume Management (LVM) is a dynamic volume management system that enables users to create, resize, and manage logical volumes without needing to modify the underlying physical partitions.

Review Question 5.74
What is the primary purpose of disk partitioning?
A) Determining partition sizes easily
B) Enhancing data security by isolating partitions
C) Increasing the complexity of managing storage
D) Combining multiple physical disks into a single unit

Review Question 5.75
Why is the allocation of partition sizes important when implementing disk partitioning?
A) To maximize the number of partitions
B) To minimize the complexity of managing partitions
C) To accommodate current data needs and future growth
D) To prevent potential fragmentation issues

Review Question 5.76

What is one of the advantages of volume management over disk partitioning?
A) Enhanced data security through isolation
B) Improved data organization and management
C) Streamlined data backup and recovery
D) Advanced features like spanning and striping

Review Question 5.77
What is RAID, and what does it provide in volume management?
A) RAID is a file system used for logical volume management.
B) RAID is a technique that combines multiple physical disks into a single unit, providing data redundancy and improved performance.
C) RAID is a method for isolating partitions to enhance data security.
D) RAID is a tool for efficient data backup and recovery.

Review Question 5.78
What is Logical Volume Management (LVM), and what is its key benefit?
A) LVM is a method for isolating partitions.
B) LVM is a dynamic volume management system that enables users to create, resize, and manage logical volumes without modifying physical partitions.
C) LVM is a tool for streamlining data backup and recovery.
D) LVM is a technique for enhancing data security through isolation.

5.5.4 File Compression

File compression involves reducing the size of files by encoding data in a more compact representation. This not only conserves storage space but also speeds up data transfer and reduces network bandwidth consumption.

In lossless compression, files are compressed without any loss of data. Popular lossless compression algorithms include ZIP, GZIP, and RAR. These algorithms achieve compression by identifying repeating patterns or redundancies in the data and replacing them with shorter codes.

Lossy compression is used primarily for multimedia files like images, audio, and video. It achieves higher compression ratios by discarding some data that is deemed less significant. JPEG for images and MP3 for audio are examples of lossy compression formats.

File compression offers several advantages that contribute to efficient data storage and transfer. One of the primary benefits is the reduction in storage requirements. Compressed files occupy less diskspace, allowing users to store a larger amount of data within the same storage capacity. Additionally, compressed files result in faster data transfer rates over networks and the internet due to their smaller file sizes. This optimization not only accelerates data exchange but also contributes to enhanced network efficiency. Moreover, file compression plays a crucial role in optimizing backup processes. Compressed files require less time and storage space during backup operations, streamlining the backup process and conserving resources.

However, there are certain challenges associated with file compression. One significant challenge is the processing overhead introduced by compression and decompression operations. These processes consume CPU resources, potentially affecting system performance during compression and extraction activities. Furthermore, file compression may have limited effectiveness for certain file formats that are already highly compressed, such as JPEG images. In such cases, attempting further compression may yield minimal reductions in file size.

Review Question 5.79
What is the primary advantage of file compression?
A) Increasing data redundancy
B) Slowing down data transfer
C) Conserving storage space and speeding up data transfer
D) Reducing data security risks

Review Question 5.80
Which type of compression algorithm discards some data to achieve higher compression ratios?
A) Lossless compression
B) ZIP compression
C) Lossy compression
D) RAR compression

Review Question 5.81
What is the primary benefit of lossless compression?
A) Achieving higher compression ratios
B) Speeding up data transfer
C) Compressing multimedia files
D) Compressing files without any loss of data

Review Question 5.82
Which type of files may have limited effectiveness with file compression, as mentioned in the book?
A) Multimedia files
B) Text files
C) Highly compressed files like JPEG images
D) Archive files

Review Question 5.83
What is one of the challenges associated with file compression mentioned in the book?
A) Increased data security risks

B) Decreased CPU resource consumption during compression
C) Limited effectiveness for text files
D) Processing overhead during compression and decompression

Review Question 5.84
How does file compression contribute to optimizing backup processes?
A) By increasing storage space requirements during backup
B) By slowing down the backup process
C) By consuming more CPU resources during backup operations
D) By requiring less time and storage space during backup operations

5.6 File System Protection and Security

File system protection and security is the process of securing files and directories from unauthorized access, modification, or deletion. This is important for protecting sensitive data from malicious actors. There are a number of different mechanisms that can be used to protect file systems, such as file permissions, encryption, and access control lists.

5.6.1 Access Control Lists (ACLs) for Authorization

Access control lists (ACLs) serve as a crucial mechanism to enforce authorization policies, determining who can access, modify, or manipulate files and directories within a computing environment. ACLs are data structures associated with files and directories that specify the permissions and access rights granted to various users or groups. Unlike traditional permission models that offer limited granularity, ACLs provide a fine-grained approach to controlling access based on user identities, roles, or groups.

An ACL consists of several components that work together to implement granular access control. The subjects specify the entities that require access, normally individual users, user groups, and running processes or applications. The objects are the resources being protected, including specific files, directories, and other data objects on the system. Actions define what activities can be performed on the objects, like read, write, execute, and delete operations. Finally, permissions tie these elements together by mapping the access levels granted to subjects for various actions on specific objects, such as read-only permission or full control. By combining subjects, objects, actions, and explicit permissions, ACLs enable precise control over resource access and help harden system security.

Access Control Lists (ACLs) offer several advantages that contribute to enhanced authorization and security mechanisms. One key advantage is the ability to achieve granular authorization. ACLs empower administrators to precisely define which users or groups have permissions to perform specific actions on individual files or directories. This fine-grained control enables organizations to tailor access permissions to meet their specific security requirements.

Additionally, ACLs facilitate role-based access, where access privileges are assigned based on users' roles or responsibilities within the organization. This approach simplifies authorization management by grouping users with similar access needs and assigning permissions accordingly.

Furthermore, ACLs are particularly suitable for handling complex access scenarios. In situations where access requirements involve intricate combinations of users, groups, and actions, ACLs provide the flexibility to define and manage permissions at a detailed level.

However, there are certain challenges and considerations associated with ACLs. One challenge is the potential complexity of ACL configurations. Fine-grained control can result in intricate permission setups, necessitating careful management and documentation to avoid confusion or errors. Moreover, ensuring consistency across ACL management for a large number of files and directories can be challenging. Maintaining uniform access control settings and permissions across various resources requires attention to detail and robust management practices.

Windows operating systems extensively use ACLs to manage permissions at both the file system and network levels. Users, groups, and system entities can be assigned various permissions using ACLs. UNIX-like systems employ POSIX ACLs, extending the traditional user, group, and others permission model with more advanced access rules.

Review Question 5.85
What is the primary purpose of Access Control Lists (ACLs)?
A) To provide system administrators with a graphical user interface
B) To define the hardware configuration of a computer system
C) To enforce authorization policies and control resource access
D) To manage software applications and their dependencies

Review Question 5.86
What components make up an ACL to implement granular access control?
A) Users, groups, and roles

B) Subjects, objects, actions, and permissions
C) Read, write, execute, and delete operations
D) File systems, directories, and data objects

Review Question 5.87
What is the benefit of role-based access facilitated by ACLs?
A) It enables users to define their own roles.
B) It simplifies resource access control by granting all users the same permissions.
C) It groups users with similar access needs and assigns permissions accordingly.
D) It allows users to modify ACL configurations without restrictions.

Review Question 5.88
What is one challenge associated with ACLs mentioned in the book?
A) Lack of fine-grained control
B) Intricate permission setups leading to confusion
C) Limited flexibility in defining access rules
D) Incompatibility with Windows operating systems

Review Question 5.89
What is the primary benefit of ACLs for organizations' security requirements?
A) Providing a graphical user interface for access control
B) Enforcing mandatory access control policies
C) Allowing users to define their own permissions
D) Enabling precise definition of user/group permissions on files and directories

5.6.2 Authentication for File Security

Authentication fortifies file security by verifying the identities of users and processes seeking access to files and resources. Authentication serves as a first line of defense against unauthorized access to files and sensitive information. By verifying the identities of individuals and processes, authentication prevents unauthorized entities from tampering with or extracting data, thereby ensuring data security and privacy. To enhance file security, various authentication methods can be implemented, each offering distinct levels of protection.

One commonly used approach is the username and password method, where users are required to provide their individual username and password combination to gain access. Despite being traditional, this method remains effective in preventing unauthorized access. Another advanced authentication method is biometric authentication, which leverages unique biological traits like fingerprints, facial features, and iris patterns to identify individuals. Biometric data offers a high degree of specificity, making it a robust option for secure access control. Additionally, two-factor authentication (2FA) provides an extra layer of security by requiring users to present two different authentication factors. This might involve combining something the user knows, like a password, with something they possess, such as a verification code received on their mobile device. The synergy of these two factors fortifies security, making it more challenging for unauthorized users to gain access.

Enhancing file security through authentication involves the implementation of various strategies. One effective approach is role-based access, where users are assigned specific roles within the system, and their access permissions are determined based on these roles. This method not only enhances security but also streamlines access management by categorizing users into distinct roles with predefined permissions.

Another valuable technique is the use of granular permissions in conjunction with authentication mechanisms. By implementing access control lists (ACLs), administrators can exert precise control over who can perform specific actions on individual files and directories. This fine-grained approach enables the customization of permissions down to the smallest level, ensuring that access is granted only to authorized users for specific resources.

Combining role-based access with granular permissions and authentication mechanisms contributes to a multi-layered security framework that safeguards files and data within an operating system. This approach addresses different levels of access needs, from broad role-based authorization to detailed permission settings, thereby bolstering the overall security posture of the system. Note that it is important to balance security and usability. Striking the right balance between robust security and user convenience is essential to prevent overly complex authentication processes.

Review Question 5.90
What is the primary purpose of authentication in file security?
A) To enhance data encryption
B) To streamline access management
C) To verify the identities of users and processes
D) To prevent data tampering during file transfers

Review Question 5.91
Which authentication method uses finger print for identification?
A) Username and password
B) Two-factor authentication
C) Role-based access control
D) Biometric authentication

Review Question 5.92

What does two-factor authentication (2FA) require users to present for access?
A) Only two things they know, like two passwords
B) Only two things they possess, like two mobile devices
C) Two pieces of biometric data
D) Two different authentication factors, like a password and a verification code

Review Question 5.93
What is the role of role-based access in file security?
A) To simplify authentication mechanisms
B) To enhance data encryption
C) To categorize users into distinct roles with predefined permissions
D) To prevent data tampering during file transfers

Review Question 5.94
How do access control lists (ACLs) contribute to file security?
A) By providing two-factor authentication
B) By preventing unauthorized access entirely
C) By fine-tuning permissions at a granular level
D) By categorizing users into specific roles

Review Question 5.95
What does a multi-layered security framework combine to safeguard files and data?
A) Biometric authentication and granular permissions
B) Role-based access and two-factor authentication
C) Username and password authentication
D) Encryption and decryption methods

Review Question 5.96
What is the key consideration when balancing security and usability in authentication processes?
A) Increasing complexity for better security
B) Prioritizing user convenience over security
C) Striking the right balance between robust security and user convenience
D) Implementing the most advanced authentication methods

Review Question 5.97
Which authentication method is considered traditional but remains effective?
A) Two-factor authentication
B) Role-based access control
C) Username and password
D) Biometric authentication

Review Question 5.98
What does granular access control help achieve in file security?
A) Two-factor authentication
B) Streamlining access management
C) Fine-grained customization of permissions
D) Encryption of file content

5.6.3 File Encryption

File encryption enhances data security by converting sensitive information into a coded format that can only be deciphered with the appropriate decryption key. Only individuals possessing the corresponding decryption key can decipher and access the original data.

Various encryption methods are available to enhance file security, each catering to specific needs. Symmetric Encryption employs a single key for both encrypting and decrypting data. This method necessitates secure distribution of the shared key among authorized parties to maintain confidentiality. For example, "HELLO" is a plain text word. By using a key of 3 (shift each letter in the plaintext 3 positions to the right in the alphabet), you get the encrypted ciphertext, "KHOOR". Now, only the individual with the key can decipher the ciphertext back to plain text. This is often called Caesar cipher.

Asymmetric Encryption, on the other hand, employs a pair of keys – a public key for encryption and a private key for decryption. Public keys can be openly shared, allowing encrypted data to be securely sent to anyone possessing the corresponding private key for decryption. For example, if Alice wants to send a message to Bob, Alice will use Bob's public key to encrypt the message. Now, only Bob who owns the private key can decipher it.

File-Level Encryption offers a more granular approach by encrypting individual files. This method provides administrators with the ability to exert fine-tuned control over which files are encrypted, ensuring that specific content remains protected.

Full Disk Encryption is a robust security measure that involves encrypting an entire storage device. This approach ensures comprehensive data protection by rendering all the data stored on the disk unreadable to unauthorized users. This method is particularly effective in preventing data exposure in the event of a lost or stolen device, as the encrypted content remains inaccessible without the proper decryption key.

Review Question 5.99
What is the primary purpose of file encryption?
A) To make data more accessible
B) To increase data transfer speed
C) To convert sensitive information into a coded format
D) To reduce the need for decryption keys

Review Question 5.100
Which encryption method uses a single key for both encryption and decryption?
A) Asymmetric Encryption
B) File-Level Encryption
C) Full Disk Encryption
D) Symmetric Encryption

Review Question 5.101
How does Asymmetric Encryption differ from Symmetric Encryption?
A) Asymmetric Encryption uses the same key for both encryption and decryption.
B) Asymmetric Encryption requires sharing the private key publicly.
C) Symmetric Encryption uses a pair of keys for encryption and decryption.
D) Asymmetric Encryption uses a pair of keys - public and private.

Review Question 5.102
What does File-Level Encryption offer that Full Disk Encryption does not?
A) Encryption for the entire storage device
B) Granular control over individual files
C) Public sharing of decryption keys
D) Reduced need for decryption keys

Review Question 5.103
Why is Full Disk Encryption effective in preventing data exposure in case of a lost or stolen device?
A) Because it doesn't require encryption keys
B) Because it makes data publicly accessible
C) Because it encrypts individual files
D) Because encrypted content remains inaccessible without the proper decryption key

5.6.4 File Systems Backup

File systems backup is a practice to ensure data preservation, offering a safety net against accidental deletions, hardware failures, and catastrophic events. File systems backup involves creating copies of data and storing them in a separate location to protect against data loss or corruption. Backups provide a means to restore data to a previous state in case of unforeseen incidents.

Backup strategies encompass various methods to ensure data preservation. Full backup involves duplicating all data, providing a comprehensive snapshot for restoration purposes. This approach guarantees that all files, regardless of changes, are included in the backup. Incremental backup selectively copies only new or modified files since the last backup (full or incremental). By capturing only the changes, this method results in smaller backups but requiring more steps to restore. Differential backup focuses on capturing the changes since the last full backup, ensuring that any modifications are included, which makes restoring data faster but increases backup size over time. This approach strikes a balance between restoration time and storage consumption, offering a viable compromise for maintaining up-to-date backups.

Implementing a robust file systems backup strategy involves careful considerations of a few factors. Setting up a backup schedule is crucial to ensure that data is regularly and consistently backed up. The frequency of backups should align with the criticality of the data and the frequency of changes. For vital data that experiences frequent updates, more frequent backups may be necessary. A backup retention policy should be defined to determine how long backup copies are retained. This policy strikes a balance between maintaining access to historical data and managing storage requirements. Retaining backups for too long can lead to excessive storage usage, while deleting them too soon might hinder recovery in case of data loss.

Review Question 5.104
What is the primary purpose of file systems backup?
A) To increase storage capacity
B) To protect against data loss or corruption
C) To speed up data access
D) To prevent hardware failures

Review Question 5.105
What does a full backup involve?
A) Duplicating all data, including changes since the last backup
B) Selectively copying new or modified files
C) Creating a comprehensive snapshot of all data
D) Backing up data incrementally

Review Question 5.106
Which backup method results in smaller backups but requires more steps to restore?
A) Full backup
B) Incremental backup
C) Differential backup
D) Backup retention policy

Review Question 5.107
Which of the following is NOT an advantage of an incremental backup?
A) Faster backup creation
B) Smaller backup size
C) Quicker data restoration
D) Greater storage efficiency

Review Question 5.108
What is the purpose of a backup retention policy?
A) To maximize storage usage
B) To minimize backup frequency
C) To manage hardware failures
D) To balance access to historical data and storage requirements

5.7 Chapter Summary

In this chapter, you have gained knowledge of fundamental file system concepts and file operations. You've also acquired an understanding of file storage organization and various file access methods. Additionally, we've explored directory structures and the traversal of file paths. We've delved into the details of four major file system types, including FAT, NTFS, ext4, and APFS. In the context of file systems management and optimization, you've learned about defragmentation, partitioning, volume management, and compression techniques. Finally, the chapter concludes by focusing on filesystem protection and security, covering topics such as authorization, authentication, encryption, and backup strategies.

5.8 Exercises

Exercise 5.1 File Size Calculation
Consider a text file named lecture_notes.txt that contains 500 characters. If each character is 1 byte, calculate the size of the file in bytes and kilobytes.

Exercise 5.2 Disk Space Utilization
Suppose a disk has a block size of 4KB. If a file of size 11KB is stored on this disk, how many blocks are used? How much space is wasted?

Exercise 5.3 File Allocation Table (FAT) Size Calculation
A file system uses a 32-bit File Allocation Table (FAT32). If each entry in the table is 4 bytes and the disk has 100,000 clusters, calculate the size of the FAT in bytes and kilobytes.

Exercise 5.4 Inode Calculation
An inode in a Unix-like system stores file attributes and disk block locations. If each disk block is 8KB and an inode can store 12 direct pointers, 1 single indirect pointer (containing 1024 direct pointers), 1 double indirect pointer (containing 1024 single indirect pointers), and 1 triple indirect pointer (containing 1024 double indirect pointers), what is the maximum file size that can be handled by the inode in theory?

5.9 Solutions to Review Questions

5.1 B; 5.2 C; 5.3 C; 5.4 C; 5.5 C; 5.6 B; 5.7 C; 5.8 D; 5.9 B; 5.10 B; 5.11 C; 5.12 C; 5.13 B; 5.14 A; 5.15 D; 5.16 C; 5.17 A; 5.18 A; 5.19 C; 5.20 A; 5.21 A; 5.22 C; 5.23 D; 5.24 C; 5.25 B;5.26 A; 5.27 C; 5.28 A; 5.29 C; 5.30 C; 5.31 B; 5.32 C; 5.33 C; 5.34 C; 5.35 B; 5.36 C; 5.37 A; 5.38 C;5.39 A; 5.40 B; 5.41 C; 5.42 C; 5.43 C; 5.44 B; 5.45 C; 5.46 A; 5.47 C; 5.48 B; 5.49 C; 5.50 C; 5.51 C;5.52 C; 5.53 C; 5.54 D; 5.55 D; 5.56 C; 5.57 C; 5.58 B; 5.59 D; 5.60 D; 5.61 C; 5.62 C; 5.63 B; 5.64 B; 5.65 B; 5.66 C; 5.67 D; 5.68 C; 5.69 D; 5.70 C; 5.71 C; 5.72 D; 5.73 C; 5.74 B;5.75 C; 5.76 D; 5.77 B; 5.78 B; 5.79 C; 5.80 C; 5.81 D; 5.82 C; 5.83 D; 5.84 D; 5.85 C; 5.86 B; 5.87 C;5.88 B; 5.89 D; 5.90 C; 5.91 D; 5.92 D; 5.93 C; 5.94 C; 5.85 B; 5.96 C; 5.97 C; 5.98 C; 5.99 C; 5.100 D; 5.101 D; 5.102 B; 5.103 D; 5.104 B; 5.105 C; 5.106 B; 5.107 C; 5.108 D;

Chapter 6: Cloud Computing Fundamentals

Chapter Learning Outcomes

6.1 Define cloud computing
6.2 Compare and contrast cloud computing and on-premise computing
6.3 Explore different cloud services and deployment models
6.4 Evaluate the shared responsibility model in cloud computing

6.1 Introduction

Businesses across various sectors are increasingly adopting cloud computing. According to the latest data, global public cloud revenue reached $415 billion in 2022, growing from $211.5 billion in 2019. It is projected to reach $690.30 billion in 2024. This significant growth underscores the importance of cloud knowledge and skills for both business managers and software developers.

Cloud computing has undeniably transformed our Internet experience and the way organizations conduct business. What might have seemed like a novelty just a few years ago is now mainstream. Many of us use cloud-based services daily, such as Gmail, Dropbox, and Office 365. There is a significant demand in the market for individuals who understand cloud computing.

The term 'cloud computing' is derived from the symbolic representation of the Internet, which is often depicted as a cloud.

6.1.1 Components of Traditional Computing

Prior to the advent of cloud computing, traditional on-premise computing was the norm. In this setup, servers are housed within the premises of companies and connected to internal networks. Let's first understand how this works before we delve into cloud computing.

The first component of traditional computing is hardware, which includes elements such as the processor, memory, hard drive, and other physical components and peripherals. Recent advancements in hardware technology have led to the development of high-performance processors and hardware accelerators, new nonvolatile memory (NVM), and high-speed networks.

The second component is the operating system, which interfaces with the hardware. The operating system is a software layer that enables the hardware to work cohesively and provides support for applications. Often referred to as a platform, the operating system examples include Windows, Linux, and MacOS. Recent trends in operating system development include edge computing, real-time operating systems (RTOS), containerization, security enhancements, and artificial intelligence integration.

Atop the operating system layer, we have the applications component. This allows users to perform specific tasks, such as drafting a term paper on a word processor or calculating total costs on spreadsheets. The latest advancements in application development for traditional computing include machine learning and deep learning methods, along with blockchain technology and the use of Big Data.

Review Question 6.1
What is the first component (bottom layer) of traditional computing?
A) Operating System
B) Applications
C) Hardware
D) Cloud Computing

Review Question 6.2
Which of the following is NOT an example of an operating system?
A) Windows
B) Linux
C) MacOS
D) Microsoft Word

Review Question 6.3
What does the operating system do?
A) It performs specific tasks for users.
B) It interfaces with the hardware and provides support for applications.
C) It includes elements such as the processor, memory, hard drive.
D) It is housed within the premises of companies and connected to internal networks.

Review Question 6.4
What is the role of applications in traditional computing?
A) They interface with the hardware.
B) They allow users to perform specific tasks.
C) They include elements such as the processor, memory, hard drive.

D) They are housed within the premises of companies and connected to internal networks.

Review Question 6.5
Which of the following is NOT a recent trend in operating system development?
A) Edge computing
B) Real-time operating systems (RTOS)
C) Containerization
D) Blockchain technology

Review Question 6.6
What is a recent advancement in hardware technology?
A) High-performance processors and hardware accelerators
B) Machine learning and deep learning methods
C) Blockchain technology
D) Use of Big Data

6.1.2 Benefits and Supports of Cloud Computing

As a company expands, the need for additional computing resources, including servers, storage, and networking hardware and software, increases. However, the rapid obsolescence of hardware and the frequent need for software upgrades can make keeping pace with innovation and change overwhelming. This is where cloud computing comes in.

Cloud computing offers several advantages over traditional computing. Firstly, it provides flexibility and scalability as computing resources can be rented as needed. Secondly, users have more immediate access to the latest technologies. Thirdly, cloud platforms generally offer better security than individual businesses can provide. Fourthly, it can lead to a reduction in IT staff and lower administration costs. Finally, cloud services are designed to ensure that users may not even notice a system failure.

These benefits of cloud computing are enabled by at least three key technologies:

Virtualization technology separates physical and logical devices, allowing users to interact with the logical or virtual aspects without needing to understand the actual physical structure of the devices.
Service-Oriented Architecture (SOA) uses a series of microservices to improve the agility of applications by creating loosely connected modules.
Distributed computing involves the study of distributed systems where components are located on different networked computers. These components communicate and coordinate their actions by passing messages to one another.

Review Question 6.7

What is one of the challenges faced by a company as it expands?
A) Decreased need for computing resources
B) Rapid obsolescence of hardware
C) Reduced need for software upgrades
D) Decreased innovation

Review Question 6.8
How does cloud computing affect IT staff requirements?
A) It increases the need for IT staff
B) It has no effect on IT staff requirements
C) It can lead to a reduction in IT staff
D) It requires specialized IT staff

Review Question 6.9
What is one of the key technologies that enable the benefits of cloud computing?
A) Virtualization technology
B) Hardware technology
C) Software technology
D) Network technology

Review Question 6.10
What does Service-Oriented Architecture (SOA) use to improve the agility of applications?
A) A series of microservices
B) A series of macroservices
C) A series of nanoservices
D) A series of megaservices

6.1.3 Key Features of Cloud Computing

Cloud computing is distinguished from traditional computing by three key features. Firstly, cloud computing must be elastic, allowing it to expand or contract to meet customer needs. This elasticity is made possible through virtualization and resource pooling, where the provider's resources are pooled together and allocated to clients as needed.

Secondly, cloud services must be self-service. This means users can access additional resources such as storage, network, or compute power automatically, 24/7, without the need for human intervention from the service provider. Essentially, the cloud must be scalable, meaning it has the ability to adjust resource usage based on demand. Most public clouds, like Amazon Web Services, offer a high degree of scalability. It's highly unlikely that your company could exhaust Amazon Web Services' storage capacity. While scalability is closely related to elasticity, they are not the same. Scalability is a prerequisite for elasticity, but not vice versa.

The third key feature of cloud computing is broad network access. This means that resources should be accessible over the network by various types of hardware, including workstations, laptops, and mobile devices, and across different operating systems such as Windows, macOS, iOS, or Android. A related concept is availability, which ensures that cloud resources are accessible and responsive whenever a client needs them.

Review Question 6.11
What is one of the key features that differentiate cloud computing from traditional computing?
A) Inelasticity
B) Elasticity
C) Rigidity
D) Flexibility

Review Question 6.12
What enables the elasticity of cloud computing?
A) Virtualization and resource pooling
B) Hardware and software upgrades
C) Network access
D) Scalability

Review Question 6.13
What does it mean when we say cloud services must be self-service?
A) Users can access additional resources automatically without human intervention.
B) Users need to manually request for additional resources.
C) Users can only access resources during business hours.
D) Users need to have technical skills to manage resources.

Review Question 6.14
What is the difference between scalability and elasticity in the context of cloud computing?
A) Scalability is a prerequisite for elasticity.
B) Elasticity is a prerequisite for scalability.
C) Scalability and elasticity are the same.
D) Neither scalability nor elasticity is important in cloud computing.

Review Question 6.15
What does broad network access in cloud computing imply?
A) Resources should be accessible over the network by various types of hardware and across different operating systems.
B) Resources should be accessible only through specific hardware and operating systems.
C) Resources should be accessible only through a wired network.
D) Resources should be accessible only through a wireless network.

Review Question 6.16
What does availability in the context of cloud computing mean?
A) Cloud resources are accessible and responsive whenever a client needs them.

B) Cloud resources are available only during business hours.
C) Cloud resources are available only to certain users.
D) Cloud resources are available only in certain regions.

6.1.4 Cloud Service Models

A cloud provider offers computing-based services and solutions to businesses and individuals, including virtual hardware, software, infrastructure, and other related services. There are three fundamental Cloud Service models:

Infrastructure as a Service (IaaS): This is virtual hardware that replaces physical on-premise IT infrastructure. It can be scaled up or down based on your needs, meaning you only pay for what you use. An example of IaaS is the Internet of Things, with sensors and internet connections that continuously transmit data. IaaS also provides the necessary resources for high-performance computing and facilitates data storage, backup, and recovery options and services to users.

Platform as a Service (PaaS): This model adds features to IaaS, including operating systems and software development tools, such as runtime environments. This allows developers to focus on apps. PaaS provides provisioning and deployment, as well as load balancing and auto-scaling.

Software as a Service (SaaS): This is a software licensing and delivery model where apps are subscribed to and accessed over the internet. It has the largest market size of the three standard services and is likely the one you are most familiar with.

Each of these service models covers different aspects:

IaaS covers compute (providing computing resources on demand), storage (for storing information), and network (all the resources required for providing users networking capabilities).
PaaS includes operating systems, middleware, DBMS (database management systems), servers, and other tools for development and business intelligence in the cloud. This is great for APIs (Application Programming Interface), DevOps, integration, and machine learning activities. PaaS covers identity, which provides a layer for dealing with user authentication. It also provides a runtime layer for applications to run on.
SaaS includes apps accessed over the internet. It charges the user a monthly or annual fee. An Internet connection is required when accessing any SaaS application. The biggest concern with the SaaS model for most users is around data security as the data is not stored on customer premises.

There are other models that cloud computing can offer, such as Function as a Service (FaaS), in which development teams provide application code as a series of functions and the cloud provider runs those functions.

Review Question 6.17
What does Infrastructure as a Service (IaaS) replace in traditional computing?
A) Physical on-premise IT infrastructure
B) Software applications
C) Internet connections
D) Data security measures

Review Question 6.18
What is a feature added by Platform as a Service (PaaS) to IaaS?
A) Virtual hardware
B) Operating systems and software development tools
C) Internet connections
D) Data security measures

Review Question 6.19
What is the typical payment model for Software as a Service (SaaS)?
A) Pay per use
B) Monthly or annual subscription
C) One-time payment
D) Free of charge

Review Question 6.20
What does IaaS cover?
A) Compute, storage, and network
B) Operating systems and software development tools
C) Apps accessed over the internet
D) User authentication

Review Question 6.21
What does PaaS include?
A) Virtual hardware
B) Operating systems, middleware, DBMS, servers, and other tools for development and business intelligence
C) Apps accessed over the internet
D) Data security measures

Review Question 6.22
What is a concern with the SaaS model for most users?
A) The cost of the service
B) The need for an internet connection
C) Data security
D) The availability of apps

6.1.5 Cloud Deployment Models

Cloud deployment models are chosen based on where the computing devices reside and who controls these devices. There are five models to consider for your business needs.

The most common model is the public cloud. All services are hosted in the cloud and are available for consumption as needed. If a client requires additional resources, they can scale up and use those resources, paying for the extra usage. Public clouds are operated by third-party companies, known as cloud providers, such as Amazon Web Services (AWS), Microsoft Azure, and Google Cloud Platform (GCP).

The second model is the private cloud, also known as on-premise cloud. This model involves purchasing virtualization software and setting up an individual cloud within a business network. It has limited scalability as resources are confined to what the company can provide internally. However, a significant advantage of a private cloud is that the company maintains control over its security.

The third model is the hybrid cloud, which combines the best features of public and private clouds. With a hybrid cloud, sensitive information can be stored privately within the private network, while still benefiting from the features of the public cloud.

The fourth model, known as the multi-cloud, involves using more than one cloud provider simultaneously. This is similar to the hybrid cloud model, but in a multi-cloud setup, you use more than one public cloud. The main benefit is redundancy. It's less likely that an incident would occur simultaneously in two different clouds, providing higher availability of your services. Multi-cloud is also useful when you need specific services from different public clouds.

The fifth model is the community cloud. This model is particularly useful for organizations with common goals and interests, such as businesses that are merging. In this model, clients are aware of the other clients on the cloud. One downside is that scalability and flexibility are much less than those found in public clouds. Therefore, with the exception of private clouds, all cloud types use the concept of shared resources.

Review Question 6.23
What is the most common cloud deployment model?
A) Private cloud
B) Public cloud
C) Hybrid cloud
D) Multi-cloud

Review Question 6.24
What is a significant advantage of a private cloud?
A) It has unlimited scalability.
B) It is operated by third-party companies.
C) The company maintains control over its security.
D) It uses more than one cloud provider simultaneously.

Review Question 6.25
What does a hybrid cloud combine?
A) The best features of public and private clouds
B) The features of multiple public clouds
C) The features of community clouds
D) The features of on-premise clouds

Review Question 6.26
What is the main benefit of a multi-cloud model?
A) It has limited scalability.
B) It provides redundancy.
C) It is useful for businesses that are merging.
D) It is operated by third-party companies.

Review Question 6.27
For which organizations is the community cloud model particularly useful?
A) Organizations with common goals and interests
B) Organizations that require high scalability
C) Organizations that need specific services from different public clouds
D) Organizations that require third-party operation

Review Question 6.28
What is a common feature of all cloud types, except private clouds?
A) They are operated by third-party companies.
B) They use the concept of shared resources.
C) They provide redundancy.
D) They have limited scalability.

6.1.6 Shared Security Responsibility

When a customer subscribes to a Platform as a Service (PaaS) from a public cloud, the cloud provider is responsible for the server security. But what happens if the customer uses a weak password?

This scenario introduces a dual role in security responsibility:

The Customer: The customer is responsible for security within the cloud. This means they are in charge of their data and how the services and resources provided by the cloud provider are used. The customer is also responsible for the configuration and setup of the operating system, network firewall configuration, network traffic, file system structure and organization, as well as data encryption and data integrity.

The Cloud Provider: The cloud provider is responsible for providing the necessary computing, storage, and database resources required for the customer to execute its operations. The provider's responsibility also extends to providing necessary networking resources, including access to different regions of the world.

In essence, running a cloud computing operation requires a commitment from both the cloud provider and the customer. The provider supplies the necessary resources for the customer to consume. Therefore, the security of the cloud is a shared responsibility.

Review Question 6.29
Who is responsible for the server security in a Platform as a Service (PaaS) from a public cloud?
A) The customer
B) The cloud provider
C) The network administrator
D) The database manager

Review Question 6.30
Who is responsible for data encryption and data integrity in the cloud?
A) The cloud provider
B) The customer
C) The network administrator
D) The database manager

Review Question 6.31
Who provides the necessary computing, storage, and database resources required for the customer to execute its operations?
A) The customer
B) The network administrator
C) The cloud provider
D) The database manager

Review Question 6.32
Who is responsible for the configuration and setup of the operating system and network firewall configuration?
A) The cloud provider
B) The customer
C) The network administrator
D) The database manager

Review Question 6.33
Who is responsible for the security of the cloud?
A) Only the customer

B) Only the cloud provider
C) Both the customer and the cloud provider
D) Neither the customer nor the cloud provider

6.2 Cloud Networking Basics

A network is a system of two or more computers or devices that are interconnected, either through wired or wireless means, enabling them to communicate with each other. There are three key components that enable computer networking.

The first component is the network adapter present in every computer or networking device. For wired networks, the network adapter features an RJ-45 port that utilizes either twisted pair or untwisted pair cable for network connectivity. Wireless adapters, on the other hand, connect to the network via a built-in or externally connected antenna.

The second component is the transmission media, which serves as the conduit for data transfer from one location to another. This can be guided media, such as copper or fiber optic cables, or unguided media, like Wi-Fi or Bluetooth.

The third component is a networking protocol. This refers to the set of rules and syntax that computers must adhere to for effective communication. For instance, the Internet Protocol (IP) establishes standards for identifying each device on the Internet with a unique logical address.

Review Question 6.34
What is a network in the context of computers and devices?
A) A system of interconnected computers or devices
B) A type of software
C) A type of computer hardware
D) A type of computer virus

Review Question 6.35
What is the role of a network adapter in a computer or networking device?
A) It stores data
B) It processes data
C) It enables network connectivity
D) It cools the device

Review Question 6.36
What does an RJ-45 port utilize for network connectivity in wired networks?
A) Twisted pair or untwisted pair cable
B) Wi-Fi or Bluetooth
C) Fiber optic cables
D) Antenna

Review Question 6.37
What is the function of transmission media in a network?
A) It serves as the conduit for data transfer
B) It stores data
C) It processes data
D) It cools the device

Review Question 6.38
What is the purpose of a networking protocol?
A) It cools the device
B) It stores data
C) It sets the rules and syntax for communication
D) It processes data

6.2.1 Connecting to the Cloud

There are several methods to connect your device to the cloud. One such method is through a web browser using Hypertext Transfer Protocol Secure (HTTPS). In the end-of-chapter exercise, you will use a browser to create a free Azure account and access the cloud. Note that HTTPS is a secure protocol that encrypts data in transmission between a web server and your browser. However, this does not necessarily mean that the data on your computer or in the cloud is encrypted.

For enhanced security, many businesses require a Virtual Private Network (VPN). The internet is a public network, and data sent over the Internet could potentially be read by hackers. HTTPS can provide some level of security, but it is not as robust as using a VPN. While HTTPS secures the connection between a browser and a web server, a VPN creates a point-to-point secure tunnel through the internet. With a VPN, you can secure a connection that is tunneled to a specific destination, such as a corporate server running a VPN server within the corporate network.

Another method to connect to the cloud is by using the Remote Desktop Protocol (RDP). Once a user is logged in, they can use cloud devices as if they were using a computer in front of them. Windows includes an RDP client called 'Remote Desktop Connection'. There are also RDP clients for other systems. Linux users can use the 'rdesktop' command, macOS users can download the 'Microsoft Remote Desktop' app from the Mac App Store, and Android and iOS users can find RDP clients in their respective app stores. To open RDP in Windows, type 'RDP' in the search box on the taskbar, and you will see the 'Remote Desktop Connection' app.

Upon opening the RDP client, a user will need to provide several pieces of information to connect, including the ID or address of the remote computer and a username and password.

Yet another way to connect is via Secure Shell (SSH). Similar to RDP, SSH allows clients to remotely connect to a virtual Linux machine securely, as if the user were sitting at the virtual computer. Recent versions of Windows come with OpenSSH, but you still need to install and configure it before using. Alternatively, you can download and install a GUI version of SSH called PuTTY.

The final connectivity method is called 'Direct Connect'. It is used to establish a physical connection between your company's private network and the cloud provider's public network. If a large number of users need persistent access to cloud services, or if there's a large amount of data transferred between the cloud and the on-site network, then Direct Connect is likely the fastest and most cost-effective option. With Direct Connect, you are literally connecting a router from your network directly to the cloud provider's router.

Review Question 6.39
What does HTTPS encrypt in a web connection?
A) Data in transmission between a web server and your browser
B) Data stored on your computer
C) Data stored in the cloud
D) Data stored on the web server

Review Question 6.40
What does a VPN provide that HTTPS does not?
A) Encryption of data in transmission
B) A point-to-point secure tunnel through the internet
C) Security between a browser and a web server
D) Encryption of data stored on your computer

Review Question 6.41
What does the 'Remote Desktop Connection' app allow you to do?
A) Connect to the internet
B) Use cloud devices as if you were using a computer in front of you

C) Encrypt data in transmission between a web server and your browser
D) Create a point-to-point secure tunnel through the internet

Review Question 6.42
What is PuTTY?
A) A VPN client
B) A web browser
C) A GUI version of SSH
D) A type of transmission media

6.2.2 Software-Defined Networking

Enterprise networks can be intricate, consisting of routers, firewalls, and other network appliances. Routers play a pivotal role in computer networks. Their primary function is to receive incoming data packets, decipher the destination address, and forward the packet to the next network that brings the data closer to its final destination.

A router operates on three major functions, also known as planes. The control plane exchanges routing information with other routers and maintains the Address Resolution Protocol (ARP) table, which maps IP addresses to physical addresses. The data plane is responsible for forwarding traffic to a router that is closer to the destination. Lastly, the management plane enables the access and management of the router through SSH or other techniques.

Traditionally, each router comes equipped with its own controller. These network devices communicate with each other, but there is no central device controlling the entire network. Software-Defined Networking (SDN) addresses this issue. The SDN controller is responsible for the control plane of the entire network. The routers, in this setup, are simplified devices that only possess a data plane, devoid of a control plane. The SDN controller feeds the data plane of the routers with information from its control plane. One of the advantages of having a central controller is the ability to configure the entire network from a single device. This controller has comprehensive access and insight into everything occurring within the network.

Review Question 6.43
What is the primary function of a router in computer networks?
A) To store data packets
B) To receive, decipher, and forward data packets
C) To encrypt data packets

D) To create data packets

Review Question 6.44
What does the control plane of a router do?
A) It forwards traffic to a router that is closer to the destination
B) It exchanges routing information with other routers and maintains the ARP table
C) It enables the access and management of the router through SSH
D) It controls the entire network

Review Question 6.45
What is a key feature of Software-Defined Networking (SDN)?
A) Each router has its own controller
B) The SDN controller is responsible for the data plane of the entire network
C) The SDN controller is responsible for the control plane of the entire network
D) The routers have both a data plane and a control plane

Review Question 6.46
In a Software-Defined Network, what do the routers possess?
A) Only a control plane
B) Both a data plane and a control plane
C) Only a data plane
D) Neither a data plane nor a control plane

Review Question 6.47
What is one advantage of having a central controller in a Software-Defined Network?
A) It allows each router to have its own controller
B) It enables the configuration of the entire network from a single device
C) It maintains the ARP table
D) It forwards traffic to a router that is closer to the destination

6.2.3 Load Balancing

Have you ever wondered how many web servers a large company like Amazon operates? Each time you enter amazon.com into your browser and press enter, your HTTP request is sent to one of Amazon's many web servers. These servers, each capable of performing the same tasks, work together to ensure a seamless shopping experience. This distribution of work across multiple servers is known as load balancing.

Load balancing employs devices known as load balancers, which are logically positioned in front of a group of web servers. Acting as a dispatcher to the outside world, the load balancer directs incoming HTTP requests to one of the many web servers behind it.

Typically, a server is located in each geographic region to enhance network performance through proximity to users.

Another common load balancing strategy involves content-based servers. This approach divides the servers so that each handles a specific type of request. For instance, one group of servers might handle web requests, while another manages streaming videos. Servers specialized to handle a specific content type are often more efficient than multi-purpose ones.

Cloud-based load balancing offers numerous benefits. It enhances performance for heavily used applications and provides scalability. In the event of traffic spikes, additional virtual servers can be quickly provisioned. Another advantage is reliability. With cloud-based load balancing, servers in different regions can host the application. If an issue arises in one region, the application in another region can take over, ensuring business continuity.

Review Question 6.48
What is the purpose of load balancing in cloud computing?
A) To ensure all servers are used equally
B) To distribute work across multiple servers
C) To increase the cost of running web servers
D) To reduce the number of servers needed

Review Question 6.49
What role does a load balancer play in a network?
A) It sends all incoming requests to a single server
B) It acts as a dispatcher, directing incoming requests to one of many servers
C) It handles all incoming requests itself
D) It blocks incoming requests to prevent server overload

Review Question 6.50
How does geographic location of servers affect network performance?
A) Servers in different regions slow down network performance
B) Geographic location of servers has no impact on network performance
C) Servers closer to users enhance network performance
D) Servers farther from users enhance network performance

Review Question 6.51
What is a common strategy for load balancing with content-based servers?
A) Each server handles all types of requests
B) Servers are divided based on the type of requests they handle
C) All servers handle only one specific type of request
D) Servers are randomly assigned requests regardless of content type

Review Question 6.52
What is one benefit of cloud-based load balancing?
A) It reduces the number of servers needed
B) It allows for quick provisioning of additional virtual servers during traffic spikes
C) It eliminates the need for load balancers
D) It ensures all servers are used equally

Review Question 6.53
How does cloud-based load balancing enhance reliability?
A) By ensuring all servers are used equally
B) By hosting the application in different regions for redundancy
C) By reducing the number of servers needed
D) By eliminating the need for load balancers

6.2.4 Firewalls

Firewalls are crucial components in networking, serving as hardware or software solutions that act as network security guards. At a basic level, firewalls filter network traffic based on rules or policies defined by the network security administrator. They protect private network resources from external hackers and can also prevent computers within the private network from accessing undesirable content on the Internet.

There are two primary types of firewalls. Network-based firewalls are designed to protect an entire business network and are typically hardware solutions with integrated software. On the other hand, host-based firewalls protect only one computer and are almost always software solutions.

Most network-based firewalls have at least two network connections: one to the internet and one to the internal or private network.

By default, most firewalls are configured as 'default deny', which means that all traffic is blocked unless specifically authorized by the administrator. A common method of configuring firewalls is to use an Access Control List (ACL). The ACL is a set of rules that determines which traffic is allowed through the firewall and which traffic is blocked. Separate ACLs are often configured for inbound and outbound network traffic, and they are often set up to block traffic by IP address. In the context of cloud firewalls, this service is often referred to as Firewall as a Service (FWaaS).

Review Question 6.54

What is the primary function of a firewall in network security?
A) To increase network traffic
B) To filter network traffic based on predefined rules
C) To redirect all network traffic to a single server
D) To block all network traffic

Review Question 6.55
What is the difference between a network-based firewall and a host-based firewall?
A) A network-based firewall protects an entire network, while a host-based firewall protects a single computer
B) A network-based firewall is a software solution, while a host-based firewall is a hardware solution
C) A network-based firewall blocks all traffic, while a host-based firewall allows all traffic
D) A network-based firewall is used for small networks, while a host-based firewall is used for large networks

Review Question 6.56
What is the default configuration of most firewalls?
A) Default allow, which allows all traffic unless specifically blocked
B) Default deny, which blocks all traffic unless specifically allowed
C) Default block, which blocks all traffic regardless of rules
D) Default redirect, which redirects all traffic to a specific server

Review Question 6.57
What is an Access Control List (ACL) in the context of firewalls?
A) A list of all users who have access to the network
B) A list of all servers protected by the firewall
C) A set of rules that determines which traffic is allowed through the firewall
D) A list of all websites blocked by the firewall

Review Question 6.58
What is Firewall as a Service (FWaaS)?
A) A type of firewall that is provided as a physical device
B) A type of firewall that is provided as a software solution
C) A type of firewall that is provided as a cloud-based service
D) A type of firewall that is provided as a network-based solution

Review Question 6.59
What is the purpose of having multiple network connections in a network-based firewall?
A) To connect to multiple internet service providers
B) To connect to the internet and to the internal or private network
C) To connect to multiple servers within the network
D) To connect to multiple devices within the network

6.3 Cloud Storage Basics

In this section, we delve into the fundamental principles of cloud storage, a cornerstone of modern cloud computing. We explore the concepts, benefits, and key considerations that underpin this essential component of digital data management in today's interconnected world.

6.3.1 Software-Defined Storage

Among all services provided on the cloud, storage is perhaps the most tangible, popular, and easily understood. Cloud storage operates on a technology called software-defined storage (SDS), which is similar to software-defined networking explored in the previous section, but applied to storage. SDS is a storage architecture that separates storage software from its hardware, unlike traditional storage which is sold as a bundle of hardware and proprietary software. SDS is independent of any specific hardware.

Decoupling storage software from its hardware allows for the expansion of storage capacity as needed. It also allows for hardware upgrades or downgrades whenever desired. Essentially, SDS provides enormous flexibility.

SDS is a layer of technology that provides many services using industry-standard servers instead of proprietary software. Essentially, SDS abstracts the controls for storage requests, not the actual stored data. It is a software layer between the physical storage and the data request, allowing manipulation of how and where data is stored. A key characteristic of SDS controller software is that it makes no assumptions about the capacity of the underlying hardware.

With a layer of software between applications and storage, the type of storage device may become somewhat irrelevant, and the devices themselves become interchangeable. The software maintains the location of each unit of data and can retrieve it, regardless of where it physically resides.

Using SDS, one logical unit of storage can be composed of many physical hard drives, enabling virtually unlimited storage. Conversely, one physical hard drive can be separated into a large number of logical storage units. Additionally, every combination in between logical and physical storage is possible.

There are many benefits to using SDS. Users can access files from anywhere in the world, facilitating easy sharing and collaboration. Most cloud storage providers offer synchronization to the desktop, ensuring that a folder on your computer always contains the most current edition of the files stored in the cloud. SDS provides scalability. Storage capacity can be added or removed without any performance issues or downtime.

A major benefit of SDS is the use of artificial intelligence (AI). SDS can monitor the access patterns of your data, storing only the most frequently accessed portion on the fastest and most expensive storage, and relegating the rest to less costly storage. Policies can be set up to retrieve data at trigger events like evening backups, monthly reports, or for training an AI application. SDS can learn to predict what data you want and retrieves it ahead of time from inexpensive tape systems, reducing wait times for the appropriate tape cartridge to load.

Review Question 6.60
What is Software-Defined Storage (SDS)?
A) A storage architecture that bundles storage software with its hardware
B) A storage architecture that separates storage software from its hardware
C) A storage architecture that depends on specific hardware
D) A storage architecture that reduces storage capacity

Review Question 6.61
What does SDS abstract in the storage process?
A) The actual data that is stored
B) The controls for storage requests
C) The physical location of the data
D) The type of storage device used

Review Question 6.62
What is a key characteristic of SDS controller software?
A) It makes assumptions about the capacity of the underlying hardware
B) It restricts the expansion of storage capacity
C) It makes no assumptions about the capacity of the underlying hardware
D) It depends on the type of storage device used

Review Question 6.63
What is one benefit of using SDS?
A) It reduces the number of servers needed
B) It allows for easy sharing and collaboration
C) It restricts access to files
D) It limits storage capacity

Review Question 6.64
How does SDS provide scalability?
A) By reducing storage capacity
B) By adding or removing storage capacity without performance issues or downtime
C) By restricting the number of servers used
D) By limiting the types of storage devices used

Review Question 6.65

How does SDS use artificial intelligence (AI)?
A) By blocking access to certain data
B) By storing all data on the fastest and most expensive storage
C) By monitoring the access patterns of data and storing frequently accessed data on the fastest storage
D) By restricting the retrieval of data to certain times

6.3.2 Storage Performance and Cost

Cloud storage is utilized by companies for various purposes. While everyone desires optimal performance, not all are willing to pay the highest price. Some businesses require cloud storage to be instantly accessible, serving as a replacement for a local hard drive. Others need long-term archival storage, while some require a combination of both. Once the business storage needs are identified, the focus can shift to the performance and price of available solutions.

Broadly, there are two major categories of cloud storage related to performance. The first is hot storage, which refers to data that is readily available at all times, allowing for frequent and rapid access. Conversely, cold storage refers to data that isn't accessed often, such as archived data. Retrieving cold data might take from several minutes to several days.

In reality, cloud providers offer a wide range of storage solutions with varying performance levels and costs. For instance, Microsoft Azure offers premium, hot, cold, and archived tiers. Google provides two hot options, multiregional storage and regional storage. AWS has two primary designations, its Simple Storage Service (S3) for hot data, and S3 Glacier for archives, each with multiple options to choose from. When a client uploads data to the cloud, the data is placed into a storage container. Cloud providers use different names for their containers. For example, AWS and Google Cloud use the term 'bucket', whereas Azure uses 'blob'. Providers allow clients to have multiple containers of varying temperatures to meet their storage needs.

When planning which container to purchase, several key performance characteristics and parameters should be considered. These include cost per GB (Gigabyte), storage capacity limits, data encryption, storage compression and/or deduplication, and finally, intelligent analysis of storage usage and/or automated optimization.

Review Question 6.66
What is the primary function of cloud storage?
A) To provide a local hard drive replacement
B) To serve as long-term archival storage
C) To offer a combination of instant access and long-term storage
D) All of the above

Review Question 6.67
What is hot storage in the context of cloud storage?
A) Data that is rarely accessed
B) Data that is available at all times
C) Data that is stored on physical hard drives
D) Data that is archived for long-term storage

Review Question 6.68
What is the advantage of decoupling storage software from its hardware in Software-Defined Storage (SDS)?
A) It restricts the expansion of storage capacity
B) It allows for the expansion of storage capacity as needed
C) It reduces the flexibility of storage management
D) It increases the dependence on specific hardware

Review Question 6.69
What does a storage container in cloud storage refer to?
A) The physical location of the data
B) The software used to manage the data
C) The place where data is stored when uploaded to the cloud
D) The network used to transfer the data

6.3.3 Storage Techniques

Data is stored at the hardware level as long sequences of 0s and 1s on a storage medium. This encompasses everything from essential operating system files to databases and personal photos. The interpretation of this data and the determination of where a relevant piece of information begins and ends is the responsibility of the device's operating system or software.

Data can be stored and retrieved from the cloud in several ways, with three primary types of cloud storage.

File Storage: This is similar to how you organize files on your personal computers. Each file has a name and a path to its folder or subfolder. The folder structure and file naming scheme make it relatively easy for humans to navigate.

Block Storage: Files are divided into equally sized chunks of data, each assigned a unique identifier, and then stored on the hard drive. Because each piece of data has a unique address, a file structure is not needed. Block storage allows files to be broken into more manageable chunks, rather than being stored as a single entity. This enables the operating system to modify a portion of a file without needing to open the entire file. Block storage has lower latency than other types of storage, and data transfers faster. It is ideal for large structured data sets that need frequent access and updates.

Object Storage: Object storage organizes and works with objects. Every object contains three components:

The data to be stored can be a photo, a research paper, or a section of a book. An object can be a portion of a file, or simply a collection of bits and bytes related to other files and not part of any file.
The metadata about the object is defined by the creator of the object storage; it contains contextual information about what the data is, what it should be used for, its confidentiality, or any other information relevant to the way the data is used.

A globally unique identifier of the object is a 128-bit unique value given to the object to enable the object to be found over a distributed system. This allows the data to be located without knowing the physical location of the data.
Cloud storage solutions offer two features to conserve space.
Compression: Compression reduces file sizes so they occupy less storage space. It works by identifying repeated information within a file and replacing that information with a shorter string.
Deduplication: Data deduplication operates at the file level or block level to eliminate duplicate data. Typically, deduplication is applied to the data first, followed by compression to each file or block.

Review Question 6.70
How is data stored at the hardware level?
A) As long sequences of 0s and 1s
B) In hexadecimal format
C) As ASCII characters
D) In binary trees

Review Question 6.71
What is the primary responsibility of a device's operating system in terms of data storage?
A) To interpret the data and determine where a relevant piece of information begins and ends
B) To compress the data
C) To deduplicate the data
D) To encrypt the data

Review Question 6.72
What is a unique feature of block storage?
A) Files are divided into equally sized chunks of data
B) Each file has a name and a path to its folder or subfolder
C) Files are organized and worked with as objects
D) Files are compressed to occupy less storage space

Review Question 6.73
What are the three components of an object in object storage?
A) The data to be stored, the metadata about the object, and a globally unique identifier of the object
B) The data to be stored, the size of the object, and the date the object was created
C) The data to be stored, the location of the object, and the owner of the object
D) The data to be stored, the type of the object, and the permissions of the object

Review Question 6.74
What is the sequence of operations in data deduplication and compression?
A) Compression first, followed by deduplication
B) Deduplication first, followed by compression
C) Both operations are performed simultaneously
D) The sequence varies depending on the type of data

6.4 Cloud Design Issues

This section discusses several factors to consider when transitioning your information technology to the cloud.

6.4.1 Redundancy and Availability

The first factor is redundancy. In the workplace, being considered redundant is negative. However, in computing, redundancy is beneficial. Redundancy implies that a device, system, or process can take over in the event of a failure, ensuring system continuity. For instance, data redundancy ensures that critical data is always accessible from any location, while network redundancy ensures that a key server or the internet is consistently available.

Incorporating redundancy into your network architecture involves additional costs, which may be a point of contention during budget discussions. It's essential to weigh the benefits against the costs by assessing your cloud needs and the risks associated with specific resources. This analysis is often encapsulated in a redundancy plan that helps mitigate issues caused by a single point of failure. Collaborate with your cloud provider to ensure that the service level agreement (SLA) includes appropriate redundancy measures. In practice, you'll need to balance the risk tolerance for a specific failure against the cost of implementing a redundant system. A comprehensive redundancy plan should cover the following areas:

Hardware Redundancy: Also known as fault tolerance, it includes components such as storage, processors, memory, or network devices.

Network Redundancy: Ensures the availability of a company's computer network even when the current infrastructure fails. It typically refers to network infrastructure such as switches and routers and may also involve guaranteeing a certain amount of network bandwidth.

Geographic Redundancy: Involves having replicas of the same resources in two or more physical locations. These locations should be sufficiently distant so that if one suffers a catastrophic natural disaster or failure, the other would remain unaffected.

Process Redundancy: Allows a business to continue operating if a process fails. As more businesses transition to e-commerce, it's crucial to map out critical business processes and identify which ones require high availability. Identifying single points of failure when setting up redundancy is vital.

Software Redundancy: Encompasses a broad range, from operating systems to applications to peripheral drivers. Software redundancy can be either redundancy of the program or redundancy within the program. Incorporating a fail-safe mechanism within software is an effective way to achieve this.

Data Redundancy: Often takes the form of data backups. Implementing data backup as part of the redundancy plan or disaster recovery plan may be legally mandated for some companies. A company that experiences data loss without a backup could potentially go out of business. With cloud computing, implementing data backups and redundancy is straightforward.

A concept closely related to redundancy is availability. While redundancy can be viewed as a "planned" operational function, availability is based on "unplanned" downtime and specifically refers to the duration the service is available. The cloud provider will specify the level of uptime guaranteed in the SLA.

Service availability is often measured in terms of nines, indicating the percentage of uptime the provider guarantees. For instance, four nines (99.99%) means the service will be available 99.99% of the time, equating to a maximum downtime of 52.6 minutes per year. The level of service SLA you should opt for depends on your company's risk tolerance and the costs of that level.

Review Question 6.75
What does redundancy imply in computing?
A) A device, system, or process can take over in the event of a failure
B) A device, system, or process is no longer needed
C) A device, system, or process is outdated
D) A device, system, or process is duplicated unnecessarily

Review Question 6.76
What does a comprehensive redundancy plan cover?
A) Hardware Redundancy
B) Network Redundancy
C) Geographic Redundancy
D) All mentioned options

Review Question 6.77
What is the purpose of geographic redundancy?
A) To ensure that a company's computer network is available even when the current infrastructure fails
B) To have replicas of the same resources in two or more physical locations
C) To allow a business to continue operating if a process fails
D) To ensure that critical data is always accessible from any location

Review Question 6.78
What does service availability refer to in the context of cloud computing?
A) The duration the service is planned to be available
B) The duration the service is available during unplanned downtime
C) The duration the service is available during planned downtime
D) The duration the service is unavailable during planned downtime

Review Question 6.79
What does four nines (99.99%) in terms of service availability mean?
A) The service will be available 99.99% of the time
B) The service will be unavailable 99.99% of the time
C) The service will be available 0.01% of the time
D) The service will be unavailable 0.01% of the time

Review Question 6.80
What could potentially happen to a company that experiences data loss without a backup?
A) The company could potentially go out of business
B) The company could potentially lose customers
C) The company could potentially face legal issues
D) The company could potentially lose data

6.4.2 Disaster Recovery and Redundancy Planning

Effective redundancy and high availability plans can mitigate service disruptions and ensure smooth business operations. However, no plan is foolproof. Disasters, whether they stem from catastrophic hardware or software failures, cyber-attacks, human error, or natural disasters, can occur. Disaster recovery is the process by which a business resumes operations following a disaster. A disaster recovery plan details the steps necessary to restore operational status in the wake of a disaster.

Disaster recovery plans must consider all facets of a corporate network infrastructure, including hardware, software, network, power, and data. The plan should also provide guidance for employees in the event of a disaster. Cloud providers can assist with disaster recovery planning, and depending on the stipulations of your Service Level Agreement (SLA), the responsibility for disaster recovery and response may fall on them. However, assuming that the cloud provider will handle everything could be a grave mistake. This is where recovery objectives come into play. A disaster recovery plan should define two recovery objectives: the Recovery Point Objective (RPO) and the Recovery Time Objective (RTO).

The RPO specifies the maximum age of data that an organization must recover from backup storage for normal operations to resume. In other words, how old can the restored data be and still be useful for running the business? Ensure that your SLA includes your RPO.

It's important to note that not all data are created equal. Different applications and databases should have different RPOs, depending on their criticality and how frequently they change. For instance, operating system core files don't change often, and you likely have the ability to restore an OS and necessary patches from installation media or online repositories. On the other hand, for medical data or financial transaction databases, the RPO should be close to zero.

The RTO is the maximum acceptable length of time that a system can be down in the event of a disaster. It defines the duration within which the cloud provider must restore full operations, including network access and data restoration.

Just as RPOs vary by system, so should RTOs. If your company has a website that doesn't handle e-commerce transactions, then a failure might be inconvenient, but it's not critical to business operations. Previously, we discussed shared responsibility, where both the client and the cloud service provider are responsible for securing cloud-based systems. Remember, the client is responsible for security in the cloud, while the cloud service provider is responsible for the security of the cloud. Redundancy and disaster planning and recovery should be thought of in the same way. Don't make assumptions about what the cloud provider will provide in these areas. While cloud providers do offer redundancy and data recovery services, these must be agreed upon in the SLA.

Review Question 6.81
What is the purpose of a disaster recovery plan?
A) To ensure high availability and redundancy
B) To detail the steps necessary to restore operational status after a disaster
C) To prevent disasters from occurring
D) To define the responsibilities of cloud providers

Review Question 6.82
What does the Recovery Point Objective (RPO) specify in a disaster recovery plan?
A) The maximum acceptable length of time that a system can be down
B) The maximum age of data that must be recovered from backups for normal operations to resume
C) The responsibilities of cloud providers
D) The steps necessary to restore operational status after a disaster

Review Question 6.83
Should all data have the same Recovery Point Objective (RPO)?
A) Yes, all data should have the same RPO
B) No, different applications and databases should have different RPOs
C) Yes, but only if they are stored in the cloud
D) No, RPOs should be defined by the cloud provider

Review Question 6.84
What does the Recovery Time Objective (RTO) define in a disaster recovery plan?
A) The maximum age of data that must be recovered from backups
B) The maximum acceptable length of time that a system can be down
C) The responsibilities of cloud providers
D) The steps necessary to restore operational status after a disaster

Review Question 6.85
Who is responsible for securing cloud-based systems?
A) Only the client
B) Only the cloud service provider
C) Both the client and the cloud service provider
D) Neither the client nor the cloud service provider

6.5 Chapter Summary

In this chapter, we explored the fundamental concepts of cloud computing. We delved into the three primary cloud service models - Infrastructure as a Service (IaaS), Platform as a Service (PaaS), and Software as a Service (SaaS), as well as the five cloud deployment models - public, private, hybrid, multi-cloud, and community. In the section on cloud networking, we discussed how to access the cloud, the principles of software-defined networking, and the roles of load balancing and firewalls.

In the cloud storage section, we examined software-defined storage and the types of cloud storage - file, block, and object. Finally, in the concluding section, we emphasized the importance of redundancy and disaster recovery plans, which are crucial components of a Service Level Agreement (SLA) with your cloud provider.

6.6 Exercises

Learn how to create a free Azure account by following the instructions provided in the 'What is the Azure free account?' section on the official Azure website. Be sure to read this section carefully, as you may incur charges for activities that are not covered by the free account. While creating an account does not require a credit card, you may need to provide one for certain activities. An email and phone number are also required.

If you're a student, you can create a student account using a specific link on the Azure website. The primary difference between a regular and a student account is that the latter offers less free credit but extends the trial period. No credit card is required as long as you have free credit remaining. A school email and phone number are also required.

After successfully creating and logging into your account, you'll be directed to a 'Get Started' page where you can begin exploring the free services available to you.

The 'Azure free services' page is divided into two main sections: 'Services free for 12 months with the Azure free account' and 'Always free services'. Be aware that there are many limitations associated with the free account. For instance, if you have a large amount of data or consume a significant amount of bandwidth, you may not have 12 months of database access. Your free credit can also deplete quickly.

6.7 References:

Statista, 2021, Public Cloud Report 2021 – Statista Technology Market Outlook,

https://www.statista.com/study/85676/public-cloud-report/

6.8 Solutions to Review Questions

6.1 A; 6.2 D; 6.3 B; 6.4 B; 6.5 D; 6.6 A; 6.7 B; 6.8 C; 6.9 A; 6.10 A; 6.11 B; 6.12 A; 6.13 A; 6.14 A; 6.15 A; 6.16 A; 6.17 A; 6.18 B; 6.19 B; 6.20 A; 6.21 B; 6.22 C; 6.23 B; 6.24 C; 6.25 A; 6.26 B; 6.27 A; 6.28 B; 6.29 B; 6.30 B; 6.31 C; 6.32 B; 6.33 C; 6.34 A; 6.35 C; 6.36 A; 6.37 A; 6.38 C; 6.39 A; 6.40 B; 6.41 B; 6.42 C; 6.43 B; 6.44 B; 6.45 C; 6.46 C; 6.47 B; 6.48 B; 6.49 B; 6.50 C; 6.51 B; 6.52 B; 6.53 B; 6.54 B; 6.55 A; 6.56 B; 6.57 C; 6.58 C; 6.59 B; 6.60 B; 6.61 B; 6.62 C; 6.63 B; 6.64 B; 6.65 C; 6.66 C; 6.67 B; 6.68 B; 6.69 C; 6.70 A; 6.71 A; 6.72 A; 6.73 A; 6.74 B; 6.75 A; 6.76 D; 6.77 B; 6.78 B; 6.79 A; 6.80 A; 6.81 B; 6.82 B; 6.83 B; 6.84 B; 6.85 C;

Chapter 7: Cloud Business Fundamentals

Chapter Learning Outcomes

7.1: Analyze business requirements for the cloud.
7.2: Utilize benchmarking tools to establish baseline performance.
7.3: Distinguish between capital expenditure and operational expenditure.
7.4: Compare pricing models for cloud services.
7.5: Evaluate various cloud service vendors based on specific criteria.
7.6: Critique different approaches to cloud adoption strategies.

7.1 Assess Business Requirements

Transitioning business computing to the cloud is a multifaceted endeavor, replete with both opportunities and challenges. In this section, we delve into the essential considerations for migrating to the cloud, guiding you through the evaluation process. We also explore performance and service level considerations, highlighting the pivotal role of benchmarking in successful cloud migration. As you conclude this section, we direct you to harness the cloud providers' frameworks to facilitate your cloud adoption journey.

7.1.1 Evaluating Business Needs

Prior to transitioning your on-premise information technology to a public cloud environment, a meticulous assessment of business requirements is imperative. In essence, why does your business necessitate cloud adoption?

The response to the question must emanate from your business stakeholders. Convene with these stakeholders to crystallize the motives behind your move to the cloud. The decision should not be driven solely by trends or popularity; rather, it should be grounded in quantitative data and well-defined objectives.

To facilitate this assessment, you can employ a feasibility study, evaluating economic, technical, and legal factors to gauge the likelihood of a successful project. Economic feasibility scrutinizes the balance between cloud computing costs, benefits, and net profit. Technical feasibility assesses your organization's capacity for cloud migration and your IT staff's proficiency in cloud technologies. Legal feasibility encompasses compliance, data certification, cybersecurity measures, and liability in the event of a security breach. Deliverables from the feasibility study encompass target metrics, including service level agreement (SLA) targets, recovery point objective (RPO), recovery time objective (RTO) targets, and high availability objectives.

An SLA is a contractual agreement specifying the level of service a cloud provider guarantees to deliver. Failure to meet these commitments results in contractual penalties. SLAs should, at a minimum, cover aspects like performance speed, application availability, data durability, support agreements, and exit terms. Basic SLAs for each cloud provider can typically be found on their respective websites.

Additionally, gap analysis can be employed to discern the disparity between your current state and the desired future state. This process entails:

Identifying the current state, which involves gathering quantitative and qualitative data about your existing IT services.
Defining the ideal future state, outlining your aspirations for your IT services.
Recognizing the gaps and comprehending their origins.
Devising and implementing a strategy to bridge these gaps.

This comprehensive analysis aids in determining whether the public cloud aligns with your business's value proposition, helping you prioritize resource allocation. The outcome of the gap analysis is a strategic roadmap highlighting your company's critical requirements and goals.

Review Question 7.1
Before you move your on-premise information technology to a public cloud, you need to assess business requirements. Which of the following is the best source for gathering the requirements?
A) IT managers
B) business managers
C) business stakeholders
D) cloud subject matter experts

Review Question 7.2
You can apply _______ to analyze economic, technical, and legal factors to ascertain the likelihood of completing a project successfully.
A) feasibility study
B) gap analysis
C) IaaS

D) cloud technology

Review Question 7.3
In _______ feasibility, you examine the benefit and cost of cloud computing and the net profit of moving to cloud.
A) economic
B) technical
C) legal
D) cloud

Review Question 7.4
In _______ feasibility, you check the business ability to migrate to the cloud and the skill levels of your IT staff on cloud technologies.
A) economic
B) technical
C) legal
D) business

Review Question 7.5
In _______ feasibility, you assess how the cloud providers follow the compliance and certification of the data.
A) economic
B) technical
C) legal
D) cloud

Review Question 7.6
The _______ is a contract that states the cloud provider offers a service at a particular level, and if it does not meet that level, then it is in violation of the contract and result in penalties.
A) cloud manual
B) user manual
C) cloud provider agreement (CPA)
D) service level agreement (SLA)

Review Question 7.7
Which of the following is NOT a gap analysis step?
A) identifying the current state
B) identifying the ideal future state
C) involving the stakeholders
D) creating and implementing a plan to bridge the gap

Review Question 7.8
You can apply _______ to determine the differences between your current state and the target state (goal) and plan a strategy to reach the goal.
A) feasibility study
B) gap analysis
C) IaaS
D) cloud technology

7.1.2 Benchmarking in Cloud Migration

In business requirement assessment, obtaining actionable assessment data is paramount. Establishing a performance baseline is essential, serving as a reference point for future comparisons post-cloud migration. For instance, you might conduct network traffic captures over days or weeks to comprehensively understand your business network's typical behavior during peak, off-peak, and regular usage periods. When you transition to the cloud, these metrics can be compared to the baseline, guiding decision-making.

Benchmarking involves utilizing tools to quantitatively evaluate your network, storage, computing resources, and existing workloads, aligning them with your current service level agreements and future goals in the cloud. The objective is to ensure that the migration does not compromise service levels.

For instance, when benchmarking servers, you assess data processing rates, service availability, incident resolution patterns, and adherence to compliance certifications, such as HIPAA for patient data handling. These requirements remain relevant even after transitioning to the cloud.

Cloud providers play a pivotal role in this process by offering benchmarking tools designed for their infrastructure. Given that physical access to the cloud vendor's devices is not feasible, these tools facilitate a comparison between the results provided by the cloud provider's benchmarking tools and your on-premise performance baseline from your business requirement assessment.

Review Question 7.9
An important part of business requirement assessment is to have _______ data.
A) actionable assessment
B) stakeholder
C) business transaction
D) cloud storage

Review Question 7.10
You must set the performance _______ to which you can compare future performance once you migrate to the cloud.
A) goal
B) plan
C) strategy
D) baseline

Review Question 7.11
The _______ is about using tools to quantitatively analyze your network, your storage, your compute, your workloads that you are offering now locally, and how they meet your existing service level agreements.
A) cloud

B) benchmark
C) performance
D) baseline

Review Question 7.12
You can compare the result provided by the cloud provider benchmarking tools to that of your on-premise performance baseline in your_______.
A) cloud portfolio
B) benchmark
C) business requirement assessment
D) own baseline

7.1.3 Frameworks for Cloud Adoption

Major public cloud providers offer comprehensive cloud adoption frameworks online. For instance, Microsoft presents the "Microsoft Cloud Adoption Framework for Azure" available at https://docs.microsoft.com/en-us/azure/cloud-adoption-framework/. This framework encompasses nine categories of guidance, spanning the entire cloud adoption journey: "get started," "strategy," "plan," "ready," "migrate," "innovate," "govern," "manage," and "organize." Regardless of where you are in your migration process, you can access a wealth of documentation, guidance, and best practices.

Within the assessments section of the Azure adoption framework, you'll find four invaluable tools designed to assist you in pinpointing the gaps between your current state and your desired state. Each tool poses specific questions and subsequently furnishes tailored, curated recommendations. For instance, the "Cloud Journey Tracker" requires approximately 15 minutes of your time to collect information through questions before proposing a suitable adoption path.

Review Question 2.13
Major public cloud providers have cloud adoption framework available online. No matter what stage you are in this migration journey, you can find a collection of documentation, guidance, and best practices to learn.
A) True
B) False

Review Question 2.14
The assessments section in "Microsoft Cloud Adoption Framework for Azure" provides tools to help you determine the gaps between the current state and the desired state. Each tool will ask you a few questions and then provide _______ recommendations for you.
A) lowest cost
B) best performance
C) personalized

D) most popular

7.2 Cloud Service Pricing Scheme

As businesses and individuals increasingly leverage cloud services, it's essential to navigate the intricate pricing models, from pay-as-you-go to reserved instances, and manage costs effectively. Unpacking these concepts, this section delves into the methodologies, best practices, and real-world applications, making it an indispensable resource for students and professionals seeking to master the art of cloud service pricing.

7.2.1 Capital and Operational Expenditure

In business information technology, there exist two distinct categories of expenditure: capital expenditure (CapEx) and operational expenditure (OpEx). CapEx involves an initial, fixed investment in assets such as computer hardware and software. The drawback of CapEx lies in its upfront lump-sum nature and the rapid depreciation of IT assets. To illustrate, consider a scenario where a business maintains an on-premise public website. To accommodate an impending traffic surge, additional server hardware must be acquired or leased. This hardware investment becomes a burden once the spike subsides. In contrast, the cloud offers an agile solution. Instead of purchasing hardware, businesses can subscribe to Platform as a Service (PaaS), eliminating concerns about provisioning, electricity costs, and physical space.

On the other hand, OpEx constitutes a company's ongoing, day-to-day expenses. In the cloud, you pay only for the services consumed, making it a "predictable" recurring cost. For instance, selecting a pay-as-you-go subscription results in monthly invoices. Unlike the fixed and upfront nature of CapEx, OpEx in the cloud can be tailored to be variable or predictable, based on contractual agreements with vendors. This section delves into the critical distinctions between these two financial models, shedding light on their applications in the world of IT.

Review Question 7.15
There are two types of capital expenditure discussed in this book: _______ expenditure and _______ expenditure.
A) cash, check
B) cash, capital
C) capital, operational
D) operational, credit

Review Question 7.16

The ______ expenditure is where you have a fixed, predictable cost upfront investment in things like computer hardware.
A) cash
B) credit
C) capital
D) operational

Review Question 7.17
The issue with ______ expenditure is that not only is it a lump sum up front, but your expenditure on information technology is going to depreciate in value quickly.
A) cash
B) credit
C) capital
D) operational

Review Question 7.18
The ______ expense, rather than an upfront cost, you're paying only for the cloud service that you use as recurring cost.
A) cash
B) credit
C) capital
D) operational

7.2.2 Cloud Pricing Models

Cloud service pricing plays a pivotal role in shaping an enterprise's decision-making process (Gupta et al., 2021). Leading public cloud providers employ a subscription-based model, offering a free service tier designed for evaluation purposes. As you might recall from the previous chapter's exercise, you created one such instance on Azure. If you're considering moving forward, running a pilot is a prudent step, allowing you to scrutinize factors such as availability, performance, user-friendliness, and overall cost.

The "pay as you go" model stands as the most prevalent option, requiring you to pay solely for the cloud services you've utilized within each payment period. This pricing structure resembles the manufacturer's suggested retail price or regular price and provides a high degree of flexibility. While it can potentially be the most expensive option, it grants you a significant level of control.

For businesses seeking to mitigate the unpredictability inherent in the pay-as-you-go model, "prepaid" arrangements offer an alternative. These typically involve multi-year contracts where you prepay for an entire year and then reevaluate the amount at the end of each 12-month period. This approach fosters predictability in cloud spending, often featuring lower costs due to loyalty-based incentives.

Spot service pricing operates on a bid-based system, where consumers bid on spare cloud resources and employ them when their bid exceeds the current spot price. However, it's essential to note that the service may be interrupted with minimal notice if the spot price surpasses your bid. The upside of this model is the potential for significantly lower costs when demand is low and supply is abundant, but it comes with the downside of unpredictable interruptions.

In their website, cloud providers equip users with tools, allowing you to visualize your spending by service or group. For instance, Azure provides a Cost Management link where you can access your bills, perform expenditure forecasting, and benefit from predictive analytics. AWS offers a closely analogous tool named Cost Explorer. Major public cloud vendors have harnessed artificial intelligence to provide valuable spending optimization recommendations, empowering you to make more cost-effective choices in your cloud operations.

Review Question 7.19
Which of the following is NOT a cloud service pricing model?
A) cash discount
B) pay as you go
C) prepaid
D) spot

Review Question 7.20
The _______ price is more like manufacturer suggested retail price, or regular price.
A) cash discount
B) pay as you go
C) prepaid
D) spot

Review Question 7.21
The _______ pricing is a way to help businesses ease the unpredictable part of pay as you go pricing scheme.
A) cash discount
B) pay as you go
C) prepaid
D) spot

Review Question 7.22
The _______ pricing scheme works when consumers bid on spare resources and employ them whenever the bid exceeds the current spot price.
A) cash discount
B) pay as you go
C) prepaid
D) spot

7.2.3 Software Licensing Models

One aspect of cloud computing cost that warrants careful consideration is the expense associated with software licenses. The licensing landscape for cloud products can be intricate, often requiring users to navigate vendor websites to explore their pricing structures. It's advisable to reach out to the vendor to ascertain whether your service subscription encompasses all costs within your per-minute usage.

Many cloud providers have established partnerships with a diverse array of independent software vendors (ISVs) who permit the utilization of their products on the cloud using a pay-as-you-go approach. In this scenario, the licensing matter becomes straightforward. Users pay a premium over the standard Infrastructure as a Service (IaaS) charges, with the additional cost directed to the ISV. This model is commonly referred to as the *utility pricing model*. If the software you need isn't readily available in the cloud, it's worthwhile to engage in discussions with your software vendor about the possibility of making their software accessible in the cloud.

Some ISVs opt not to participate in the utility pricing model and instead offer their software as a service with a monthly subscription fee. They typically provide standard APIs and web-based interfaces, making implementation a swift and hassle-free process. This option often serves as the most straightforward and rapid route for migrating your existing on-premise installations to a vendor-hosted, on-demand offering. This pricing model is known as the ISV SaaS-based Cloud Service pricing model.

For those who possess traditional software licenses, the "Bring Your Own License" (BYOL) pricing model provides an avenue to either procure new licenses conventionally or leverage existing, highly discounted multi-year licenses and apply them to pre-configured cloud product images. It's important to note that major cloud providers commonly accommodate the BYOL approach.

Review Question 7.23
Many cloud providers have teamed with variety of independent software vendors (ISV) who have permitted the use of their product on the cloud with pay-as-you-go. What is this pricing model called?
A) low cost
B) utilities
C) ISV SaaS-based Cloud Service
D) bring your own license (BYOL)

Review Question 7.24
Some ISVs do not join the utility pricing model and offer their software as a service and charge a monthly subscription fee. What is this pricing model called?
A) low cost
B) utilities
C) ISV SaaS-based Cloud Service
D) bring your own license (BYOL)

Review Question 7.25
The _______ pricing model allows you to purchase a new license the traditional way or use your existing multi-year highly-discounted license and apply it to the product which is available as a pre-configured image in cloud.
A) low cost
B) utilities
C) ISV SaaS-based Cloud Service
D) bring your own license (BYOL)

7.3 The Need for Cloud Knowledge

In today's digital landscape, the need for a deep understanding of cloud computing is paramount. As organizations increasingly migrate their operations to cloud environments, professionals across diverse industries must grasp the fundamental concepts and intricacies of this transformative technology. Cloud computing offers unmatched scalability, flexibility, and cost-efficiency, but harnessing its potential demands a comprehensive knowledge base.

7.3.1 IT Skills and Certification Essentials

Cloud computing fundamentally diverges from on-premise computing in a pivotal way. The latter entails in-house hosting, with an organization managing its own infrastructure, while the former delegates this responsibility to a third-party provider. This shift empowers companies to adopt a pay-as-needed approach, enabling dynamic scaling in response to usage patterns, user demands, and the company's growth trajectory.

These disparities necessitate adjustments within your IT department, either through new hires or by facilitating the professional development of existing employees. Pursuing professional certifications (Hulshof and Daneva, 2021) proves instrumental in this endeavor.

All three major cloud providers—Microsoft Azure, Amazon AWS, and Google GCP—offer comprehensive certification programs. For instance, if your organization is a Microsoft partner, it may mandate a specific number of certified staff members. Each provider presents a range of certifications, distinguished by professional levels (e.g., entry, associate, professional) and specialized domains, encompassing networking, security, databases, analytics, and more.

Review Question 7.26
Some cloud providers require enterprises using their services to have a number of _______ staff members.
A) experienced
B) newly graduated
C) certified
D) subject matter expert (SME)

Review Question 7.27
The differences between on-premise and cloud means that enterprises need _______.
A) new hires
B) help employees with professional development
C) new hires and/or help employees with professional development
D) to move the business to a different region

Review Question 7.28
Each cloud provider has several certifications with different _______, such as entry, associate, professional and _______, such as networking, security, database, analytics.
A) persons, costs
B) persons, specialties
C) levels, costs
D) levels, specialties

7.3.2 Key Challenges and Leveraging Support

As you've already discovered, transitioning to the cloud promises a swifter time-to-market for your services. This is exemplified by the ability to rapidly render your applications geo-available. However, this enhanced agility brings forth a crucial requirement: proficiency in cloud computing technology.

Approaching the cloud in the same manner as on-premise IT is a misstep. To fully unlock the potential of cloud technology, a shift in perspective is essential. According to the Flexera 2021 State of the Cloud Report (McLellan, 2021), the foremost challenges in cloud adoption encompass security, effective cloud spend management, and a shortage of resources and expertise. Fortunately, major cloud providers offer guidance and support to help address these challenges. One effective approach is to secure a support agreement as part of your subscription, recognizing that it is a service in itself.

Review Question 7.29

One trade-off for cloud computing is the business ________ and demand on ________.
A) agility, employee cloud skills
B) market, employee cloud skills
C) profit, market share
D) agility, market share

Review Question 7.30
According to Flexera 2021 State of the Cloud Report, what are the top three challenges of the cloud?
A) customer support, security, and managing cloud spend
B) security, managing cloud spend, and lack of resources/expertise
C) managing cloud spend, lack of resources/expertise, and customer support
D) security, managing cloud spend, and customer support

Review Question 7.31
There are many challenges for an enterprise to move onto cloud. One way to meet the challenges is to buy support agreement with your subscription.
A) True
B) False

7.4 Cloud Adoptions

In today's rapidly evolving digital landscape, cloud computing has emerged as a transformative force for businesses of all sizes and industries. The adoption of cloud technology offers unparalleled opportunities for efficiency, scalability, and innovation.

7.4.1 Managed Service Providers (MSPs)

When embarking on the journey to the cloud, one viable option to contemplate is partnering with a Managed Service Provider (MSP) (Issa, 2021). An MSP offers an alternative to traditional IT outsourcing and can play a pivotal role in your cloud strategy. In a typical MSP-cloud architecture arrangement, you may grant the MSP direct oversight of your environment. This can manifest in two ways: allowing the MSP to assume full control of your cloud operations permanently or, in many cases, facilitating a transitional approach where they assume 100% control initially and gradually train your in-house IT personnel to assume full responsibility. The latter approach is often favored in most scenarios.

A fundamental document an MSP will typically furnish is the Statement of Work (SOW). This contract delineates the precise scope of responsibilities, distinguishing between what the MSP will manage and your own obligations, aligning with the shared responsibility model we discussed in an earlier chapter. While the MSP provides the tools and infrastructure, it's your responsibility to leverage these resources effectively.

Within the SOW, you'll find Service Level Agreements (SLAs), which define specific quantifiable metrics. For instance, SLAs establish parameters like the maximum permissible response time between reporting an issue to your MSP and its resolution. Another critical metric is high availability. Importantly, the SLAs and high availability commitments from your MSP are distinct from those of the cloud vendor.

When collaborating with an MSP, you have the flexibility to opt for paying the MSP for cloud usage and service consumption, as opposed to direct billing from the cloud provider. If you're in search of a reliable MSP, you may consider initiating a Request for Proposal (RFP). An RFP is a formal business document that signals your intent to seek assistance while providing project specifics. Interested MSPs then submit their bids, detailing the services they offer and the associated costs. You can subsequently select the most suitable MSP and proceed from there.

Review Question 7.32
A(n) _______ is an alternative to a traditional IT outsourcing.
A) internet service provider (ISP)
B) managed service provider (MSP)
C) outsourcing service provider (OSP)
D) contract service provider (CSP)

Review Question 7.33
If you contract an MSP, it will be in control of your business cloud completely.
A) True
B) False

Review Question 7.34
In a contract with an MSP, ideally, you want the MSP _______.
A) to be completely in control of your cloud business
B) to stay away from your cloud business as much as possible
C) to handle only non-critical part of the cloud business
D) to be completely in control at the beginning and train your IT employees to eventually take control the cloud of your business

Review Question 7.35
Which of the following statements is true about SLA when you contracting an MSP?
A) you have only one SLA with your MSP
B) you have only one SLA with your MSP and your MSP has only one SLA with the cloud provider
C) You have only one SLA with your cloud provider
D) You have one SLA with your MSP and one SLA with your cloud provider

Review Question 7.36
Some elements that a managed service provider will typically offer are the _______.
A) request for proposal (RFP)

B) statement of work (SOW)
C) work load statement (WLS)
D) MSP statement

Review Question 7.37
When looking for a more reliable MSP, you may consider using a _______. It is a business document that announces that you're looking for help and provide some details about what the project is.
A) request for proposal (RFP)
B) statement of work (SOW)
C) work load statement (WLS)
D) MSP statement

7.4.2 Evaluating Cloud Vendors

When choosing the right cloud vendor(s) for your needs, consider three key criteria. First, investigate whether the vendor offers a free or evaluation service tier. These tiers require minimal to no investment, allowing for a preliminary deployment to gauge the environment. While similarities may exist among various vendors, it's worthwhile for your team to express their preferences and pinpoint the option that best aligns with your business objectives.

Secondly, the transition from on-premise software can be met with resistance from your team. Avoid unnecessary changes that might disrupt operations. For example, if you predominantly use proprietary on-premise software (e.g., Windows), your team may be resistant to a full switch to open-source (e.g., Linux) in the cloud, or vice versa.

The third crucial consideration is steering clear of vendor lock-in. Adopting a cloud-first architecture, which is vendor-neutral and portable, is one solution. Utilizing containers allows applications to run on any cloud or on-premise environment with minimal to no modifications. Another strategy is a multi-cloud approach, wherein your business workload spans across multiple cloud platforms.

Total Cost of Ownership (TCO) in cloud computing is a comprehensive financial metric used to assess the complete cost associated with adopting and maintaining cloud services or infrastructure over a specified period. TCO takes into account not only the visible, direct costs, such as subscription fees, but also the indirect expenses related to operating, managing, and supporting cloud-based resources.

You can also evaluate a cloud provider through Proof of Value (PoV) analysis, similar to TCO calculations.

PoV quantifies the cost savings accrued over time by migrating to the cloud. Major cloud providers offer online TCO calculators, which you can utilize for comparative analysis.

Furthermore, consider conducting a Proof of Concept (PoC) analysis. This involves using the cloud provider's free or trial tier to execute small projects that demonstrate the feasibility of specific workloads. Define your success criteria, encompassing both business and technical metrics, and compare the PoC analysis results against these criteria.

Lastly, perform a pilot test, which entails a limited-scale deployment of a workload in a production cloud environment. This might temporarily disrupt your business services, so it should be executed with the involvement of subject matter experts (SMEs) who can facilitate a rollback if necessary. Pilots offer a valuable opportunity to gather user feedback. Begin with a small pilot and gradually expand, using load balancers to direct a portion of traffic to the pilot environment (canary deployment).

Review Question 7.38
Consider three criteria when you evaluate which cloud vendor(s) to work with. Which of the following is not one of the criteria?
A) try a free or evaluation service tier
B) change from on-premise software
C) avoid vendor lock-in
D) lowest cost first

Review Question 7.39
Using a multi-cloud approach, where a business may want their workload running in multiple clouds, is a possible solution to ________.
A) try a free or evaluation service tier
B) change from on-premise software
C) avoid vendor lock-in
D) lowest cost first

Review Question 7.40
The ________ analysis is where you quantify your cost savings over time in migrating to the cloud.
A) proof of value (PoV)
B) proof of concept (PoC)
C) proof of cost (PoC)
D) proof of total cost (POTC)

Review Question 7.41
The ________ is where you use the cloud provider's free or trial tier to conduct small projects that demonstrate the feasibility of a particular workload.
A) proof of value (PoV)
B) proof of concept (PoC)

C) proof of cost (PoC)
D) proof of total cost (POTC)

Review Question 7.42
The _______ refers to a small-scale rollout of a workload to a production cloud environment.
A) proof of value (PoV)
B) proof of concept (PoC)
C) pilot
D) experiment

7.5 User Management and Software Development

This section delves into the profound shifts and evolving paradigms that have come to define modern application architectures. As businesses migrate to the cloud, the landscape of software development undergoes a metamorphosis, from traditional monolithic structures to the dynamic realm of cloud-native applications. The core elements of user management, encompassing authentication, authorization, and accounting, are central in this journey.

7.5.1 User Management

User management in cloud computing closely aligns with the AAA security model, encompassing Authentication, Authorization, and Accounting.

Authentication serves as the process for verifying a user's identity or a process. It's akin to validating who you are. When you log in to check your email, your password acts as your authentication. If you walk into a classroom to take a final exam, your face is authenticated because your professor recognizes you. At an airport, your driver's license is your authentication.

Authentication is a fundamental requirement for most enterprise applications. It involves confirming the identity of a user or process. Multi-factor authentication (MFA) is a common technique, which entails using an additional factor beyond a password. Password knowledge is one factor (something you know), and the system might also send a verification code or a one-time password (OTP) as a second factor (another thing you know). Alternatively, biometric authentication methods like facial scans or fingerprint scans can be used as a second or third factor.

For those offering Software as a Service (SaaS) apps on the cloud, Single Sign-On (SSO) is worth considering. It's a concept you've likely encountered as a user when websites offer the option to sign in with your Facebook, Twitter, or LinkedIn account, sparing you from creating new credentials. SSO on-premises can be intricate due to Identity Federation requirements, but major cloud providers typically offer this service.

Authorization pertains to the specific permissions assigned to authenticated identities. Having a driver's license and a flight ticket doesn't automatically grant permission to board – if your name is on the no-fly list, you're denied access. The principle of least privilege is vital, ensuring that authenticated users possess only the necessary privileges for their tasks. Role-Based Access Control (RBAC) is a commonly used authorization scheme, where roles like administrator, developer, or analyst can be assigned to users, each role granting specific resource privileges.

Accounting is the audit of user or process activities, measuring resource consumption. This includes tracking the time spent on a process or the data viewed. Accounting involves logging session statistics and usage information, serving purposes like authorization control, billing, trend analysis, resource utilization, and capacity planning.

Review Question 7.43
The _______ is the process of verifying the identity of a user or process.
A) authentication
B) authorization
C) accounting
D) automatic

Review Question 7.44
The _______ refers to the specific permissions that are assigned to an authenticated identity.
A) authentication
B) authorization
C) accounting
D) automatic

Review Question 7.45
The _______ is auditing user or process activities. It measures the resources a user consumes.
A) authentication
B) authorization
C) accounting
D) automatic

Review Question 7.46
Single sign-on (SSO) on-premises can be complex because the requirement of involving _______.
A) identity federation

B) identity partnership
C) authentication
D) authorization

7.5.2 Application Architectures

As businesses increasingly transition to the cloud, software developers must adapt to new application architectures. In the pre-cloud era, the prevalent model was the monolithic architecture, often referred to as the 3-tier application architecture.

The presentation layer, the user interface, encompasses what users see when they interact with a website. The application layer manages business logic and data access, handling tasks such as credit card validation and inventory management in the case of an online store. The database layer serves as the repository for application data, storing information like customer shipping addresses.

With the advent of cloud computing, developers have the option to create cloud-first or cloud-native applications. A modern approach gaining traction in the public cloud realm is microservices, where applications are decomposed into independent, self-contained components. Supporting cloud-native applications is containerization, a topic we will delve into later in this book.

However, transitioning to cloud-native application development does come with added complexity. If your current application operates as a monolith, it can still be hosted within a series of virtual machines even in a cloud environment. You have the option to refactor a monolithic application into microservices by breaking down the layers and establishing connections via APIs.

Another technology well-suited for cloud computing is Virtual Desktop Infrastructure (VDI). VDI involves creating and managing desktop environments and applications, enabling employees to access their work and applications from anywhere. This is facilitated by virtual machines (VMs), where multiple applications and operating systems can run on a single physical machine. In contrast to traditional PCs, which rely on physical, portable devices, VDI allows resources to be dedicated to specific users, offering flexibility and remote accessibility.

Review Question 7.47
Before the cloud era, the most popular application architecture is probably monolithic architecture, also

known as _______ architecture.
A) application
B) 1-tier
C) 2-tier
D) 3-tier

Review Question 7.48
A more modern approach to software development and one that suites to public cloud is _______ where your application is decomposed into freestanding parts by using containers.
A) application
B) macro services
C) microservices
D) 3-tier

Review Question 7.49
The _______ is different from remote desktop services (RDS). It allows the resources to be dedicated to a particular user.
A) personal desktop services (PDS)
B) virtual desktop services (VDI)
C) micro desktop service (MDS)
D) logical desktop services (LDS)

7.6 Cloud Migration Strategies

Before embarking on the journey of cloud migration, it's imperative to grasp the unique facets of cloud computing. At its core, cloud technology relies on virtualization, enabling applications to run virtually in the cloud. Cloud resources are inherently elastic, facilitating parallel and cluster-based execution. This elasticity may pose challenges for applications not originally designed for parallel or cluster modes, impacting their optimal performance in the cloud environment.

There are four primary cloud migration strategies (Wang et al., 2020). The first, "Whole Migration," involves migrating the entire application workload and data to the cloud as is. Often referred to as "lift and shift," "rehosting," or "re-platforming," this classic approach requires minimal modification to the workload. However, it might perpetuate existing architectural issues without leveraging the full potential of cloud features.

In contrast, "Mixed Migration" (or "Phased Migration") involves migrating some application components to the cloud while retaining others on-premise. This strategy is well-suited for 3-tier applications with distinct service objects and business process logics in separate layers. Unlike "Whole Migration," it doesn't overlook the internal architecture of applications.

The "Component Replacement" strategy, also known as "Hybrid Migration," entails using cloud service components offered by cloud providers to replace specific components of existing applications. These components often automate elastic expansion, load balancing, fault detection and processing, and provide enhanced security layers.

Lastly, the "Cloud-First Migration" (or "Rip and Replace") strategy advocates the complete redesign of an application with a cloud-first architecture. This approach acknowledges the significant disparities between cloud and on-premises environments, prompting a reconfiguration for maximal availability, security, and performance. While the initial redesign may incur costs, it can potentially avert complications down the line.

Review Question 7.50
One of the core technology of cloud computing is _______.
A) cloud
B) condensed water
C) networking
D) virtualization

Review Question 7.51
The cloud computing resources are ______.
A) elastic
B) rich
C) scarcity
D) abundant

Review Question 7.52
Which of the following is the simplest migration strategy that is suitable for small applications?
A) whole migration
B) mixed migration
C) component replacement migration
D) cloud-first migration

Review Question 7.53
Which of the following is NOT a cloud migration strategy discussed in the book?
A) whole migration
B) mixed migration
C) constant migration
D) cloud-first migration

Review Question 7.54
The _______ strategy refers to where the entire workload of your application and your data, are migrated to the cloud as is.

A) whole migration
B) mixed migration
C) hybrid migration
D) cloud enabled migration

Review Question 7.55
The _______ refers to moving some applications or components to the cloud while keeping other parts on-premise.
A) whole migration
B) mixed migration
C) hybrid migration
D) cloud enabled migration

Review Question 7.56
The _______ refers to using cloud service components provided by the cloud providers to replace one or more components of current applications.
A) whole migration
B) mixed migration
C) hybrid migration
D) cloud enabled migration

Review Question 7.57
The _______ migration, also called rip and replace, strategy where you're redesigning your app from scratch with cloud-first architecture.
A) whole migration
B) mixed migration
C) hybrid migration
D) cloud-first migration

Review Question 7.58
The _______ strategy works well with 3-tier applications where different service objects and business process logics exists in different layers.
A) whole migration
B) mixed migration
C) hybrid migration
D) cloud-first migration

Review Question 7.59
The _______ strategy can be expensive due to the redesign of the existing applications, but may save a lot of trouble later on.
A) whole migration
B) mixed migration
C) component replacement migration
D) cloud-first migration

7.7 Chapter Summary

The initial step in migrating to the cloud is to identify the business requirements from your stakeholders. We have examined two types of IT expenditures: capital and operational. We have explored various cloud service purchasing models, ranging from free-tier options to spot pricing. Our knowledge extends to user management and the attributes of cloud software development. We have analyzed vendor relationships with cloud providers and managed service providers. In the preceding section, we delved into the four cloud migration strategies available for consideration when transitioning your IT to the cloud.

7.8 Exercise

Create a free static web app on Azure.

Step 0: You will need a GitHub account to store your app. Create a GitHub account if you don't have one before continuing. https://github.com/

Step 1: Login to azure with the account you created in the last chapter exercise
(https://portal.azure.com/#home). Find the "Static Web Apps" inside the "Azure Services"
If you don't see it, click on "Create a resource" link
And search for "static web apps".
On the "Static Web Apps" page, click on "create" to start the process.
In the "Resource Group" field, click on "Create new" and give any new name for the group (you can call it MyBook to match the screenshots later). Next, give a name for the required "Name" field.
Select "free" plan type to avoid any bills.
Select any time zone that is closest to your customer. For our exercise, it does not matter.
Check "GitHub" for deployment source. Click on "Sign in with GitHub". If you don't have an account on GitHub, create one. It is free.

Step 2: After login to GitHub, you will be asked to give azure permission to access your GitHub storage. Next, create a new repository in your GitHub. Give a name to your new repository (Mine is called MyBook). Leave everything else default. Click on "Create Repository" button to create a new repository.
On the new page, click on "creating a new file" link.
On the new page, name the file "index.html" (no quotation marks). And type in the following lines into the text area:

```
<!DOCTYPE html>
<html>
<head>
<meta charset = "utf-8">
<title>My Website</title>
</head>
<body>
<h1>Welcome to the cloud!</h1>
</body>
</html>
```

Scroll down to the bottom of the page. Click "Commit new file" to save the file. You just created an html file on your GitHub account.

Step 3: Back to the azure, you will see a new section has been added (Organization, Repository, Branch): Wait for a few second if necessary, then select from the dropdown. The "Organization" is your GitHub account name. The "Repository" is the repository you just created in Step 2, and the "Branch" is "main" (unless you use a different branch in GitHub when you create the index.html file.).

Fill out the content. Click on "Review+create" to create the app. The "tags" step is optional. We don't recommend it at this time.

Step 4: On the "Summary" page, click on the "Create" button. You will see the page (It may take a few seconds for the green check icon to show up), "Your deployment is complete".

Click on "Go to resource" button.

You will see information on top of the new page, something like "Thank you for using Azure Static Web Apps!"

You can ignore that and wait for a few minutes, no typos here, it can take a few minutes. Or you can click on it to visit the GitHub and see if the action is completed (green check icon) or failed (red error icon not shown here).

Step 5: Go back to Azure if you are not already there. Click on the URL provided on the page. A browser new tap will open and you should see the following: "Welcome to the cloud!"

If you click on the URL too early, you will see the "waiting for your content" message instead of your webpage (Remember in Step 4 GitHub can take a few minutes to process the html file. This is necessary only for the first time you view the page.).

7.9 References

Gupta, B., Mittal, P., & Mufti, T. (2021). A Review on Amazon Web Service (AWS), Microsoft Azure & Google Cloud Platform (GCP) Services. http://eprints.eudl.eu/id/eprint/2890/

Hulshof, M., & Daneva, M. (2021, July). Benefits and Challenges in Information Security Certification–A Systematic Literature Review. In International Symposium on Business Modeling and Software Design (pp. 154-169). Springer, Cham.

Issa, N. G. (2021). "Cloud Computing Security and Privacy Preservation: Using multi-level encryption". IJEIT on Engineering and Information Technology, Vol.7, No. 2, June 2021.

McLellan, C. (2021), Cloud computing in the real world: The challenges and opportunities of multicloud, ZDNet, https://www.zdnet.com/article/research-multicloud-deployment-increases-among-enterprises/

Wang, Z., Yan, W., & Wang, W. (2020, June). Revisiting Cloud Migration: Strategies and Methods. In Journal of Physics: Conference Series (Vol. 1575, No. 1, p. 012232). IOP Publishing.

7.10 Solutions to Review Questions

7.1 C; 7.2 A; 7.3 A; 7.4 B; 7.5 C; 7.6 D; 7.7 C; 7.8 B; 7.9 A; 7.10 D; 7.11 B; 7.12 C; 7.13 A; 7.14 c; 7.15 C; 7.16 C; 7.17 C; 7.18 D; 7.19 A; 7.20 B; 7.21 C; 7.22 D; 7.23 B; 7.24 C; 7.25 D; 7.26 C; 7.27 C; 7.28 D; 7.29 A; 7.30 B; 7.31 A; 7.32 B; 7.33 B; 7.34 D; 7.35 D; 7.36 B 7.37 A; 7.38 D; 7.39 C; 7.40 A; 7.41 B; 7.42 C; 7.43 A; 7.44 B; 7.45 C; 7.46 A; 7.47 D; 7.48 C; 7.49 B; 7.50 D; 7.51 A; 7.52 A; 7.53 C; 7.54 A; 7.55 B; 7.56 C; 7.57 D; 7.58 B; 7.59 D;

Chapter 8: Cloud Operations

Chapter Learning Outcomes

8.1 Analyze business continuity in cloud environments
8.2 Identity key areas for cloud optimization
8.3 Utilize DevOps practices
8.4 Examine the relationship between DevOps and CI/CD processes
8.5 Understand IaC and orchestration in DevOps

8.1 Performance and Expenses

This section delves into key factors for unlocking the potential of cloud computing. It first discusses challenges related to cloud availability and business continuity. It then explores cloud elasticity and resource scaling, highlighting how to optimize usage and ensure continuity. Lastly, it underscores the importance of monitoring and logging, addressing challenges with data streams and service models to maintain cloud performance and security.

8.1.1 Availability and Business Continuity

One of the primary advantages of cloud computing is high availability (Tsai, 2021). Cloud availability pertains to the uptime of the cloud and its ability to operate without interruption (Aziz et al, 2021). Offering highly available services in cloud computing is crucial for maintaining customer trust and satisfaction, averting revenue losses, and, most importantly, ensuring business continuity.

Service outages in cloud computing can significantly impact enterprise system workloads and consumer data and applications. Business continuity relies on service providers delivering services to businesses in line with the service level agreements (SLA). When drafting SLAs with a cloud provider, it's essential to define business continuity processes that meet the business's availability requirements.

Cloud vendors segment the world into regions, each further divided into zones with one or more data centers. This structure ensures that if an incident, such as a natural disaster, affects one region or zone, another can take over and maintain service availability. Some vendors also support region pairs, which are two regions within the same geography. These pairs never undergo platform updates simultaneously to minimize the risk of an update failure impacting both platforms at once.

Disaster recovery is the coordinated process of restoring IT infrastructure, including data necessary to support ongoing business services, following a disaster. The fundamental concept of disaster recovery involves having a secondary resource at a pre-planned level of operational readiness.

Replication is a process that duplicates data and services between data centers in different regions and zones. Besides serving disaster recovery purposes, it reduces latency by bringing data closer to the user. Replication is a continuous process that must keep the data synchronized at all times. Geo-redundancy is the replication between two geographically distant locations and forms the backbone of disaster recovery. It employs automatic failover to swiftly reroute requests to a secondary data center, often so quickly that the consumer may not realize anything went wrong. For instance, Azure allows you to check which regions are available for the type of service you want.

Replication services between these physically separated zones ensure that if one goes down, another can take over, effectively eliminating a single point of failure.

In replication, your services can be deployed to a primary region and automatically replicated to a secondary region by the cloud provider's geo-redundant services. The two regions should be far enough apart that a natural disaster won't affect both. A traffic manager service directs requests through your application to the primary region. If the primary region becomes unresponsive for any reason, failover activates and redirects traffic to the secondary region. This mechanism ensures maximum availability of resources.

Review Question 8.1
What does cloud availability refer to?
A) The cost of cloud services
B) The uptime of the cloud and its ability to operate without interruption
C) The number of users a cloud service can support
D) The geographical coverage of cloud services

Review Question 8.2
What is the primary purpose of dividing the world into regions and zones by cloud vendors?
A) To increase the cost of cloud services

B) To ensure service availability in case of an incident in one region or zone
C) To limit the number of users in a particular region
D) To increase latency

Review Question 8.4
What is the fundamental concept of disaster recovery?
A) Increasing the cost of recovery
B) Having a secondary resource at a pre-planned level of operational readiness
C) Reducing the number of users
D) Increasing latency

Review Question 8.5
What is the purpose of replication in cloud computing?
A) To increase the cost of cloud services
B) To duplicate data and services between data centers in different regions and zones
C) To limit the number of users in a particular region
D) To increase latency

Review Question 8.6
What is geo-redundancy?
A) A method to increase the cost of cloud services
B) A process to limit the number of users in a particular region
C) The replication between two geographically distant locations
D) A method to increase latency

Review Question 8.7
What happens when the primary region becomes unresponsive in a replication process?
A) The secondary region is shut down
B) Traffic is redirected to the secondary region
C) The primary region is restarted
D) The replication process is stopped

Review Question 8.8
What is the role of a traffic manager service in the replication process?
A) To shut down the primary region
B) To direct requests through your application to the primary region
C) To restart the primary region
D) To stop the replication process

Review Question 8.9
What is the benefit of having region pairs in cloud computing?
A) To increase the cost of cloud services
B) To ensure that platform updates are not done simultaneously
C) To limit the number of users in a particular region
D) To increase latency

8.1.2 Resource Optimization and Scaling

As previously discussed, cloud elasticity, made possible by the virtualization characteristic of the cloud, is a significant benefit of cloud computing. Infrastructure, platform, software, and other resources are virtualized, allowing for allocation and deallocation as needed.

However, without the right services and tools (CloudZero, 2021), the cost of subscribing to these resources can spiral out of control. Over-provisioning resources can be costly, while under-provisioning can negatively impact performance (Bhatti et al., 2020). Cloud optimization involves eliminating cloud resource waste by appropriately selecting, provisioning, and right-sizing resources. It describes the process of scalable provisioning, where cloud resources are added or removed in response to changes in demand and consumption.

Cloud optimization is about scaling the correct amount of resources to meet your business requirements. Scaling can be done manually or automatically. For instance, you manually added a static web app resource in the previous chapter's exercise. Automatic scaling allows you to define policies that adjust the number of resources based on constantly monitored needs.

When it comes to scaling, you have two options: vertical and horizontal. Vertical scaling, or scaling up, involves adding more resources to an existing deployment, such as configuring more memory or processing power for a virtual machine. The opposite, scaling down, involves reducing these resources.

Horizontal scaling, or scaling out, involves adding more instances of a deployment. A common scenario is when you have a web application in the cloud, and you spin up more instances of the web application to handle additional user requests. Reducing the number of instances is referred to as scaling in.

In addition to scaling, right-sizing is crucial for optimizing resource usage, as cloud providers bill you for the services you provision rather than what you consume. Right-sizing is the process of analyzing the utilization and performance of your resources, assessing efficiency, and adjusting services as needed. It is a continuous process (Burke, 2020) aimed at saving costs by preventing over-provisioning. Given the ever-changing usage and requirements in the cloud, it's important to continuously monitor needs and adjust limits as necessary.

Review Question 8.10
What is cloud elasticity?
A) The ability to control costs in the cloud

B) The ability to allocate and deallocate resources as needed
C) The ability to increase the performance of cloud services
D) The ability to reduce latency in cloud services

Review Question 8.11
What is the purpose of cloud optimization?
A) To increase the cost of cloud services
B) To increase latency in cloud services
C) To reduce the performance of cloud services
D) To eliminate cloud resource waste by appropriately selecting, provisioning, and right-sizing resources

Review Question 8.12
What is vertical scaling?
A) Adding more instances of a deployment
B) Adding more resources to an existing deployment
C) Reducing the number of instances of a deployment
D) Reducing the resources of an existing deployment

Review Question 8.13
What is horizontal scaling?
A) Adding more instances of a deployment
B) Adding more resources to an existing deployment
C) Reducing the resources of an existing deployment
D) Reducing the number of instances of a deployment

Review Question 8.14
What is right-sizing in the context of cloud computing?
A) Increasing the cost of cloud services
B) Increasing latency in cloud services
C) Reducing the performance of cloud services
D) Analyzing the utilization and performance of your resources, assessing efficiency, and adjusting services as needed

Review Question 8.15
What is the main goal of right-sizing?
A) To increase the cost of cloud services
B) To reduce the performance of cloud services
C) To save costs by preventing over-provisioning
D) To increase latency in cloud services

8.1.3 Monitoring and Logging

Businesses utilizing cloud services require detailed, real-time monitoring to keep track of all aspects of their platform (Pourmajidi et al., 2021). This requirement can pose challenges, particularly when dealing with high volumes of data. For instance, Netflix generates more than 10 billion records a day (Anwar, 2015), and processing and storing such data can be computationally expensive.

Different cloud service models necessitate varying levels of monitoring (Rodrigues et al., 2016). Infrastructure as a Service (IaaS) provides consumers with full control over the entire lifecycle of virtual machines (VMs), necessitating comprehensive monitoring systems that cover infrastructure, operating systems, and application metrics.

Platform as a Service (PaaS) consumers control one or more scalable application development and deployment environments and require access to the operating metrics of such platforms. Hence, PaaS requires less extensive monitoring than IaaS. In contrast, Software as a Service (SaaS) consumers, who only use applications hosted on the cloud, require minimal monitoring resources.

Major cloud providers offer comprehensive monitoring solutions that allow you to detect and diagnose issues across all your services. These solutions also identify misaligned resource allocations where deployments have either too few or too many resources provisioned, leading to poor performance or unnecessary costs.

A robust monitoring solution enables near real-time visualization of monitoring metrics. A common example is a graph displaying the CPU and memory utilization of a virtual machine or a database. Additionally, you can set alerts for customizable thresholds and receive notifications when these alerts are triggered. For instance, you might want to receive an SMS message when a virtual machine shuts down. Any suspicious activity or threats to your deployments should be detected immediately.

In the context of the cloud, logging refers to the recording of system events and messages exchanged between services and components. The cloud's capabilities enable near real-time logging while managing high-volume application and system outputs. It's scalable and designed to grow with applications and data. The cloud offers a variety of services, and logging data can originate from hundreds of different sources. However, it must be manageable and searchable from a central location.

Review Question 8.16
What is a significant challenge when monitoring cloud services?
A) The lack of data
B) The high volume of data
C) The low cost of data storage
D) The slow speed of data processing

Review Question 8.17
Which cloud service model requires the most comprehensive monitoring systems?
A) Software as a Service (SaaS)
B) Platform as a Service (PaaS)
C) Infrastructure as a Service (IaaS)
D) Database as a Service (DBaaS)

Review Question 8.18
What do major cloud providers offer to help detect and diagnose issues across all your services?
A) Comprehensive monitoring solutions
B) Detailed user manuals
C) Advanced data encryption
D) Unlimited data storage

Review Question 8.19
What is a common example of a monitoring metric visualized in near real-time?
A) The number of users accessing a service
B) The CPU and memory utilization of a virtual machine or a database
C) The geographical location of users
D) The amount of data stored in the cloud

Review Question 8.20
What does logging refer to in the context of the cloud?
A) The process of storing data in the cloud
B) The recording of system events and messages exchanged between services and components
C) The process of encrypting data
D) The process of deleting old data

Review Question 8.21
What is a key feature of cloud logging?
A) It is slow and difficult to manage
B) It is scalable and designed to grow with applications and data
C) It is limited to a small number of sources
D) It is only available for certain cloud services

Review Question 8.22
What is a requirement for logging data in the cloud?
A) It must be manageable and searchable from a central place
B) It must be encrypted and stored in a secure location
C) It must be deleted after a certain period of time
D) It must be accessible to all users

8.2 Utilizing DevOps in the Cloud

In the ever-evolving landscape of cloud computing, the integration of DevOps and cloud technology has emerged as a significant advantage for businesses and organizations worldwide. This section explores the powerful combination of DevOps practices within cloud environments. DevOps, a methodology anchored in collaboration and automation, is perfectly suited for the agility and scalability of the cloud. Together, they redefine the way software is developed, deployed, and managed, enabling rapid innovation, enhanced quality, and optimized resource utilization. Discover how DevOps principles integrate seamlessly with cloud infrastructure, empowering teams to orchestrate applications, scale resources, and deliver continuous value in this transformative alliance.

8.2.1 DevOps

Transitioning your information technology from on-premise to the cloud is often driven by the belief that the cloud is a superior environment for your databases and applications. This section focuses on software development. DevOps is a mindset that extends the agile software development philosophy. It aims to deliver high-quality software through continuous integration, delivery, improvement, faster feedback, and enhanced security (Gokarna & Singh, 2021). It unifies software development and operations, eliminating their existence as separate entities. The automation capabilities of the cloud provide an ideal environment for DevOps. When discussing DevOps, the context is often assumed to be the cloud (Nair, 2021).

One issue that DevOps addresses is the independent operation of development and operations teams, a common problem in the traditional Systems Development Life Cycle (SDLC).

In the traditional waterfall SDLC, it's common for a development team to work on an application for months before releasing it in its entirety to operations. This approach often leads to customer dissatisfaction as they don't receive incremental updates and can't provide feedback. Moreover, software testing is less effective because operational constraints, which are limitations derived from business requirements and enterprise policies, are not fully implemented due to the lack of customer involvement.

DevOps employs short release cycles to push updates and bug fixes to production in short time intervals, enhancing productivity with faster services. It is frequently used, but not exclusively, to develop and deploy microservices. These services are highly scalable, lightweight, and loosely coupled. Because microservices are modular and easier to test, they align well with DevOps.

DevOps heavily relies on automated testing to identify software issues at an early stage. Teams working independently tend to use their own architectures and tools, configuring their components in a way that best suits them, not necessarily the customers. This amalgamation of solutions from different teams makes it challenging to track configurations. DevOps centralizes configuration in a repository and uses orchestration to automatically configure services upon deployment.

Review Question 8.23
What is a significant advantage for businesses and organizations in the landscape of cloud computing?
A) The integration of DevOps and cloud technology
B) The use of traditional SDLC
C) The separation of development and operations teams
D) The use of waterfall SDLC

Review Question 8.24
What does DevOps aim to deliver?
A) High-security software
B) High-quality software through continuous integration, delivery, improvement, faster feedback, and enhanced security
C) Software with no feedback system
D) Software developed in long release cycles

Review Question 8.25
What is one issue that DevOps addresses?
A) The collaboration of development and operations teams
B) The independent operation of development and operations teams
C) The use of agile software development philosophy
D) The use of cloud technology

Review Question 8.26
What often leads to customer dissatisfaction in the traditional waterfall SDLC?
A) Receiving incremental updates
B) The ability to provide feedback
C) Working on an application for months before releasing it in its entirety to operations
D) Effective software testing

Review Question 8.27
What does DevOps employ to enhance productivity?
A) Long release cycles
B) Independent operation of teams
C) Short release cycles
D) Ineffective software testing

Review Question 8.28
What type of services does DevOps frequently develop and deploy?
A) Highly scalable, heavyweight, and tightly coupled services
B) Microservices
C) Services that are difficult to test
D) Services developed in long release cycles

Review Question 8.29
What does DevOps heavily rely on to identify software issues at an early stage?
A) Automated testing
B) Manual testing
C) Long release cycles
D) Independent operation of teams

Review Question 8.30
What makes it challenging to track configurations in teams working independently?
A) The use of their own architectures and tools
B) The use of a centralized configuration repository
C) The use of orchestration to automatically configure services upon deployment
D) The use of microservices

8.2.2 CI/CD

DevOps embodies a set of principles designed to deliver high-quality software in small, frequent increments. Continuous Integration and Continuous Delivery (CI/CD) are practical implementations of these principles. Continuous Integration (CI) is a process that automatically compiles, builds, and tests code changes with the aim of identifying bugs as they are introduced into the code base (Latendresse et al., 2021). Given the critical and increasingly expensive task of bug fixing in software development, the software community has embraced CI as a strategy to mitigate this issue and enhance the quality of their software products. CI employs software tools, including cloud services, to automate the implementation of DevOps principles within a pipeline. A CI pipeline consists of a series of steps necessary to prepare the increment for deployment.

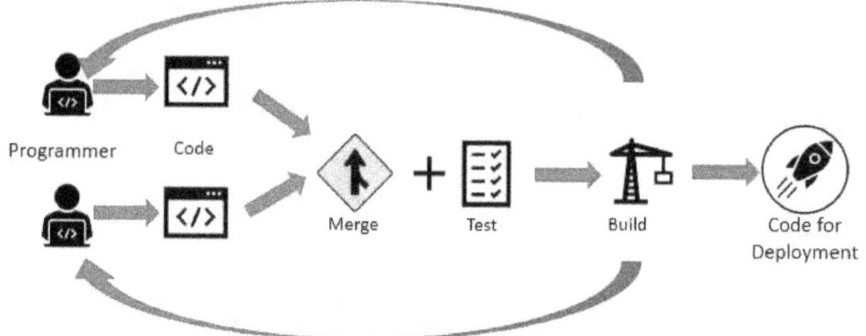

Figure 8.1 Stages in Continuous Integration (CI)

The build part of the pipeline is central to continuous integration. It revolves around a source code management repository with frequent merges of code changes. The process begins with programming the planned changes or bug fix, which are then merged with the main code branch in the source code repository. This is followed by tests to ensure all features continue to function as expected. The entire application (original + changes) is then built to check if it still compiles. Any issues in the build or test process trigger notifications and result in the rejection of the code changes. Programmers address these issues and initiate another CI cycle.

Upon successful merging, testing, and building phases, a new version of the application can be deployed in the Continuous Delivery (CD) stage of the CI/CD. Humble and Farley (2010) define continuous delivery as a set of practices designed to expedite, automate, and optimize the delivery of software to the customer with superior quality and minimal risks in a continuous manner.

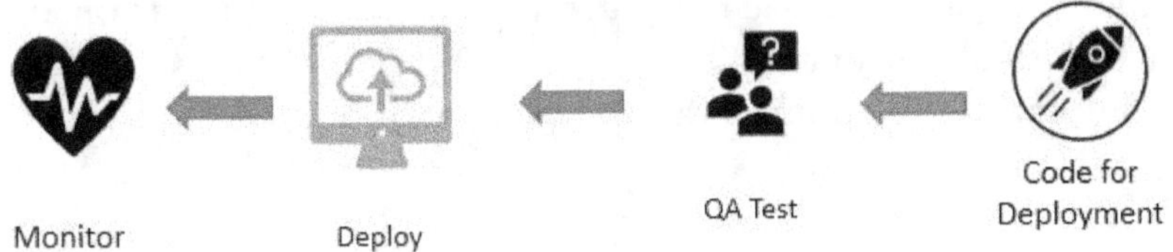

Figure 8.2 Stages in Continuous Delivery (CD) (read from right to left)

Like continuous integration, continuous delivery employs a deployment pipeline to automate the delivery process (Sabau et al., 2021). Code for deployment enters the deployment pipeline and results in a new software increment

Review Question 8.31
What is the aim of Continuous Integration (CI)?
A) To delay the identification of bugs
B) To automatically compile, build, and test code changes to identify bugs as they are introduced
C) To manually compile, build, and test code changes
D) To introduce bugs into the code base

Review Question 8.32
What does a CI pipeline consist of?
A) A series of steps necessary to prepare the increment for deployment
B) A single step to prepare the increment for deployment
C) A series of steps to introduce bugs into the code base
D) A single step to introduce bugs into the code base

Review Question 8.33
What triggers notifications and results in the rejection of code changes in CI?
A) Successful merging, testing, and building phases
B) The introduction of bugs into the code base
C) Issues in the build or test process

D) The completion of the CI cycle

Review Question 8.34
What happens upon successful merging, testing, and building phases in CI/CD?
A) A new version of the application can be deployed in the Continuous Delivery (CD) stage
B) The CI cycle is initiated again
C) Notifications are triggered and code changes are rejected
D) The CI cycle is completed

Review Question 8.35
How is continuous delivery defined according to Humble and Farley (2010)?
A) A set of practices designed to delay the delivery of software to the customer
B) A set of practices designed to expedite, automate, and optimize the delivery of software to the customer with superior quality and minimal risks in a continuous manner
C) A single practice designed to expedite, automate, and optimize the delivery of software to the customer with superior quality and minimal risks in a continuous manner
D) A set of practices designed to expedite, automate, and optimize the introduction of bugs into the code base

Review Question 8.36
What does continuous delivery employ to automate the delivery process?
A) A deployment pipeline
B) A CI pipeline
C) A source code management repository
D) A series of steps necessary to prepare the increment for deployment

Review Question 8.37
What happens when code for deployment enters the deployment pipeline in continuous delivery?
A) It results in a new software increment
B) It triggers notifications and results in the rejection of code changes
C) It initiates another CI cycle
D) It completes the CI cycle

Review Question 8.38
What is the relationship between DevOps and CI/CD?
A) They are the same
B) They are unrelated
C) DevOps is a CI/CD implementation
D) CI/CD is a DevOps implementation

8.2.3 Infrastructure as Code (IaC)

Within the realm of cloud computing, a resource refers to any service or component managed by the cloud infrastructure. The success of a CI/CD pipeline hinges on automatic resource provisioning, which enables consistent and repeatable deployment of applications. Provisioning is a term used by operations to describe the process of preparing computers or virtual hosts for use by installing necessary libraries or services on the infrastructure.

Automatic resource provisioning is underpinned by a concept known as Infrastructure as Code (IaC) (Morris, 2021). IaC is an approach to infrastructure automation that draws from software development practices. It emphasizes consistent, repeatable routines for provisioning and modifying systems and their configurations. Changes are made to the code, which are then tested and applied to your systems through automation. In practice, cloud infrastructure is defined in machine-readable files, often in JSON format, that describe a resource hierarchy.

JSON, or JavaScript Object Notation, is a language-independent data format that consists of attribute-value pairs, as shown in Figure 3.10. One of the advantages of using these files is that they can be maintained in a code repository, similar to application code, complete with versioning and change history.

IaC plays a pivotal role in the CI/CD pipeline, which needs to respond swiftly to code changes and repeatedly deploy resources to various environments such as test, acceptance, and production. DevOps aims to solve the problem of configuration complexity, which arises from using disparate methods for configuring and deploying resources, often involving automation. This is where configuration management through orchestration comes into play.

Orchestration is a process that automates a series of tasks running on multiple servers or hosts to work in unison. An integral part of continuous delivery is the automated configuration, management, and coordination of resources and services. This relies on IaC templates and settings retrieved from a repository. Orchestration facilitates complex workflows where a series of automated steps are executed to provision and patch fully configured resources. For instance, you can automatically create and configure a virtual machine with applications installed and user access granted, all without human intervention.

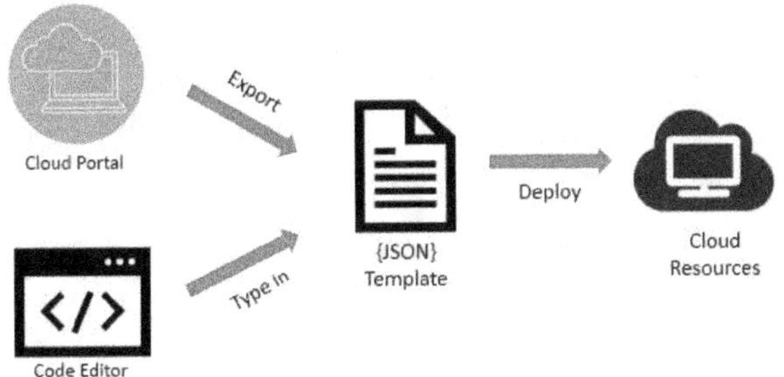

Figure 8.3 Cloud automation template

You have the option to create an IaC template from scratch using a code editor or use command-line tools on the cloud portal to export based on an existing resource. The file contains a hierarchy describing all properties and dependencies, along with parameters and variables that you can customize. Once you deploy the modified template back to the cloud, your resource is created. In the CI/CD pipeline, these templates are stored in a repository, and the parameters are automatically filled in upon deployment. This enables quick and consistent recreation of complete environments.

Review Question 8.39
What does a resource refer to within the realm of cloud computing?
A) Any service or component managed by the cloud infrastructure
B) The process of preparing computers or virtual hosts for use
C) The concept known as Infrastructure as Code (IaC)
D) A series of tasks running on multiple servers or hosts

Review Question 8.40
What is Infrastructure as Code (IaC)?
A) A language-independent data format
B) An approach to infrastructure automation that draws from software development practices
C) A process that automates a series of tasks running on multiple servers or hosts
D) A method for creating an IaC template from scratch

Review Question 8.41
What is JSON?
A) A language-independent data format that consists of attribute-value pairs
B) A concept known as Infrastructure as Code (IaC)
C) A process of preparing computers or virtual hosts for use
D) A series of tasks running on multiple servers or hosts

Review Question 8.42
What role does IaC play in the CI/CD pipeline?
A) It creates an IaC template from scratch
B) It automates a series of tasks running on multiple servers or hosts
C) It prepares computers or virtual hosts for use
D) It responds swiftly to code changes and repeatedly deploys resources to various environments

Review Question 8.43
What problem does DevOps aim to solve?
A) Configuration complexity
B) The creation of an IaC template from scratch
C) The preparation of computers or virtual hosts for use
D) The automation of a series of tasks running on multiple servers or hosts

Review Question 8.44
What is orchestration?

A) A process that automates a series of tasks running on multiple servers or hosts to work in unison
B) A language-independent data format that consists of attribute-value pairs
C) A concept known as Infrastructure as Code (IaC)
D) A method for creating an IaC template from scratch

Review Question 8.45
What can you do with an IaC template?
A) Respond swiftly to code changes and repeatedly deploy resources to various environments
B) Automate a series of tasks running on multiple servers or hosts
C) Prepare computers or virtual hosts for use
D) Create it from scratch using a code editor or use command-line tools on the cloud portal to export based on an existing resource

Review Question 8.46
What happens when you deploy the modified template back to the cloud?
A) Computers or virtual hosts are prepared for use
B) A series of tasks running on multiple servers or hosts are automated
C) Your resource is created
D) Code changes are responded to swiftly and resources are repeatedly deployed to various environments

8.2.4 DevOps Automation

DevOps solutions are fundamentally centered around automation. The Application Programming Interface (API) plays a crucial role in this process. An API is a contract that outlines how two or more components and services, whether on the cloud or on-premise, can interact with each other. In fact, every action and visual element in the cloud portal is facilitated by APIs.

For instance, when you log into the Azure portal to view your existing resources, a call is made through the Resource Manager API to retrieve the list of resources. APIs utilize industry standards to expose their contracts in a manner that allows them to be used across any programming language. One of the most commonly used standards is Representational State Transfer (REST). REST employs HTTP/HTTPS methods like GET and POST to indicate the actions to be performed on the resources. Attribute values can be passed within the URL if the GET method is used.

By exposing a REST API with standardized HTTP methods, any application can interact with your service without needing to understand how the service is implemented in the backend. For example, in the case of Data USA, your web browser sends an HTTP GET request to Data USA's API with the attribute values (nation, population, latest). The service returns a JSON response with the latest year (2019) and population (328,239,523) among other information. As long as the URL remains the same, changes in the backend won't affect the consuming applications or users.

To simplify the use of their APIs, many API publishers provide Software Development Kits (SDKs) in various programming languages. These SDKs act as a convenient wrapper around the HTTP calls.

Review Question 8.47
What is the role of the Application Programming Interface (API) in DevOps solutions?
A) It sends an HTTP GET request to Data USA's API
B) It acts as a convenient wrapper around the HTTP calls
C) It outlines how two or more components and services can interact with each other
D) It provides Software Development Kits (SDKs) in various programming languages

Review Question 8.48
What happens when you log into the Azure portal to view your existing resources?
A) A JSON response is returned with the latest year and population
B) An HTTP GET request is sent to Data USA's API
C) A call is made through the Resource Manager API to retrieve the list of resources
D) Software Development Kits (SDKs) are provided in various programming languages

Review Question 8.49
What is one of the most commonly used standards that APIs utilize to expose their contracts?
A) Software Development Kits (SDKs)
B) Application Programming Interface (API)
C) Representational State Transfer (REST)
D) Resource Manager API

Review Question 8.50
What do many API publishers provide to simplify the use of their APIs?
A) Software Development Kits (SDKs) in various programming languages
B) A JSON response with the latest year and population
C) An HTTP GET request to Data USA's API
D) A call through the Resource Manager API to retrieve the list of resources

8.2.5 DevOps for Application Quality

DevOps places a strong emphasis on continuous testing to ensure applications function as expected. Currently, there are three main types of application testing that are widely utilized (Khan et al., 2020; Rastogi, 2021).

The first type, unit testing, involves running tests in an isolated environment. This ensures that any issues that arise during testing won't impact other systems.

The second type, Test-Driven Development (TDD), is a process where automated tests are defined before coding begins (de Souza et al., 2021). In complex systems, it's not uncommon for a change in one part of a program to inadvertently introduce a bug in another part. To validate that existing functionality remains intact after an update, a regression test is performed. This involves a combination of automated tests and manual tests, where a tester follows scenarios from a test script to validate application functionality.

The third type, Behavior-Driven Development (BDD), tests the system's actual behavior from the end user's perspective (Aghayi et al., 2021). For instance, load testing can be used to test the software by simulating realistic loads. Load testing ensures that your application can handle the demands of a production environment. Many unforeseen performance problems in live services could have been prevented with load tests.

Review Question 8.51
What does DevOps place a strong emphasis on to ensure applications function as expected?
A) Continuous testing
B) Continuous integration
C) Continuous delivery
D) Continuous deployment

Review Question 8.52
What does unit testing involve?
A) Running tests in a shared environment
B) Running tests in an isolated environment
C) Running tests in a production environment
D) Running tests in a development environment

Review Question 8.53
What is Test-Driven Development (TDD)?
A) A process where automated tests are defined after coding begins
B) A process where automated tests are defined before coding begins
C) A process where manual tests are defined after coding begins
D) A process where manual tests are defined before coding begins

Review Question 8.54
What does Behavior-Driven Development (BDD) test?
A) The system's expected behavior from the developer's perspective
B) The system's expected behavior from the end user's perspective
C) The system's actual behavior from the end user's perspective
D) The system's actual behavior from the developer's perspective

Review Question 8.55
What does load testing ensure?

A) Your application can handle the demands of a development environment
B) Your application can handle the demands of a test environment
C) Your application can handle the demands of a production environment
D) Your application can handle the demands of an isolated environment

8.3 Financial Considerations

This section delves into the financial dimensions of cloud computing, with a focus on cost-effectiveness and efficiency. It provides an analysis of cloud software licensing, elucidating its complexities and its impact on the overall cost structure of cloud-based solutions. This is essential reading for anyone seeking to understand the economics of the cloud.

8.3.1 Key Financial Aspects of Cloud Usage

This subsection examines the primary financial considerations associated with cloud usage. It is crucial for all stakeholders to understand the main sources of expenses and how to allocate resources cost-effectively. Transitioning operations to the cloud shifts costs from capital expenditures (CapEx) to operating expenditures (OpEx). CapEx encompasses traditional costs for physical assets such as buildings and hardware, which are typically paid upfront and depreciated over several years for tax purposes. Conversely, OpEx covers charges for services and licenses, which are usually billed periodically and can be deducted in the current tax year.

Cloud provider bills typically fall under three categories. The first is storage, with cloud vendors offering various types such as file, block, object storage, and databases. Generally, online storage is more affordable than on-premise solutions, although high-performance databases in the cloud can still be costly.

The second category is network traffic to and from resources. While inbound data transfers to the cloud are usually free, cloud vendors will charge for outbound data transfers.

The third and most costly category is compute, which includes CPU power, memory, and licenses for virtual machines and containers. Even if a virtual machine is turned off when not in use, it may still be considered active by your cloud provider and billed accordingly. To avoid this, you should deallocate it through the cloud portal or with a script, freeing up the hardware and networking resources for others to use.

Two types of service instances can help reduce costs. Reserved instances are ideal when you have predictable needs and can commit to them for an extended period, typically one or more years. With reserved instances, you select a specific performance level upfront. Although you generally cannot change the level during the reservation period, the agreement may allow for some modifications.

Spot instances are another option. These are instances you can purchase when the provider has a pool of unused compute capacity. Providers maintain this extra capacity to ensure elasticity. The main drawback is that there is no guarantee you can obtain or retain the instance. However, spot instances are well-suited for non-critical batch processing.

Review Question 8.56
What is the primary difference between capital expenditures (CapEx) and operating expenditures (OpEx) in the context of cloud computing?
A) CapEx covers charges for services and licenses, while OpEx covers costs for physical assets.
B) CapEx is usually billed periodically, while OpEx is typically paid upfront.
C) CapEx encompasses costs for physical assets, while OpEx covers charges for services and licenses.
D) CapEx is deducted in the current tax year, while OpEx is depreciated over several years.

Review Question 8.57
Which category of cloud provider bills is typically the most costly?
A) Storage
B) Network traffic
C) Compute
D) Database

Review Question 8.58
What type of cloud service instance is ideal when you have predictable needs and can commit to them for an extended period?
A) Spot instances
B) Reserved instances
C) Elastic instances
D) Scalable instances

Review Question 8.59
What is a major drawback of using spot instances?
A) They are more expensive than reserved instances.
B) There is no guarantee you can obtain or retain the instance.
C) They cannot be used for non-critical batch processing.
D) They require a long-term commitment.

Review Question 8.60
What should you do to avoid being billed for a virtual machine that is not in use?
A) Turn it off

B) Deallocate it through the cloud portal or with a script
C) Delete it
D) Upgrade it

Review Question 8.61
Which type of data transfer is usually free with cloud vendors?
A) Outbound data transfers
B) Inbound data transfers
C) Both inbound and outbound data transfers
D) Neither inbound nor outbound data transfers

8.3.2 Cloud Software Licensing

Understanding software licensing can help reduce costs. There are numerous license types available in the cloud. A perpetual license never expires, allowing you to use the licensed resource indefinitely. Typically, you pay once upfront.

A subscription license requires periodic payments for temporary access. For instance, the Office 365 subscription requires annual payments to maintain usage. In some cases, cloud vendors allow the transfer of existing licenses to save costs, a process known as Bring Your Own License (BYOL). For example, if you have an SQL Server license for an on-premise server, it's often possible to transfer that license when migrating the server to the cloud.

Volume licensing authorizes the use of multiple copies of an application with one license. This is typically used to license operating systems for a collection of virtual machines.

There are also open source licenses, which allow you to freely use, modify, and share software. However, some open sources only permit use in non-commercial environments, so it's important to examine all conditions.

When planning deployments, always include a cost estimate. Understand all the different licensing options. Depending on your vendor, there might be more options available than the ones discussed. Inquire about bundles and discounts, as consuming a large amount of resources can often lead to better pricing deals. Your cloud portal will have a license manager available. It provides an overview of all the licenses you are using. Regularly check this list to discover unexpected costs and find ways to optimize the number of licenses. Most providers, like Microsoft Azure, also offer a trial license that gives you free access for a limited time.

A cloud license manager should include the resource type, description, license type, allowed installations, and number of licenses in use. Instances where the number of purchased licenses greatly exceeds those installed might indicate over-provisioning and unnecessary expenses.

Review Question 8.62
What is a perpetual license?
A) A license that requires periodic payments for temporary access.
B) A license that never expires and allows you to use the licensed resource indefinitely.
C) A license that authorizes the use of multiple copies of an application with one license.
D) A license that allows you to freely use, modify, and share software.

Review Question 8.63
What is the process of transferring existing licenses to save costs known as?
A) Volume Licensing
B) Subscription Licensing
C) Bring Your Own License (BYOL)
D) Perpetual Licensing

Review Question 8.64
What does a cloud license manager include?
A) Resource type, description, license type, allowed installations, and number of licenses in use.
B) Only the number of licenses in use.
C) Only the resource type and description.
D) Only the license type and allowed installations.

Review Question 8.65
What is the purpose of volume licensing?
A) To authorize the use of multiple copies of an application with one license.
B) To require periodic payments for temporary access.
C) To allow the transfer of existing licenses to save costs.
D) To allow the use of the licensed resource indefinitely.

Review Question 8.66
What is a characteristic of open source licenses?
A) They require periodic payments for temporary access.
B) They allow you to use the licensed resource indefinitely.
C) They allow you to freely use, modify, and share software.
D) They authorize the use of multiple copies of an application with one license.

Review Question 8.67
What is a subscription license?
A) A license that never expires and allows you to use the licensed resource indefinitely.
B) A license that authorizes the use of multiple copies of an application with one license.

C) A license that requires periodic payments for temporary access.

D) A license that allows you to freely use, modify, and share software.

8.4 Chapter Summary

In this chapter, we explored various aspects of cloud operations. We delved into the issues of cloud availability and disaster recovery, which are typically outlined in service level agreements. We also introduced DevOps, continuous integration, and continuous delivery - concepts that are gaining popularity in the cloud era. Lastly, we discussed the major categories of resources that incur costs in cloud computing: storage, compute, and network.

8.5 Exercise

Develop a dynamic website with php on Azure.

Step 1: Login to Azure portal with the account you created in Chapter One's exercise.

Step 2: Create a blank php app.

First click on "Create a resource" link to start.

Search for "Web App" and click on "Create" link to create a new web app.

In the "Create Web App" page, find the "Project Details" section.

Inside the "Project Details" section, click on "Create new" link

Give a name for the resource group.

Inside the "Instance Details" section, give a name that is unique in Azure. Check "Code" for the "Publish".

Select a recent version of PHP for "Runtime stack". Check "Linux" for "Operating System". Pick a "Region" for your location.

Your new website will have the URL of https://youruniquename.azurewebsites.net

In the "App Service Plan" section, pick "Free F1" size. This is free for 60 minutes compute time per day.

Click on "Review + Create" button on the bottom.

In the next page, click on the "Create" button to create the app.

Wait until you see "Your deployment is complete" check mark.

Now you have a website, but nothing of your own on the site.

Click on "Go to resource" button.

You will see the URL for your website. If you click on it, Azure will have some suggestions for you.

Step 3: Your first cloud PHP website.

Go to "Development Tools" on the side navigation panel.

Click on "Advanced Tools" then click on "Go"

On the menu of the new page, click "SSH"

You will see this window (Linux command line):

Type in the command at the prompt and push enter (no quotation marks): "cd site/wwwroot"

You will see the current directory changes to "home/site/wwwroot".

Next, add a file called index.php to the wwwroot directory as explained in the next line:

Type in the command at the prompt and press enter (no quotation marks): "nano index.php".

A blank editor window will display:

In the text editor that shows up, type in the following php code:

```php
<!DOCTYPE html>
<html>
<head>
<meta charset = "utf-8">
<title>My PHP Website</title>
</head>
<body>
<h1>Welcome to the cloud!</h1>
<form action = "" method = "post">
Your name:
<br><input type = "text" name = "name" size = "30" maxlength = "30">
<br>
<input type = "submit" name = "submit" value = "Submit">
</form>
<?php
if(isset($_POST['submit']))
{
$yourName = $_POST['name'];
echo "<p>Hi, $yourName, welcome to my cloud.</p>";
}
?>
</body>
</html>
```

After finishing typing, press Ctrl and X on keyboard to exit. You will see a dialog on the bottom of the screen. It prompts if you want to save the modified buffer.

Press Y on keyboard to confirm. Still another dialog will show on the bottom.

Press the Enter key on the keyboard to save the content to the file in the Linux default format.

Step 4: Run your website anywhere in the world.

Open your browser, enter https://youruniquename.azurewebsites.net

If you don't remember your unique name, go back to the resources page on the "overview" and click on the URL. You will see a webpage with a textbox and a submit button.

Type in any name. Click on the submit button on the website, your will see something like:

Hi, xxx, welcome to my cloud.

If you have some knowledge of PHP, you can play it here.

8.6 References:

Aghayi, E., LaToza, T. D., Surendra, P., & Abolghasemi, S. (2021). Crowdsourced behavior-driven development. Journal of Systems and Software, 171, 110840.

Anwar, A., Sailer, A., Kochut, A., and Butt, A.R. 2015. Anatomy of cloud monitoring and metering:A case study and open problems. InProceedings of the 6th Asia-Pacific Workshop on Systems, APSys'15, pages 6:1–6:7, New York, NY, USA, ACM. ISBN 978-1-4503-3554-6. doi: 10.1145/2797022.2797039. URLhttp://doi.acm.org/10.1145/2797022.2797039.

Aziz, W. A., Babulak, E., & Al-Dabass, D. (2021). Network Function Virtualization over Cloud-Cloud Computing as Business Continuity Solution. https://www.intechopen.com/online-first/76746

Bhatti, R., Luitjens, P., & Sobhani, P. (2020). When Engineers and Lawyers Talk: Right-Sizing Your Data Protection Risk Profile. In 2020 {USENIX} Conference on Privacy Engineering Practice and Respect ({PEPR} 20).

Burke, M. (2020). Rightsizing: The Foundation for Optimizing Your Cloud Infrastructure. Published Dec. 18, 2020. https://www.cloudhealthtech.com/blog/rightsizing-foundation-optimizing-your-cloud-infrastructure

CloudZero (2021). What is Cloud Optimization? (And Why Is It Important?). https://www.cloudzero.com/blog/cloud-optimization

de Souza, P. L., de Souza, W. L., & Pires, L. F. (2021). ScrumOntoBDD: Agile software development based on scrum, ontologies and behaviour-driven development. Journal of the Brazilian Computer Society, 27(1), 1-45.

Gokarna, M., & Singh, R. (2021, February). DevOps: A Historical Review and Future Works. In 2021 International Conference on Computing, Communication, and Intelligent Systems (ICCCIS) (pp. 366-371). IEEE.

Humble, J., & Farley, D. (2010). Continuous delivery: reliable software releases through build, test, and deployment automation. Pearson Education.

Khan, M. O., Jumani, A. K., & Farhan, W. A. (2020). Fast Delivery, Continuously Build, Testing and Deployment with DevOps Pipeline Techniques on Cloud. Indian Journal of Science and Technology, 13(05), 552-575.

Latendresse, J., Abdalkareem, R., Costa, D. E., & Shihab, E. (2021, May). How Effective is Continuous Integration in Indicating Single-Statement Bugs?. In 2021 IEEE/ACM 18th International Conference on Mining Software Repositories (MSR) (pp. 500-504). IEEE.

Morris, K. (2021). Infrastructure as code: dynamic systems for the cloud age. 2nd edition. O'Reilly Media, Inc.

Nair, A. (2021). DevOps-Driven Approach to Development in Cloud. https://www.techrxiv.org/articles/preprint/DevOps-Driven_Approach_to_Development_in_Cloud/14184716

Pourmajidi, W., Zhang, L., Miranskyy, A., Steinbacher, J., Godwin, D., & Erwin, T. (2021). The Challenging Landscape of Cloud Monitoring. Knowledge Management in the Development of Data-Intensive Systems, 157-189.

Rastogi, S. (2021). A Comparative Study on Testing Techniques of Software. International Journal of Innovative Science and Research Technology 6(7), 114-119.

Rodrigues, G. D. C., Rodrigo N. Calheiros, Vinicius Tavares Guimaraes, GledersonLessa dos Santos, M´arcio Barbosa de Carvalho, Lisandro Zambenedetti Granville, Liane Mar-garida Rockenbach Tarouco, and Rajkumar Buyya. Monitoring of cloud computing environments:Concepts, solutions, trends, and future directions. InProceedings of the 31st Annual ACM Symposiumon Applied Computing, SAC '16, pages 378–383, New York, NY, USA, 2016. ACM. ISBN 978-1-4503-3739-7. doi: 10.1145/2851613.2851619. URLhttp://doi.acm.org/10.1145/2851613.2851619.

Sabau, A. R., Hacks, S., & Steffens, A. (2021). Implementation of a continuous delivery pipeline for enterprise architecture model evolution. Software and Systems Modeling, 20(1), 117-145.

Tsai, W. L. (2021). Constructing assessment indicators for enterprises employing cloud IaaS. Asia Pacific Management Review, 26(1), 23-29.

8.7 Solutions to Review Questions

8.1 B; 8.2 B; 8.3 B; 8.5 B; 8.6 C; 8.7 B; 8.8 B; 8.9 B; 8.10 B; 8.11 D; 8.12 B; 8.13 A; 8.14 D; 8.15 C; 8.16 B; 8.17 C; 8.18 A; 8.19 B; 8.20 B; 8.21 B; 8.22 A; 8.23 A; 8.24 B; 8.25 B; 8.26 C; 8.27 C; 8.28 B; 8.29 A' 8.30 A; 8.31 B; 8.32 A; 8.33 C; 8.34 A; 8.35 B; 8.36 A; 8.37 A; 8.38 D; 8.39 A; 8.40 B; 8.41 A; 8.42 D; 8.43 A; 8.44 A; 8.45 D; 8.46 A; 8.47 C; 8.48 C; 8.49 C; 8.50 A; 8.51 A; 8.52 B; 8.53 B; 8.54 C; 8.55 C; 8.56 C; 8.57 C; 8.58 B; 8.59 B; 8.60 B; 8.61 B; 8.62 B; 8.63 C; 8.64 A; 8.65 A; 8.66 C; 8.67 C;

Chapter 9: Cloud Compliance and Security

Chapter Learning Outcomes

9.1 Summarize the key points of cloud policies.
9.2 Comprehend the concept of cloud risk management.
9.3 Discuss the criteria for assessing cloud security.
9.4 Explain the relationship between ITIL and cloud service management.

9.1 Cloud Compliance

In this section, we navigate the complex landscape of cloud compliance, discussing the shift of responsibilities from on-premise environments to cloud providers. We'll explore how cloud services simplify compliance processes, leveraging a foundation of security certifications to boost transparency and trust. While cloud providers manage the certification of architecture and services, organizations must uphold their part of the shared responsibility model.

9.1.1 Data Sovereignty

Businesses face increasing regulation. Regulatory compliance is a significant concern for top management (Kulkarni et al., 2021). Non-compliance can lead to substantial fines and reputational risk. The current practice of regulatory compliance is document-centric and heavily dependent on human experts.

Considering the size of modern enterprises, their multi-geographical operations, increasing dynamics, and frequent changes in regulations, a cloud-based solution is an effective technology to address these challenges.

Cloud computing, while virtual, operates on physical servers, networks, and data centers located somewhere in the world. The physical location could be in one or multiple countries. Until now, we have not focused on the specific locations of these countries. However, this can lead to legal complications. Data sovereignty implies that when you generate or collect data through cloud services, that data must remain within certain boundaries (Hummel et al., 2021). These boundaries could be a country, indigenous populations, or the consumers of a product. Violating these laws could result in fines and other penalties. However, data sovereignty isn't always legislated. It can also relate to information technology architecture or research. Data sovereignty can also be defined as giving data owners complete control over their data and digital identities (Braud et al., 2021). This includes determining who can do what with the data shared by the data owner, and in which context.

As you venture into the cloud and your organization expands globally, it's crucial to adhere to data sovereignty laws and understand their implications. Fortunately, major cloud providers offer data sovereignty options to facilitate this process for you and your organization.

Major cloud providers have a global presence with regions worldwide. They likely have a region in the country where you operate and where data sovereignty laws apply. In cases where the providers do not have a region in the country, they have the technology to operate on-premise or at a colocation data center at your physical location. Azure refers to this as Stack Hub, AWS as Outposts, and GCP as a hybrid cloud platform.

For global organizations, there are international compliance requirements and latency issues to consider. The cloud makes it easier for a business to expand globally. Major cloud providers may have a region in the area where you wish to conduct business.

Review Question 9.1
What is a significant concern mentioned in the book for top management in businesses?
A) Employee satisfaction
B) Regulatory compliance
C) Marketing strategies
D) Product development

Review Question 9.2
What does data sovereignty imply?
A) Data must be encrypted at all times.
B) Data must remain within certain boundaries.
C) Data must be accessible to all users.
D) Data must be stored in a physical location.

Review Question 9.3
What could be the result of violating data sovereignty laws?
A) Increased sales
B) More data storage

C) Improved reputation
D) Fines and other penalties

Review Question 9.4
What does data sovereignty also relate to, apart from legislation?
A) Information technology architecture
B) Marketing strategies
C) Employee satisfaction
D) Product development

Review Question 9.5
What do major cloud providers offer to facilitate the process of adhering to data sovereignty laws?
A) Data sovereignty options
B) Marketing strategies
C) Employee training
D) Product development tools

Review Question 9.6
What does Azure refer to the technology to operate on-premise or at a colocation data center at your physical location as?
A) Stack Hub
B) Outposts
C) Hybrid cloud platform
D) Data center

Review Question 9.7
What are the international considerations for global organizations when using the cloud?
A) Compliance requirements and latency issues
B) Marketing strategies and product development
C) Employee satisfaction and data storage
D) Sales and reputation

Review Question 9.8
What makes it easier for a business to expand globally?
A) Marketing strategies
B) The cloud
C) Product development
D) Employee satisfaction

9.1.2 Industry-Specific Standards

Each industry has unique needs, compliance, and regulatory requirements that must be addressed by the technology stack. Major cloud providers cater to these needs by offering industry-specific solutions. For instance, Azure offers a policy resource that can assist in meeting some industry-specific requirements.

Companies in the financial sector have numerous compliance requirements to fulfill, ranging from The Sarbanes-Oxley Act (SOX) to the Gramm-Leach-Bliley Act (GLBA). Similarly, businesses in healthcare need to comply with the Health Insurance Portability and Accountability Act (HIPAA) and the Health Information Technology for Economic and Clinical Health Act (HITECH), among others.

In addition to these industry-specific standards, there are international policies to adhere to in the cloud. The International Organization for Standardization (ISO) has published a set of standards for cloud computing, which can be found in the ISO/IEC 17788 document (2014). This document provides an overview of cloud computing, a glossary of cloud-related terms and definitions, as well as security best practices for cloud computing. As you venture into the cloud, it's crucial to understand and adhere to these standards and best practices.

Review Question 9.9
What do major cloud providers offer to cater to the unique needs and compliance requirements of each industry?
A) Industry-specific solutions
B) Marketing strategies
C) Employee training programs
D) Product development tools

Review Question 9.10
What does Azure offer to assist in meeting some industry-specific requirements?
A) A policy resource
B) A marketing strategy
C) An employee training program
D) A product development tool

Review Question 9.11
What is one of the compliance requirements that companies in the financial sector need to fulfill?
A) The Marketing Strategy Act (MSA)
B) The Health Insurance Portability and Accountability Act (HIPAA)
C) The Health Information Technology for Economic and Clinical Health Act (HITECH)
D) The Sarbanes-Oxley Act (SOX)

Review Question 9.12
What organization has published a set of standards for cloud computing?
A) The United Nations (UN)
B) The International Organization for Standardization (ISO)
C) The World Health Organization (WHO)
D) The International Monetary Fund (IMF)

Review Question 9.13

What does the ISO/IEC 17788 document provide?
A) A product development tool for cloud computing
B) A marketing strategy for cloud computing
C) An employee training program for cloud computing
D) An overview of cloud computing, a glossary of cloud-related terms and definitions, and security best practices for cloud computing

9.1.3 Regulatory and Compliance Certifications

Enterprises must meet specific regulatory and compliance standards for their business operations. In on-premise environments, IT and security teams are responsible for ensuring that their data centers and workloads meet these regulatory and compliance certifications. The current certification process can be complex and suboptimal, often proving expensive and heavily reliant on the auditor's skills (Hulshof and Daneva, 2021).

In the cloud, providers shoulder most of these requirements. They rely on security certifications to enhance transparency and trustworthiness (Orue-Echevarria et al., 2021). A cloud certification scheme employs specific rules, procedures, and management systems that may apply to one or more systems (Tsvilii, 2021). Cloud providers regularly audit their resources and processes, updating these certifications as required by regulations.

Running your workloads on the cloud streamlines the process of achieving regulatory and compliance certification. This is because the data centers and services of cloud providers are already certified, having undergone audits and checks to ensure they meet those certifications. Your workloads run on top of their data centers and within their services, thereby meeting regulatory and compliance standards.

However, it's important to remember the shared responsibility model. While cloud providers certify the architecture and services running in the cloud, your organization must ensure that your staff and processes also adhere to these certifications.

Major cloud providers publish a comprehensive list of their certifications, which you will benefit from when running your workloads on their cloud. For instance, Azure lists all the certifications they meet through their cloud and the various services that comply with those regulatory and compliance certifications.

Many cloud providers also offer on-demand reporting for you to present to your auditors. Some providers have services that scan your environment to check if your workloads meet regulatory and compliance needs.

For example, Azure Security Center continually scans your environment. You can use it in conjunction with Azure Policy to enforce policies that help you maintain compliance and meet regulatory needs.

Review Question 9.14
Who is responsible for ensuring that data centers and workloads meet regulatory and compliance certifications in on-premise environments?
A) The CEO
B) The marketing team
C) IT and security teams
D) The sales team

Review Question 9.15
What do cloud providers rely on to enhance transparency and trustworthiness?
A) Marketing strategies
B) Security certifications
C) Sales tactics
D) Employee training programs

Review Question 9.16
What does running your workloads on the cloud streamline?
A) The process of achieving regulatory and compliance certification
B) The process of marketing your products
C) The process of training your employees
D) The process of developing your products

Review Question 9.17
What must your organization ensure in addition to the certifications provided by cloud providers?
A) That your sales tactics are working
B) That your marketing strategies are effective
C) That your staff and processes also adhere to these certifications
D) That your product development tools are up-to-date

Review Question 9.18
What do major cloud providers publish?
A) A comprehensive list of their certifications
B) A comprehensive list of their marketing strategies
C) A comprehensive list of their sales tactics
D) A comprehensive list of their product development tools

9.2 Cloud Policies

Cloud computing success hinges on the development and implementation of robust policies. This section explores the complex landscape of regulations, standards, and guidelines that govern cloud technologies. These policies, which cover everything from security and compliance to resource management and data governance, form the bedrock of cloud computing strategies. By delving into the various facets of cloud policies, this section provides readers with a thorough understanding of how these regulations influence the adoption, operation, and expansion of cloud-based solutions.

9.2.1 ITIL Service Value System

Governance plays a crucial role in the adoption and operation of the cloud. This section guides you through the many aspects of cloud governance, covering a range of cloud policy and procedure topics. The Information Technology Infrastructure Library (ITIL) is a widely used IT service management methodology that aids in the planning, design, delivery, operation, and continuous improvement of IT services (Cartlidge and Steria, 2020). ITIL procedures are employed to gauge the effectiveness of IT service management processes and their correlation with accelerated system development in the cloud.

Challenges in IT deployment and maintenance management can significantly limit the reliability of cloud computing services (Wang et al., 2021). Every enterprise aims to remain competitive in the market and deliver the services its customers demand in a cost-effective manner. ITIL provides a framework for effectively executing and supporting cloud applications. By adhering to ITIL, a business can prevent cloud sprawl and instability, minimize the risk of service disruption, and enhance customer loyalty by integrating people, processes, and technology into hybrid environments.

A central component of ITIL is the Service Value System (SVS). The SVS illustrates how all elements of IT service management collaborate as a system to create value through stakeholder collaboration. The inputs to the SVS are opportunity and demand, while the key elements include guiding principles, governance, service value chain, practices, and continual improvement. The outputs of the SVS are the values delivered to stakeholders.

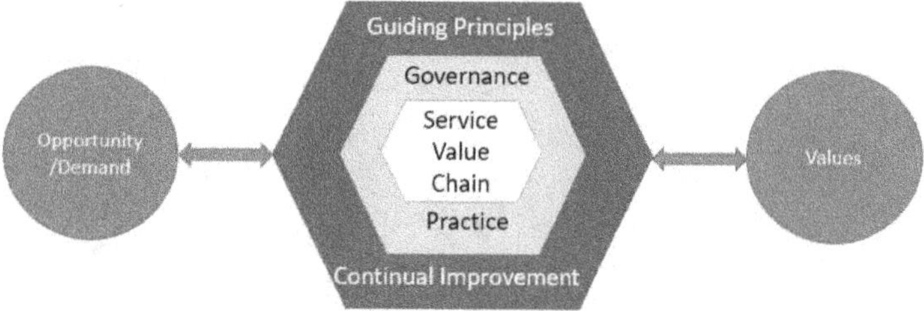

Figure 9.1: ITIL's Service Value System (SVS)

Within the SVS, guiding principles offer recommendations that steer an organization in its objectives, strategies, work types, or management structure. Governance refers to the methods by which the organization is directed and controlled. The service value chain comprises a series of interconnected activities that an organization undertakes to deliver value to its customers and facilitate value realization. Practices are sets of organizational resources designed to perform work or achieve a goal. Continual improvement is a constant organizational activity carried out at all levels to ensure performance meets stakeholder expectations.

Review Question 9.19
What is the Information Technology Infrastructure Library (ITIL)?
A) A cloud computing service.
B) A hardware management technique.
C) An IT service management methodology.
D) A data storage system.

Review Question 9.20
What does ITIL provide for businesses?
A) A framework for effectively executing and supporting cloud applications.
B) A method for creating cloud applications.
C) A platform for marketing cloud applications.
D) A system for pricing cloud applications.

Review Question 9.21
What is the Service Value System (SVS) in ITIL?
A) A set of guidelines for cloud application development.
B) A system illustrating how all elements of IT service management collaborate to create value.
C) A database of all IT services provided by a company.
D) A tool for measuring the effectiveness of IT services.

Review Question 9.22
What are the inputs to the Service Value System (SVS)?
A) Demand and supply.
B) Opportunity and demand.
C) Supply and opportunity.
D) Demand and performance.

Review Question 9.23
What does the service value chain in the SVS represent?
A) A series of interconnected activities to deliver value to customers.
B) A chain of command in IT service management.
C) A sequence of cloud applications offered by a company.
D) A timeline of a company's IT services.

Review Question 9.24
What are practices within the SVS?
A) Sets of organizational resources designed to perform work or achieve a goal.
B) Guidelines for using cloud applications.
C) Policies governing the use of IT services.
D) Procedures for maintaining IT hardware.

Review Question 9.25
What is continual improvement in the context of the SVS?
A) A one-time organizational activity to improve performance.
B) An ongoing organizational activity performed at all levels to ensure performance meets stakeholder expectations.
C) A periodic review of IT services.
D) A strategy for improving cloud application functionality.

9.2.2 Service Value System Components

Among the five components of the Service Value System (SVS), the central element is the Service Value Chain (SVC). The SVC is an operating model that outlines the key activities necessary to respond to demand and facilitate value realization through the creation and management of cloud resources and services (O'Loughlin, 2019). The SVC comprises six value chain activities that contribute to value creation.

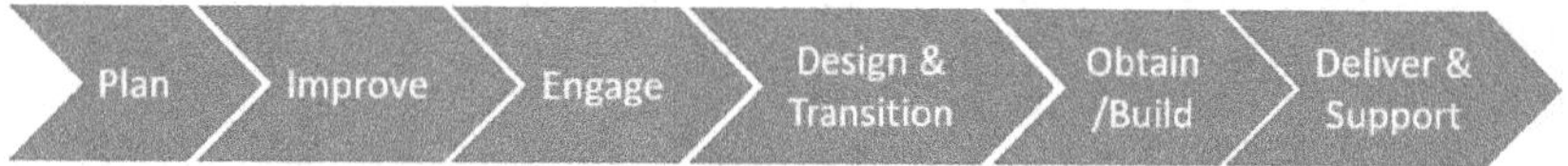

Figure 9.2: SVS Service Value Chain

The Cloud *Plan* activity aims to align the company's cloud strategy with its business strategy. It encompasses business needs, policy, vision, business objectives, adoption drivers, and risks.
The Cloud *Improve* activity ensures the continual improvement of products, services, and practices across all value chain activities. This activity can involve improving the cloud service or enhancing existing services, applications, and IT components by integrating them with the cloud.
The Cloud *Engage* activity involves engaging with stakeholders to understand their strategy, needs, and requirements, as well as end-user expectations. A critical aspect of this activity is engaging with cloud service providers, which can range from creating a customer account and providing credit card billing details to navigating a Request for Proposal (RFP) process.
The *Design and Transition* activities ensure that products and services consistently meet stakeholder expectations for quality, cost, and time to market. Once established, ongoing design and transition activities for cloud-based services can be managed using DevOps or Agile methodologies.
The *Obtain/Build* activity ensures that cloud service components are available when and where needed and meet agreed specifications. The cloud enables rapid resource expansion and provisioning. It also automates build activities, including testing and validation, using relevant Continuous Integration/Continuous

Deployment (CI/CD) toolchains.

The *Deliver and Support* activities ensure that services are delivered and supported according to agreed specifications and stakeholder expectations. Major cloud vendors manage incidents, problems, changes, and levels of availability and capacity as part of their service delivery. You will have Service Level Agreements (SLAs) from the cloud provider and SLAs that you need to meet as an internal IT department. While the cloud provider supports the services provided from the cloud, they do not support the actual workloads running in the cloud. Therefore, an IT team, Subject Matter Experts (SMEs), and network experts are still needed to support the business and end users.

Review Question 9.26
What is the central element of the Service Value System (SVS)?
A) Cloud Plan Activity
B) Service Value Chain (SVC)
C) Cloud Improve Activity
D) Cloud Engage Activity

Review Question 9.27
What is the aim of the Cloud Plan activity?
A) To engage with stakeholders
B) To align the company's cloud strategy with its business strategy
C) To ensure that services are delivered and supported according to agreed specifications
D) To ensure the continual improvement of products, services, and practices

Review Question 9.28
What does the Cloud Improve activity ensure?
A) The alignment of the company's cloud strategy with its business strategy
B) The delivery and support of services according to agreed specifications
C) The engagement with stakeholders to understand their strategy, needs, and requirements
D) The continual improvement of products, services, and practices across all value chain activities

Review Question 9.29
What is a critical aspect of the Cloud Engage activity?
A) Engaging with cloud service providers
B) Aligning the company's cloud strategy with its business strategy
C) Ensuring the continual improvement of products, services, and practices
D) Ensuring that services are delivered and supported according to agreed specifications

Review Question 9.30
What do the Design and Transition activities ensure?
A) That products and services consistently meet stakeholder expectations for quality, cost, and time to market
B) The alignment of the company's cloud strategy with its business strategy
C) The engagement with stakeholders to understand their strategy, needs, and requirements
D) The continual improvement of products, services, and practices

Review Question 9.31
What does the Obtain/Build activity ensure?

A) That cloud service components are available when and where needed and meet agreed specifications
B) The alignment of the company's cloud strategy with its business strategy
C) The engagement with stakeholders to understand their strategy, needs, and requirements
D) That products and services consistently meet stakeholder expectations for quality, cost, and time to market

Review Question 9.32
What do the Deliver and Support activities ensure?
A) The engagement with stakeholders to understand their strategy, needs, and requirements
B) The alignment of the company's cloud strategy with its business strategy
C) That services are delivered and supported according to agreed specifications and stakeholder expectations
D) That cloud service components are available when and where needed and meet agreed specifications

Review Question 9.33
Who is still needed to support the business and end users even with the support from the cloud provider?
A) The company's customers
B) The company's board of directors
C) The company's shareholders
D) An IT team, Subject Matter Experts (SMEs), and network experts

9.2.3 Centralized Cloud Governance

Individual business units and teams within an organization have the capability to independently purchase their own cloud services from a cloud provider, thereby bypassing the IT department. However, when a business unit or team procures their own cloud services, they may not prioritize security or be equipped to handle security issues. Moreover, as business needs evolve, cloud resources require maintenance and adaptation, tasks that are more efficiently managed through centralized cloud governance. With a cloud governance structure in place, business units and teams will coordinate with central IT, reducing risk. It's crucial to ensure that your governance can keep pace with the speed of business. Many organizations base their on-premise operating procedure governance on ITIL. Continuing to follow this framework for managing information technology in the cloud is a recommended practice.

Review Question 9.34
According to the book, what actions can individual business units and teams within an organization take independently that could potentially lead to security concerns?
A) They can bypass the IT department and purchase their own cloud services from a cloud provider.
B) They can create their own IT department.
C) They can establish their own cloud provider company.
D) They can prioritize security over all other aspects.

Review Question 9.35

What is a potential issue when a business unit or team procures their own cloud services?
A) They may become a cloud provider.
B) They may prioritize security over all other aspects.
C) They may not prioritize security or be equipped to handle security issues.
D) They may establish their own IT department.

Review Question 9.36
What is the purpose of centralized cloud governance?
A) To ensure that business units and teams coordinate with central IT, reducing risk.
B) To allow business units and teams to bypass the IT department.
C) To prioritize security over all other aspects.
D) To establish a separate IT department for each business unit and team.

Review Question 9.37
What is a recommended practice for managing information technology in the cloud?
A) Bypassing the IT department and purchasing cloud services independently.
B) Prioritizing security over all other aspects.
C) Establishing a separate IT department for each business unit and team.
D) Continuing to follow the ITIL framework.

9.2.4 ITIL's Change Enablement

Change management is a critical aspect of information technology within organizations. ITIL incorporates a service management practice known as change enablement, which can be applied to cloud change management. Compared to traditional change management, change enablement allows IT services to operate in more flexible and less rigid environments. Change enablement aims to maximize the number of successful product and service changes while minimizing the risks associated with these changes. A change is defined as any addition, modification, or removal of anything that could have a direct or indirect effect on services (Agutter, 2020).

For instance, a DevOps environment on the cloud automates change enablement. If code is released frequently, automated integration and delivery pipelines with staged tests are used to ensure there is no negative impact on the production environment. If a test fails, the code is withdrawn. Despite automation, change enablement still generates logs to document what changes have been made, and the tests being used will require ongoing review.

Change enablement should be employed to ensure that application teams, business owners, and business units are all aligned before making changes to any applications or workloads running in the cloud.

Review Question 9.38
What is the purpose of change enablement in ITIL?
A) To operate IT services in rigid environments.
B) To minimize the number of successful product and service changes.
C) To maximize the number of successful product and service changes while minimizing the risks associated with these changes.
D) To remove anything that could have a direct or indirect effect on services.

Review Question 9.39
How does a DevOps environment on the cloud handle change enablement?
A) It manually handles change enablement.
B) It automates change enablement.
C) It ignores change enablement.
D) It minimizes change enablement.

Review Question 9.40
What happens if a test fails in a DevOps environment on the cloud?
A) The code is promoted.
B) The code is withdrawn.
C) The code is ignored.
D) The code is minimized.

Review Question 9.41
Who should be aligned before making changes to any applications or workloads running in the cloud?
A) Application teams, business owners, and business units
B) Only application teams
C) Only business owners
D) Only business units

9.2.5 Resource Management and Change Tracking

Cloud providers offer a variety of robust options to assist businesses in managing their resources. These can be accessed through a cloud portal, APIs via programming, or command-line tools. Automation tools such as Azure Resource Manager (ARM) templates for implementing Infrastructure as Code (IaC) on Azure, and CloudFormation templates on AWS, are available. Additionally, major cloud providers offer native tools to aid resource management. For instance, Azure's Update Management streamlines patch management.

Cloud providers offer change tracking capabilities, enabling you to monitor changes on servers. For instance, if you discover an issue with a server, you can review all service changes from the previous day, such as moved or deleted files, through change management. Change tracking aids in identifying the root cause of issues and provides visibility into activities across servers and environments.

Another advantage of change tracking is the inventory management it provides for your Infrastructure as a Service (IaaS) virtual machines. Having an inventory simplifies the management of these resources.

Review Question 9.42
How can businesses manage their resources in cloud computing?
A) Through a cloud portal, APIs via programming, or command-line tools.
B) Through physical servers only.
C) Through manual tracking only.
D) Through paper documentation.

Review Question 9.43
What is the purpose of Azure's Update Management?
A) To implement Infrastructure as Code (IaC) on Azure.
B) To streamline patch management.
C) To monitor changes on servers.
D) To provide inventory management for IaaS virtual machines.

Review Question 9.44
What does change tracking in cloud computing enable you to do?
A) Monitor changes on servers.
B) Implement Infrastructure as Code (IaC) on Azure.
C) Streamline patch management.

Review Question 9.45
What is an advantage of change tracking for Infrastructure as a Service (IaaS) virtual machines?
A) It provides inventory management.
B) It streamlines patch management.
C) It monitors changes on servers.
D) It implements Infrastructure as Code (IaC) on Azure.

9.2.6 Identity and Access Control

Cloud access is typically managed by an identity provider and a role-based access control (RBAC) service for authorization. For instance, Azure employs Azure Active Directory as an identity provider and has built-in RBAC in Azure Resource Manager for authorization. These services work together to identify the user and assign appropriate access privileges.

RBAC manages access based on the roles that users hold within the system and rules that define what access is permitted for users in specific roles. A role is similar to a group in the directory system. For instance, with RBAC, a user in the accounts payable (AP) clerk role would automatically be added (i.e., dynamic membership) to the AP Role, granting them access to AP functions in the accounting system. In this example, Azure Active Directory provides the user accounts, groups, and service accounts, while RBAC controls access permissions. AWS offers a similar service with its Identity and Access Management (IAM). Major cloud providers offer policy services that can help define and enforce policies. For example, Azure Policy can be used for various purposes.

Use for Azure Policy	Example
Requiring tags for resources	Facilitates easier resource location for chargeback.
Geo-compliance	Prevents resources from being deployed to specific regions.
Cost control	Restricts service usage.
Configuration	Ensures HIPAA compliance.
Security	Establishes rules for database management.

Table 9.1: Uses and examples of Azure Policy.

Review Question 9.46
What is the primary function of an identity provider in cloud access management?
A) To manage user roles
B) To enforce policies
C) To identify the user
D) To control costs

Review Question 9.47
What is the role of Azure Active Directory in the given context?
A) It provides user accounts, groups, and service accounts.
B) It controls access permissions.
C) It manages user roles.
D) It enforces policies.

Review Question 9.48
What is an example of a use for Azure Policy?
A) To add users to roles
B) To identify the user
C) To ensure HIPAA compliance
D) To provide user accounts

Review Question 9.49
What is the equivalent of a role in the directory system?
A) A group
B) A user
C) A policy
D) A service account

Review Question 9.50
What service does AWS offer that is similar to Azure Active Directory and RBAC in Azure?

A) AWS Lambda
B) AWS S3
C) AWS IAM
D) AWS EC2

9.2.7 Security Communication Policies

Security communication policies dictate the who, what, when, and how of announcing an incident or service outage. It's crucial that these policies are well-documented and communicated to all stakeholders to ensure a coordinated and effective response.

Your security communication policy should encompass several key elements:

Stakeholder Identification: Identify the application owner and users, and clearly define their roles and responsibilities. Establish guidelines for when these individuals should be notified, taking into account the severity and potential impact of the incident.
Alert Conditions: Define the specific conditions or thresholds that trigger alerts. These could be based on system metrics, unusual activity, or other indicators that suggest a potential issue.
Notification Channels: Determine the most effective communication channels for delivering alerts. These could include SMS messages, emails, automated phone calls, or even physical mail, depending on the urgency and nature of the incident.
Incident Response: Outline the steps to be taken in response to an incident. This could range from automatic system remediation and logging for minor issues, to immediate, direct communication and coordinated response for major incidents.

In scenarios where the cloud system can automatically rectify the issue and maintain normal operation, a comprehensive log of the incident may suffice. However, in more severe scenarios, such as a major disaster, it may be necessary to initiate immediate communication through a phone call, involving key stakeholders and initiating a well-coordinated response plan.

Remember, the goal of a security communication policy is not just to respond to incidents, but to do so in a way that minimizes disruption, maintains trust, and learns from each incident to improve future responses."

Review Question 9.51
What is the primary purpose of a security communication policy?
A) To define user roles and responsibilities
B) To announce an incident or service outage
C) To define alert conditions
D) To determine notification channels

Review Question 9.52
What is the role of 'Stakeholder Identification' in a security communication policy?
A) To define the specific conditions that trigger alerts
B) To identify the application owner and users, and define their roles and responsibilities
C) To determine the most effective communication channels for delivering alerts
D) To outline the steps to be taken in response to an incident

Review Question 9.53
What could be a potential 'Alert Condition' in a security communication policy?
A) An employee logs in on work
B) Unusual activity
C) An email notification
D) A well-coordinated response plan

Review Question 9.54
What is meant by 'Notification Channels' in a security communication policy?
A) The steps to be taken in response to an incident
B) The conditions that trigger alerts
C) The communication channels for delivering alerts
D) The roles and responsibilities of users

Review Question 9.55
What is the goal of a security communication policy?
A) To respond to incidents in a way that minimizes disruption, maintains trust, and learns from each incident to improve future responses
B) To define user roles and responsibilities
C) To define the specific conditions that trigger alerts
D) To determine the most effective communication channels for delivering alerts

Review Question 9.56
In a severe scenario, such as a major disaster, what action might be necessary according to a security communication policy?
A) Initiate immediate communication through a phone call
B) Define user roles and responsibilities
C) Define the specific conditions that trigger alerts
D) Determine the most effective communication channels for delivering alerts

9.3 Cloud Risk Management

Cloud computing has transformed how organizations manage their data and IT infrastructure. It offers numerous benefits, such as scalability and cost efficiency, but also introduces unique risks and challenges. Managing these risks is critical to ensuring the security, resilience, and compliance of cloud-based operations. In this section, we delve into the vital domain of cloud risk management. We will explore various risk dimensions, from data security and compliance to service availability and vendor dependencies.

Through strategic risk assessment, mitigation, and response strategies, organizations can confidently navigate the complex landscape of cloud computing.

9.3.1 Risk Management

Risk management is a process that involves the identification, assessment, and prioritization of the likelihood of assets being exposed to danger. This process is followed by the coordination of actions and allocation of resources to minimize, monitor, and control the probability and impact of such danger (Bowers, 2016).

The first step in risk management is asset inventory. It's essential to know what assets are in your environment before you can secure them effectively. Assets can be either physical or logical.

The second step is to rank the assets in order of importance. You assign a value to each asset, which helps you understand the level of risk you have and how you're going to manage it.

The third step is to identify the owners of those assets. This step helps determine who is responsible for securing those assets.

The final step is to assess the risk associated with these assets. An asset that is accessible via the Internet poses more risk than one that is only available on-premise.

After working through all these steps, you can proceed to secure the asset using the tools available in the cloud. For instance, AWS provides a "Systems Manager" that can assist you with inventory management.

Just like AWS, Azure offers the Data Discovery & Classification tool, which can be found under the Security heading in your Azure SQL Database pane.

Review Question 9.57
What is the first step in risk management?
A) Identifying the owners of the assets
B) Assessing the risk associated with the assets
C) Asset inventory
D) Ranking the assets in order of importance

Review Question 9.58

Which asset poses more risk?

A) An asset that is only available on-premise

B) An asset that is accessible via the Internet

C) An asset that is ranked low in importance

D) An asset that is not owned by anyone

Review Question 9.59

What is the purpose of ranking assets in order of importance in risk management?

A) To identify the owners of the assets

B) To understand the level of risk and how to manage it

C) To assess the risk associated with the assets

D) To inventory the assets

Review Question 9.60

What tool does Azure offer similar to AWS Systems Manager?

A) Azure Risk Manager

B) Azure Asset Inventory

C) Azure Data Discovery & Classification tool

D) Azure Security Manager

9.3.2 Risk Documentation and Management Tools

Risk documentation is a crucial aspect of risk management. It aids in identifying company assets, understanding the security posture, and consolidating knowledge. It provides a central repository for IT components and assets, IT security, and emergency management. It documents responsibilities, roles, and contact persons, thereby shortening response times in the event of a security breach, emergency, or disaster. Numerous tools are available for documentation. A robust tool should offer features such as diagram capabilities, documentation, monitoring, and automation.

For instance, Azure offers a tool called Azure Resource Graph that enables you to query, explore, and analyze cloud resources across all your subscriptions. You can apply filters to view everything in a specific subscription or certain types of assets. You can export this information into spreadsheets or include it in documentation. Additionally, third-party tools like Cloudockit can provide significant benefits for documentation.

Cloudockit is a tool that generates an automated view of your current cloud architecture with editable diagrams. It allows you to specify how your cloud components are arranged and automatically refreshes the information without altering your diagram layouts.

A risk register is an essential tool for risk management documentation (Ryu et al., 2016). It helps stay on top of potential issues that could derail intended outcomes. A typical risk register includes the following fields:

Field name	Explanation
Risk ID	Uniquely identifies each risk
Risk	Name or a brief description of the risk
Category	Internal or external, material-related or labor-related, etc.
Probability	Likelihood of the risk occurring, a number between 0 and 1
Impact	The severity of the impact on your asset if the risk occurs
Rating	Where this risk falls on your priority list, on a 1 to 10 scale
Mitigation	Steps involved if a breach happens, e.g., antimalware, continuous updates

Table 9.2 Fields of a typical risk register

Review Question 9.61
What is the purpose of risk documentation in risk management?
A) To provide a central repository for IT components and assets
B) To document responsibilities, roles, and contact persons
C) To shorten response times in the event of a security breach
D) All of the other options are correct

Review Question 9.62
What is a risk register used for in risk management documentation?
A) To stay on top of potential issues that can derail intended outcomes
B) To uniquely identify each risk
C) To provide a name or a brief description of the risk
D) To determine the likelihood of the risk occurring

9.3.3 Data Portability

When selecting a cloud provider, it's crucial to consider data portability. This is the ability for data owners to move data into and out of the cloud with ease. Data portability facilitates the management of multi-cloud or hybrid cloud environments and can help avoid vendor lock-in.

There are three primary technologies that support data portability in the cloud:

Open API: APIs are sets of requirements that dictate how one application can communicate and interact with another. An open API is a publicly available and free API for developers. If a business uses an open API on-premise, it will be easier to migrate to a cloud provider that also uses an open API (McKenzie, 2020).
Containerization: Containers are self-contained packages that may include all the dependencies needed to run an application. These self-contained packages are portable, making it easy to move a container between on-

premise and cloud environments.

Everything as Code (EaC): EaC involves managing all aspects of software development, delivery, and management by defining and codifying the infrastructure, schema, and pipelines used to create, maintain, iterate, or expand app development (Tozzi, 2020). It uses policy template files to govern the way software is built, deployed, configured, and monitored automatically. When moving an application, you only need to move the template.

Review Question 9.63

What is data portability in the context of cloud computing?

A) The ability to move data into and out of the cloud with ease

B) The ability to store large amounts of data in the cloud

C) The ability to access data from any location

D) The ability to encrypt data stored in the cloud

Review Question 9.64

What is an open API?

A) A private API for developers

B) A set of requirements that dictate how one application can communicate and interact with another

C) A type of cloud storage

D) A method of encrypting data

Review Question 9.65

What is containerization in the context of cloud computing?

A) A method of data encryption

B) A type of cloud storage

C) Self-contained packages that may include all the dependencies needed to run an application

D) A type of API

Review Question 9.66

What does Everything as Code (EaC) involve?

A) Managing all aspects of software development, delivery, and management by defining and codifying the infrastructure, schema, and pipelines used to create, maintain, iterate, or expand app development

B) Encrypting all data stored in the cloud

C) Storing all data in the cloud

D) Communicating and interacting with other applications

9.3.4 Risks of Vendor Lock-In

Vendor lock-in is a situation that an organization faces when it encounters significant challenges or incurs high costs while attempting to switch from its current vendor to another for its products and services. This issue can prevent the organization from migrating to another provider, even if the current cloud provider experiences downtime or decides to increase costs.

To mitigate the risks associated with vendor lock-in, several strategies can be employed:

Multi-Cloud Strategy: Utilize more than one cloud service for your information technology needs. This approach not only provides redundancy but also offers flexibility in choosing the best features from different providers.
Data Backups: Maintain internal backups of your data outside of the cloud provider. This could mean running an application on one cloud with a backup application on a different cloud. This ensures that your data is safe and accessible, even if one provider experiences issues.
Data Portability: Choose providers that support data portability technologies. These technologies allow you to easily move your data from one provider to another, providing flexibility and reducing dependency on a single provider.
Adoption of Portable Technologies: Use portable technologies that are not tied to a specific vendor. These technologies, discussed earlier in this section, allow for easier migration between different platforms and reduce the risk of vendor lock-in.

By implementing these strategies, organizations can reduce their dependency on a single vendor, thereby mitigating the risks associated with vendor lock-in. This allows for greater flexibility and control over their IT infrastructure.

Review Question 9.67
What is vendor lock-in?
A) A situation where an organization faces difficulties in switching vendors due to high costs or significant challenges.
B) A situation where a vendor locks an organization into a long-term contract.
C) A situation where an organization is unable to find a suitable vendor for its needs.
D) A situation where a vendor refuses to provide services to an organization.

Review Question 9.68
What is the purpose of a multi-cloud strategy?
A) To increase the cost of cloud services.
B) To provide redundancy and flexibility in choosing the best features from different providers.
C) To reduce the speed of data transfer.
D) To limit the organization's options to a single cloud service.

Review Question 9.69
What is the benefit of maintaining internal backups of data outside of the cloud provider?
A) It ensures that data is lost if one provider experiences issues.
B) It ensures that data is safe and accessible, even if one provider experiences issues.
C) It increases the risk of data loss.
D) It reduces the flexibility of data access.

Review Question 9.70
What is the advantage of choosing providers that support data portability technologies?
A) It increases dependency on a single provider.
B) It reduces flexibility.
C) It allows you to easily move your data from one provider to another.

D) It makes data transfer more difficult.

Review Question 9.71
How does the adoption of portable technologies help mitigate the risks of vendor lock-in?
A) It increases the risk of vendor lock-in.
B) It ties the organization to a specific vendor.
C) It allows for easier migration between different platforms.
D) It makes it more difficult to switch vendors.

9.3.5 Risk Response Strategies

Risk response refers to the strategic process of managing and controlling identified risks. It involves

stakeholders deciding on the best course of action to handle the risks associated with their activities.

There are several types of risk response strategies:

Risk Acceptance: This strategy involves acknowledging the associated risk and continuing with the activity regardless. For instance, an organization might recognize the potential risk of a cloud provider going out of business but chooses to migrate to the cloud regardless. This decision is often made when the benefits outweigh the potential risks, or when the risk is deemed manageable.

Risk Transfer: This strategy involves outsourcing the risk to a third party. For example, an organization can acquire cyber insurance to cover potential cybersecurity risks, effectively transferring the risk to the insurance company. This strategy is often used when the potential risk could result in significant financial loss.

Risk Avoidance: This strategy involves choosing not to engage in the risky activity at all. For instance, an organization might decide not to migrate its services to the cloud to avoid any risks related to cloud computing. This strategy is often used when the potential risks outweigh the benefits of the activity.

Risk Mitigation: This strategy involves implementing security controls to reduce or even completely eliminate the risks, thereby avoiding negative impacts. For instance, an organization might implement automated disaster recovery on critical servers across cloud regions. If a server in one region goes down, another one in a different region automatically takes its place, ensuring continuity of service.

By understanding and implementing these strategies, organizations can better manage their risks, allowing

for more informed decision-making and greater control over their IT infrastructure.

Review Question 9.72
What does risk response refer to?
A) The process of identifying risks.
B) The process of managing and controlling identified risks.
C) The process of ignoring identified risks.
D) The process of creating risks.

Review Question 9.73

What is the risk acceptance strategy?
A) Ignoring the associated risk and discontinuing the activity.
B) Acknowledging the associated risk and continuing with the activity regardless.
C) Transferring the associated risk to a third party.
D) Implementing security controls to reduce the associated risk.

Review Question 9.74
What does the risk transfer strategy involve?
A) Ignoring the risk.
B) Continuing the activity despite the risk.
C) Outsourcing the risk to a third party.
D) Avoiding the risky activity altogether.

Review Question 9.75
What is the risk avoidance strategy?
A) Choosing to engage in the risky activity.
B) Transferring the risk to a third party.
C) Choosing not to engage in the risky activity at all.
D) Acknowledging the risk and continuing the activity.

Review Question 9.76
What does the risk mitigation strategy involve?
A) Ignoring the risk.
B) Transferring the risk to a third party.
C) Continuing the activity despite the risk.
D) Implementing security controls to reduce or even completely eliminate the risks.

9.4 Cloud Security

In this course, we will examine the various security threats prevalent in the cloud environment. We will delve into the practices of vulnerability scanning and penetration testing. Lastly, we will discuss effective strategies for enhancing security, ensuring your cloud infrastructure remains robust against potential threats.

9.4.1 Cloud Security Threats

Over the past decade, cloud computing has evolved from a promising business concept to one of the fastest-growing sectors in the IT industry. However, with its widespread adoption, critical security issues have emerged, causing concern among organizations.

Understanding security begins with identifying the sources of threats (Alouffi et al., 2021). Data tampering and leakage are significant concerns for both clients and cloud vendors. These threats originate from attackers, hackers, or unauthorized users who attempt to access cloud computing services. The increasing use of APIs exacerbates these threats. Other potential sources include malicious insiders and disgruntled employees.

Inadequate communication between clients and cloud providers is another major threat. Many businesses operate on hybrid and multi-cloud models. Insufficiently secured communication between on-premise and cloud, as well as between different clouds, can pose significant risks. According to the weakest link principle, robust cloud security can be compromised by weak on-premise security.

Other identified threats to cloud computing security include issues related to data storage, confidentiality, and availability in cloud services. For instance, if you lose the encryption keys for your data at rest, you cannot retrieve the data, and even the cloud vendor cannot regenerate the lost keys.

Threat intelligence is a proactive approach to identify and mitigate these threats in the cloud early on. Major vendors offer threat intelligence solutions that can be integrated into their cloud services to detect suspicious activities, alert security teams, and neutralize threats promptly.

Review Question 9.77
What is a significant concern for both clients and cloud vendors in cloud security?
A) API usage
B) Data tampering and leakage
C) Hybrid cloud models
D) Encryption key8

Review Question 9.78
What happens if you lose the encryption keys for your data at rest in cloud services?
A) The cloud vendor can regenerate the lost keys
B) You can retrieve the data
C) You cannot retrieve the data
D) The data is automatically decrypted

Review Question 9.79
What is the purpose of threat intelligence in cloud security?
A) To increase API usage
B) To identify and mitigate threats early on
C) To generate encryption keys
D) To facilitate communication between clients and cloud providers

9.4.2 Vulnerability Scanning and Penetration Testing

Vulnerability scanning is the systematic identification, analysis, and reporting of security weaknesses in a computer system. It provides an organization with the necessary information to understand and react to the security threats it faces.

In the context of cloud computing, vulnerability scanning becomes even more important due to the shared responsibility model of cloud security. While the cloud provider ensures the security of the cloud, security in the cloud is the responsibility of the user. There are several tools available for vulnerability scanning in the cloud, such as Nessus, OpenVAS, and Qualys among others.

Penetration testing, also known as pen testing or ethical hacking, is the practice of testing a computer system, network, or web application to find security vulnerabilities that an attacker could exploit.

Penetration testing is crucial in the cloud environment to ensure the robustness of the security measures in place. It helps in validating the efficiency of defensive mechanisms and adherence to security policies. Some of the popular tools used for penetration testing in the cloud include Metasploit, Wireshark, and Kali Linux.

Both vulnerability scanning and penetration testing are essential to maintain a secure cloud environment. They help in identifying potential security threats and provide ways to mitigate them effectively. The goal is not just to secure the system, but to understand the ongoing process of maintaining security in the face of evolving threats.

Review Question 9.80
What is vulnerability scanning?
A) The practice of testing a computer system to find security vulnerabilities
B) The systematic identification, analysis, and reporting of security weaknesses in a computer system
C) The process of maintaining security in the face of evolving threats
D) The practice of ensuring the robustness of security measures in place

Review Question 9.81
What is the purpose of penetration testing?
A) To identify potential security threats
B) To test a computer system, network, or web application to find security vulnerabilities
C) To ensure the security of the cloud
D) To report security weaknesses in a computer system

Review Question 9.82
Which of the following is not a tool used for vulnerability scanning in the cloud?

A) Nessus
B) OpenVAS
C) Qualys
D) Metasploit

9.4.3 Enhancing Cloud Security

Cloud security is a blend of traditional security strategies and cloud-specific techniques. It can be broadly categorized into three aspects: core architecture, authentication and access, and data management.

In terms of core architecture, data can be encrypted either at rest or in transit for added security. For those utilizing Infrastructure as a Service (IaaS), it's recommended to implement an anti-malware solution and maintain consistent patching. The Zero Trust security approach, which includes strategies like network segmentation, should be applied to the infrastructure.

When it comes to authentication and access, it's advisable to use strong passwords and two-factor authentication for all users. Role-Based Access Control (RBAC) should be employed, and a least privilege approach should be taken for all accounts and groups, meaning users should only have access to the resources they need to perform their tasks.

As for data management, it's best to avoid storing sensitive data in the cloud whenever possible. If it's necessary, ensure that you meet all compliance requirements. Most major cloud providers offer services that comply with most certification standards. Data sanitation, which refers to how vendors handle the physical media that once stored your data, is crucial for sensitive data. It's important to ensure that your cloud providers have standard procedures in place for sanitizing your data in their cloud environments. Always check their websites for their specific policies and procedures.

Review Question 9.83
What does the core architecture aspect of cloud security involve?
A) Using strong passwords and two-factor authentication
B) Encrypting data at rest or in transit, implementing an anti-malware solution, maintaining consistent patching, and applying the Zero Trust security approach
C) Avoiding the storage of sensitive data in the cloud
D) Checking the websites of cloud providers for their specific policies and procedures

Review Question 9.84

What is the least privilege approach in the context of authentication and access in cloud security?
A) Using two-factor authentication for all users
B) Ensuring that users only have access to the resources they need to perform their tasks
C) Implementing an anti-malware solution
D) Encrypting data at rest or in transit

Review Question 9.85
What is data sanitation in the context of data management in cloud security?
A) Avoiding the storage of sensitive data in the cloud
B) How vendors handle the physical media that once stored your data
C) Using strong passwords and two-factor authentication
D) Applying the Zero Trust security approach

Review Question 9.86
According to the book, what is a recommended practice when storing sensitive data in the cloud?
A) Use two-factor authentication
B) Implement an anti-malware solution
C) Ensure that you meet all compliance requirements
D) Apply the Zero Trust security approach

9.5 Chapter Summary

In this chapter, we began by exploring the complexities of cloud compliance. These requirements can stem from international standards, state laws, or industry-specific regulations. Compliance in the cloud can pose more challenges than traditional on-premise solutions due to the inability to physically access the machines hosting the services. Next, we delved into the Information Technology Infrastructure Library (ITIL) as a framework for IT service management and discussed its role in cloud risk management. We concluded the chapter by addressing security issues pertinent to cloud computing, emphasizing the importance of understanding and mitigating these risks in the cloud environment.

9.6 Exercise

Building a MySQL Database on Azure
Step 1: Set Up MySQL
1.1 Navigate to the Azure portal page and click on "Create a resource".
1.2 In the "Search services and marketplace" search box, type "MySQL Flexible Server".
1.3 Select "Azure Database for MySQL Flexible Server" from the search results and click on "Create".
1.4 On the "Flexible Server" page, under the "Project Details" section, select the existing project from the "Resource Group" dropdown menu. Note the "Estimated Costs" panel on the right side of the screen.
1.5 In the "Authentication" section, create your admin username and password.
1.6 Click on "Next: Networking".

1.7 On the following page, ensure that "Public Access" and "Firewall Rules" are checked.
1.8 Click on "Review + Create".
1.9 After reviewing the details, click on "Create". This process may take a few minutes.
1.10 Once you see "Your deployment is complete" with a green checkmark, note down your server name, admin username, and password. Keep this information in a secure place.

Step 2: Add a Database
2.1 In the "Resources" section of the portal, locate the "Azure Database for MySQL Flexible Server" that you created in Step 1.
2.2 Click on this resource to open its details.
2.3 On the left panel, under the "Settings" group, click on the "Databases" menu.
2.4 At the top of the right panel, click on the "+Add" button.
2.5 In the popup, name your new database "visitordb" and click on the "Save" icon to close the popup.
2.6 On the left panel, under the "Settings" group, click on "Server Parameters". In the search box at the top, type in "SSL". You should see "require_secure_transport". Change the "VALUE" from "ON" to "OFF" by clicking on the dropdown. (Note: This turns off the encryption between your browser and the database server for learning purposes. You may want to enable it for other applications.)

Step 3: Add a Table to the Database
3.1 Create a PHP file named 'createdb.php'. Paste the following code into the editor and replace the values for the $host, $user, and $password variables with the information you noted down in Step 1.5. Save the file.

```php
<!DOCTYPE html>
<html>
<head>
<meta charset = "utf-8">
<title>Create MySQL DB on Azure</title>
</head>
<body>
<?php // replace the host, user and password with your credentials
$host = "yourServerName.mysql.database.azure.com";
$user = "yourusername";
$password = "yourpassword";
$db = "visitordb";
// connect to the database
$conn = mysqli_init();
mysqli_real_connect($conn, $host, $user, $password, $db, 3306);
// Create a table
$query = "CREATE TABLE visitor
(
  visitorid INTEGER AUTO_INCREMENT,
  visitorName VARCHAR(100) NOT NULL,
  visitTime TIMESTAMP DEFAULT NOW(),
  PRIMARY KEY(visitorid)
)";
if(mysqli_query($conn, $query))
echo "<p>Table created.</p>";
// Close the connection
```

```
mysqli_close($conn);
?>
</body>
</html>
```

Save this PHP file as instructed in Chapter 8. Run 'createdb.php' on your browser as you ran 'index.php' in Chapter 8, this time by appending '/createdb.php' to the URL.
If the table was created successfully, you should see "Table created" displayed on your browser.

Step 4: Build User Interface
4.1 Open 'index.php' using the command `nano index.php`.
4.2 Replace the existing content with the following code:

```
<!DOCTYPE html>
<html>
<head>
<meta charset = "utf-8">
<title>My PHP Website</title>
</head>
<body>
<h1>Welcome to the cloud!</h1>
<form action = "" method = "post">
Your name:
<br>
<input type = "text" name = "name" size = "30" maxlength = "30">
<br>
<input type = "submit" name = "submit" value = "Submit">
<input type = "submit" name = "view" value = "View All">
</form>
<?php // replace the host, user and password with your credentials
$host = "youripaddressandportnumber";
$user = "yourusername";
$password = "yourpassword";
$db = "visitordb";
// connect to the database
$conn = mysqli_init();
mysqli_real_connect($conn, $host, $user, $password, $db, 3306);
// If the "Submit" button is clicked
if (isset($_POST['submit']))
{
$yourName = $_POST['name'];
// SQL statement
$query = "INSERT INTO visitor (visitorName) VALUES('$yourName')";
if(mysqli_query($conn, $query))
echo "<p>Hi, $yourName, welcome to my cloud.</p>";
else
echo "<p>Hi, $yourName, please try again.</p>";
}
```

```php
// if the "view all" button is clicked
if(isset($_POST['view']))
{
$query = "SELECT * FROM visitor";
$result = mysqli_query($conn, $query);
if(mysqli_num_rows($result) > 0)
{
$display = "<h2>All Visitors</h2>";
while($row = mysqli_fetch_assoc($result)){
$display .="Name: ".$row["visitorName"]."<br>";
$display .="Date Time: ".$row["visitTime"]."<br>";
}
}
echo $display;
}
// close the connection
mysqli_close($conn);
?>
</body>
</html>
```

4.3 Save the file following the same steps outlined in Chapter 8.

4.4 Open a new tab in your browser and enter your URL, which should be in the format YourResourceGroupName.azurewebsites.net. Replace YourResourceGroupName with the name of your resource group.

4.5 Enter a name and click on the "Submit" button. You should see a welcome message similar to your exercise in Chapter 8.

4.6 Try entering more names and clicking "Submit" each time.

4.7 Finally, click on the "View All" button. You should see a list of all visitors you've entered.

9.7 References:

Agutter, C. (2020). ITIL® 4 Essentials: Your essential guide for the ITIL 4 Foundation exam and beyond. IT Governance Ltd.

Alouffi, B., Hasnain, M., Alharbi, A., Alosaimi, W., Alyami, H., & Ayaz, M. (2021). A Systematic Literature Review on Cloud Computing Security: Threats and Mitigation Strategies. IEEE Access, 9, 57792-57807.

Bowers, D. (2016). Risk Management: Past, Present and Future Directions. Nova Science Publishers, Inc.

Braud, A., Fromentoux, G., Radier, B., & Le Grand, O. (2021). The Road to European Digital Sovereignty with Gaia-X and IDSA. IEEE Network, 35(2), 4-5.

Cartlidge, A. and Steria, S. (2020). An Introductory Overview of ITIL4. itSMF UK, AXELOS Limited.

Hulshof, M., & Daneva, M. (2021, July). Benefits and Challenges in Information Security Certification–A Systematic Literature Review. In International Symposium on Business Modeling and Software Design (pp. 154-169). Springer, Cham.

Hummel, P., Braun, M., Tretter, M., & Dabrock, P. (2021). Data sovereignty: A review. Big Data & Society, 8(1), 2053951720982012

ISO/IEC 17788:2014 (2014) Information technology — Cloud computing — Overview and vocabulary https://standards.iso.org/ittf/PubliclyAvailableStandards/c060544_ISO_IEC_17788_2014.zip

Kulkarni, V., Sunkle, S., Kholkar, D., Roychoudhury, S., Kumar, R., & Raghunandan, M. (2021). Toward automated regulatory compliance. CSI Transactions on ICT, 1-10.

McKenzie, C. (2020). Open API (Public API). TechTarget. https://searchapparchitecture.techtarget.com/definition/open-API-public-API

O'Loughlin, M. (2019). ITIL 4 and the Cloud., AXELOS Limited. February.

Orue-Echevarria, L., Garcia, J. L., Banse, C., & Alonso, J. (2021). MEDINA: Improving Cloud Services trustworthiness through continuous audit-based certification. In CEUR Workshop Proceedings. CEUR-WS.

Ryu, C., Lim, S. Y., & Suh, M. (2016). Project Risk Management in R&D Organizations: A Survey on Risk Register from Korean companies. The Journal of Modern Project Management, 4(2).

Spacey, J. (2017). 8 Types of Risk Response. Simplicable. https://simplicable.com/new/risk-response

Tozzi, C. (2020). Everything As Code: What It Is and Why It's Gaining Traction. ITPro Today. https://www.itprotoday.com/development-techniques-and-management/everything-code-what-it-and-why-its-gaining-traction

Tsvilii, O. (2021). Cyber Security Regulation: Cyber Security Certification of Operational Technologies. Technology audit and production reserves, 1(2), 57.

Wang, D., Zhong, D., & Li, L. (2021). A comprehensive study of the role of cloud computing on the information technology infrastructure library (ITIL) processes. Library Hi Tech (accepted, pre-publishing paper).

9.8 Solutions to Review Questions

9.1 B; 9.2 B; 9.3 D; 9.4 A; 9.5 A; 9.6 A; 9.7 A; 9.8 B; 9.9 A; 9.10 A; 9.11 D; 9.12 B; 9.13 D; 9.14 C; 9.15 B; 9.16 A; 9.17 C; 9.18 A; 9.19 C; 9.20 A; 9.21 B; 9.22 B; 9.23 A; 9.24 A; 9.25 B; 9.26 B; 9.27 B; 9.28 D; 9.29 A; 9.30 A; 9.31 A; 9.32 C; 9.33 D; 9.34 A; 9.35 C; 9.36 A; 9.37 D; 9.38 C; 9.39 B; 9.40 B; 9.41 A; 9.42 A; 9.43 B; 9.44 A; 9.45 A; 9.46 C; 9.47 A; 9.48 C; 9.49 A; 9.50 C; 9.51 B; 9.52 B; 9.53 B; 9.54 C; 9.55 A; 9.56 A; 9.57 C; 9.58 B; 9.59 B; 9.60 C; 9.61 D; 9.62 A; 9.63 A; 9.64 B; 9.65 C; 9.66 A; 9.67 A; 9.68 B; 9.69 B; 9.70 C; 9.71 C; 9.72 B; 9.73 B; 9.74 C; 9.75 C; 9.76 D; 9.77 B; 9.78 C; 9.79 B; 9.80 B; 9.81 B; 9.82 D; 9.83 B; 9.84 B; 9.85 B; 9.86 C;

Chapter 10: Introduction to Linux

Chapter Learning Outcomes

10.1 Explain the key features and principles of an open source ecosystem.
10.2 Describe the implications and variations of major types of open source software licenses.
10.3 Demonstrate an understanding of the roles and functionalities of components within the Linux.
10.4 Identify different Linux distributions (distros).
10.5 Demonstrate the ability to use the command line interface to manage and manipulate files.

10.1 Discovering Linux

This chapter introduces the principles of Linux, the Free and Open Source Software (FOSS) licensing, the operating system's core concepts, and its software ecosystem. It also presents a variety of Linux distributions for different purposes. Whether you're a beginner or an IT enthusiast, this chapter lays a solid foundation for understanding Linux's role in the digital world.

10.1.1 Essential Knowledge for IT Success

To thrive in the modern IT landscape, a firm grasp of Linux is essential. Linux stands as the reigning operating system in domains such as cloud computing, Internet of Things (IoT), DevOps, and enterprise server environments.

While Linux may not replace Windows and macOS on the desktop front, it exerts significant influence far beyond personal computers. If your career path intersects with enterprise server management, cloud operations, mobile computing, DevOps practices, or network administration – all areas where Linux holds sway – then acquainting yourself with the fundamental Linux administration tools is a strategic advantage.

Linux excels as a desktop environment, known for its speed, efficient resource utilization, and robust stability, with rare occurrences of the notorious "blue screen of death." Furthermore, Linux boasts the noteworthy attribute of being freely accessible.

Whether you're contemplating a future in Linux system administration, seeking to gain insights into the server environments where your code will reside, evaluating a migration of your office infrastructure to Linux, or simply curious about Linux, this chapter serves as a valuable resource for you. It equips you with the foundational knowledge you need to navigate the world of Linux effectively.

Review Question 10.1
What domains is Linux the reigning operating system in?
A) Personal computers
B) Cloud computing, IoT, DevOps, and enterprise server environments
C) Mobile computing
D) Network administration

Review Question 10.2
What is a strategic advantage if your career path intersects with areas where Linux holds sway?
A) Learning Windows administration tools
B) Acquainting yourself with the fundamental Linux administration tools
C) Focusing solely on macOS
D) Ignoring Linux

Review Question 10.3
What is Linux known for in a desktop environment?
A) Frequent "blue screen of death"
B) Slow speed
C) Inefficient resource utilization
D) Speed, efficient resource utilization, and robust stability

10.1.2 Free and Open Source Software (FOSS)

There are numerous approaches to licensing free and open source software (FOSS). Various organizations, including the Free Software Foundation (FSF), the Open Source Initiative (OSI), and Creative Commons (CC), curate approved lists of licenses.

The Free Software Foundation (FSF) advocates for software freedom, championing users' rights to use, modify, and distribute software. The FSF is known for the GNU General Public License (GPL), which allows extensive user rights, including the freedom to modify and distribute software, provided the original license conditions are maintained. For example, the Linux kernel is distributed under the GPL.

The Open Source Initiative (OSI) promotes the influence of open source software by endorsing flexible licensing options. It emphasizes open access to source code and community-driven development. Licenses that align with OSI principles include the Berkeley Software Distribution (BSD) licenses, which require minimal attribution when redistributing the software.

Creative Commons (CC) provides creators of various intellectual properties, including software, music, films, and books, the flexibility to determine the specific rights they wish to retain. Under the Creative Commons system, creators can choose from four key elements:

Attribution: Allows redistribution and modification as long as the original creator is credited.
Share-Alike: Requires that the original license conditions be preserved in all future distributions and copies.
Non-Commercial: Permits use for non-commercial purposes only.
No Derivative Works: Allows redistribution, but only of unmodified copies.

The copyleft approach, seen in the FSF's GPL and Creative Commons Share-Alike, mandates that subsequent distributions maintain the original permissions. This is preferred by authors who want their software to remain free and open.

In contrast, non-copyleft open source licenses, often called permissive licenses, place fewer restrictions on derivatives, typically requiring only attribution. Examples include the BSD, MIT, and Apache licenses.
Business Models for Open Source

Companies can release software as open source while offering premium services and support to paying customers. An example of this approach is the Ubuntu Linux distribution, supported by Canonical.

Understanding the license governing open source software is essential for users. However, finding this information can sometimes be challenging. Desktop applications often provide license details in the help menu. The most reliable method is to visit the product's website, where licensing information is readily available. For example, Ubuntu maintains its licensing data on ubuntu.com/licensing. It's advisable to consult with legal counsel before making decisions regarding open source software.

Review Question 10.4
What is the Free Software Foundation (FSF) known for?
A) The Linux kernel
B) The GNU General Public License (GPL)
C) The Berkeley Software Distribution (BSD) licenses
D) The Creative Commons system

Review Question 10.5
What does the Open Source Initiative (OSI) emphasize?

A) Software freedom
B) Open access to source code and community-driven development
C) The flexibility to determine the specific rights creators wish to retain
D) The copyleft approach

Review Question 10.6
What does the Creative Commons (CC) system allow creators to do?
A) Choose from four key elements for their intellectual properties
B) Use, modify, and distribute software
C) Release software as open source while offering premium services and support
D) Maintain the original license conditions in all future distributions and copies

Review Question 10.7
What is the copyleft approach?
A) It allows redistribution and modification as long as the original creator is credited
B) It mandates that subsequent distributions maintain the original permissions
C) It permits use for non-commercial purposes only
D) It allows redistribution, but only of unmodified copies

Review Question 10.8
What are non-copyleft open source licenses often called?
A) Permissive licenses
B) Copyleft licenses
C) Creative licenses
D) General licenses

Review Question 10.9
What is an example of a company releasing software as open source while offering premium services and support?
A) The Free Software Foundation
B) The Open Source Initiative
C) Canonical
D) Creative Commons

Review Question 10.10
Where can users often find license details for desktop applications?
A) In the help menu
B) On the product's website
C) In the software's source code
D) In the software's settings

Review Question 10.11
What is the most reliable method for finding licensing information for a product?
A) Consulting with legal counsel
B) Visiting the product's website
C) Checking the help menu
D) Reading the software's source code

Review Question 10.12

What does the Berkeley Software Distribution (BSD) licenses require?
A) Redistribution and modification as long as the original creator is credited
B) That the original license conditions be preserved in all future distributions and copies
C) Use for non-commercial purposes only
D) Minimal attribution when redistributing the software

Review Question 10.13
What does the GNU General Public License (GPL) allow?
A) Redistribution and modification as long as the original creator is credited
B) Redistribution, but only of unmodified copies
C) Use for non-commercial purposes only
D) Extensive user rights, including the freedom to modify and distribute software

10.1.3 Software Ecosystem

In the early 1990s, Linus Torvalds developed the original Linux kernel and generously made it open source. This means that the source code for every Linux component is available for anyone to download, modify, and use as they see fit, even for creating custom versions that could potentially be profitable.

An operating system is a crucial software component within a computer that manages hardware and orchestrates the operation of other software. It governs tasks related to files, devices, memory, processors, and also regulates user access and permissions (McHoes and Flynn, 2018).

The Linux environment consists of three essential elements: the Linux kernel, the desktop interface, and customizations unique to your chosen distribution, such as Red Hat or Ubuntu. The installation and update processes for the Linux kernel are typically managed by your distribution. In the interest of stability, distributions often delay incorporating non-critical new kernel releases for several months.

All desktop operating systems provide two primary interfaces for accessing their tools: a graphical user interface (GUI) and a command-line interface (CLI).

Many Linux distributions simplify software management through third-party software repositories and package management tools that handle updates seamlessly. For instance, on Ubuntu, you can choose how updates are applied to your system.

Beyond the core operating system, Linux offers a vast array of free software packages, covering an extensive range of computing tasks. Whether you need office productivity suites, web server applications, or security utilities, Linux seamlessly integrates these software packages into its ecosystem through package managers.

Review Question 10.14
Who developed the original Linux kernel?
A) Richard Stallman
B) Linus Torvalds
C) Bill Gates
D) Steve Jobs

Review Question 10.15
What does an operating system manage within a computer?
A) Hardware and the operation of other software
B) Internet connectivity
C) User interface design
D) Software installation processes

Review Question 10.16
What are the three essential elements of the Linux environment?
A) The Linux kernel, the desktop interface, and customizations unique to your chosen distribution
B) The Linux kernel, the command-line interface, and the graphical user interface
C) The Linux kernel, the desktop interface, and third-party software repositories
D) The Linux kernel, the desktop interface, and the operating system

Review Question 10.17
What are the two primary interfaces for accessing tools in all desktop operating systems?
A) A graphical user interface (GUI) and a command-line interface (CLI)
B) A desktop interface and a mobile interface
C) A user interface and a developer interface
D) A hardware interface and a software interface

Review Question 10.18
How do many Linux distributions simplify software management?
A) Through cloud-based storage solutions
B) Through automatic updates
C) Through user-friendly interfaces
D) Through third-party software repositories and package management tools

Review Question 10.19
What does Linux offer beyond the core operating system?
A) A proprietary software store
B) A built-in antivirus program
C) A vast array of free software packages
D) A unique desktop interface

10.1.4 The Linux Distributions

The open-source nature of Linux has led to the creation of numerous customized versions of the operating system, known as distributions or distros for short. Each distro is crafted to address specific needs. Notable among these is the widely recognized Android OS, which is tailored for mobile devices. Additionally, enterprise-focused deployments have their own distros, such as Red Hat Enterprise Linux. For those involved in scientific and advanced mathematical applications, there's Scientific Linux. Network security enthusiasts often turn to Kali Linux, while Raspberry Pi users rely on Raspberry Pi OS for their Internet of Things (IoT) devices. Docker containers share the OS kernel with their Linux host environments, and even the most popular cloud instances leverage specialized Linux distributions.

Distributions are often organized into families. Rather than reinventing the wheel, various communities may fork derivative versions of a parent distro, introduce their customizations, and distribute them under new names. This efficient approach ensures that updates and patches from the upstream parent are effortlessly delivered downstream to all its children. Among the well-known distribution families is Debian, which supports an extensive ecosystem, encompassing the versatile Ubuntu, the user-friendly Mint, and the security-focused Kali Linux.

Specialized distros often come with built-in functionalities that seamlessly integrate with specific cloud host environments. Examples include AWS's Amazon Linux 2 and purpose-built Long-Term Support (LTS) Ubuntu releases. LTS releases prioritize stability through rigorous testing of software and configurations, enabling distro managers to provide security and feature updates for up to five years. This long-term support alleviates concerns about the need for frequent rebuilds. For instance, Ubuntu releases new versions every six months, with LTS releases every two years.

Whether your project resides on a physical machine, within a server rack in your local data center, within a cloud computing platform like AWS, or as a virtual machine briefly brought to life through virtualization technologies like Docker, Linux is an ideal choice for the task at hand. Its adaptability and diverse distributions cater to a wide spectrum of computing needs.

Review Question 10.20
What is a Linux distribution (distro)?
A) A version of Linux tailored for specific needs
B) A type of Android OS

C) A cloud host environment
D) A type of Docker container

Review Question 10.21
Which Linux distribution is used for scientific and advanced mathematical applications?
A) Android OS
B) Red Hat Enterprise Linux
C) Scientific Linux
D) Kali Linux

Review Question 10.22
What is the purpose of Long-Term Support (LTS) releases?
A) To provide security and feature updates for up to five years
B) To release new versions every six months
C) To create a new Linux distribution
D) To introduce customizations to a parent distro

Review Question 10.23
Which Linux distribution is tailored for mobile devices?
A) Android OS
B) Red Hat Enterprise Linux
C) Scientific Linux
D) Kali Linux

Review Question 10.24
What is the Debian distribution family known for?
A) Being used for network security
B) Being used for IoT devices
C) Supporting an extensive ecosystem
D) Being used for enterprise-focused deployments

Review Question 10.25
What technology do Docker containers share with their Linux host environments?
A) The OS kernel
B) The cloud host environment
C) The LTS releases
D) The Android OS

10.2 Installing Linux

In this section, we will create a Virtual Machine with Ubuntu on Azure:

Step 1: Logging In and Initial Setup

Log in to the Azure portal. Click "Create a resource." Search for "Ubuntu Server." Pick the most recent

LTS and free one. Click on "Create" to proceed.

Step 2: Project Details: Use an existing project or create a new one for the "Resource group." Give a name, such as "Ubuntu" for the "Virtual machine name". Pick a Region and Availability Zone also.

Step 3:   Select the latest LTS image and opt for the most cost-effective plan for the machine size.

Step 4: Administrator Account: Choose "Password" for authentication type. Fill out the username and password you will use them later on.

Step 5: Inbound Port Rules: Keep the default values for inbound port rules. This is for testing only.

Step 6: Review and Create: Click "Review + Create."

Step 7: Deployment: After review, click "Create."
Wait a few minutes for the deployment to complete.

Step 8: Accessing Cloud Shell by clicking "Go to resource."

Step 9: Using Cloud Shell by clicking the "Connect" icon at the top of the page.
Select "SSH using Azure CLI"
This will take several minutes the first time you connect in this way.

Step 10: Practice simple Linux commands

Practice two commands: cd which stands for "change directory" and "/" stands for root directory. The "ls" command makes a list of the content in the current directory:

```
$ cd /
$ ls
```
Finally, type "exit" to log out of the cloud shell.

Review Question 10.26
What is the first step in creating a Virtual Machine with Ubuntu on Azure?
A) Select the latest LTS image
B) Log in to the Azure portal
C) Accessing Cloud Shell

D) Practice simple Linux commands

Review Question 10.27
According to the instructions in this book, what type of authentication is chosen for the Administrator
Account when setting up the Virtual Machine?
A) SSH keys
B) Biometric
C) Password
D) Two-factor authentication

Review Question 10.28
How do you access the Cloud Shell after the deployment is complete?
A) Clicking "Go to resource" and clicking the "Connect" icon
B) Clicking "Review + Create"
C) Clicking "Create"
D) Clicking the "Connect" icon

Review Question 10.29
What does the "cd" command stand for in Linux?
A) Create directory
B) Change directory
C) Copy directory
D) Clear directory

10.3 Configuring the Linux Environment

In this section, we explore the Ubuntu file system, understand its structure, and learn to adjust locale,

navigation, and timezone settings. This knowledge is crucial for efficient and effective Linux environment

management.

10.3.1 Navigating the Ubuntu File System

Connect to the virtual machine running Ubuntu, as created in the previous section. Once you see the

prompt ($) on your terminal, enter the following command without the quotation marks: "cd /boot".

```
$ cd /boot
```

In this command:

"cd" is short for "change directory," a command used to switch between directories.
"/" represents the top-level root directory.
"boot" is a subdirectory under the root directory.

To view the contents of the "boot" directory, use the command "ls -l," which stands for "list in long

format." Inside the "boot" directory, you'll find a file named "vmlinuz," which is a compressed version of a functional Linux kernel. The version with the latest timestamp is likely the one currently in use by your system.

Next, examine the contents of the 'grub' subdirectory, which houses files utilized by the GRUB bootloader. Issue the following command:

```
$cd grub
$ls
```

Note that in this instance, the 'cd' command is used without the '/' character since 'grub' is not a subdirectory directly under the top-level root directory; rather, it is located directly within the current directory.

To view the 'grub.cfg' file, execute the following command:

```
cat grub.cfg
```

The 'cat' command is a command-line utility that displays the contents of a file or command output. It is commonly employed for examining large files. After reviewing the file, exit the display by pressing 'Ctrl + C.'

This file serves as the configuration file read during startup, determining the options presented by GRUB. It's essential to note the advisory against direct edits to this file. The contents are automatically generated based on information stored in other files elsewhere in the file system.

Review Question 10.30
What does the "/" symbol represent in Linux?
A) Home directory
B) Current directory
C) Top-level root directory
D) User directory

Review Question 10.31
What is the purpose of the 'ls -l' command?
A) To list files in a directory in long format
B) To locate a file in a directory
C) To link files in a directory
D) To load files from a directory

Review Question 10.32
What is the 'vmlinuz' file found in the 'boot' directory?
A) A text file containing boot configurations
B) A compressed version of a functional Linux kernel
C) A directory containing boot scripts
D) A file containing the GRUB bootloader

Review Question 10.33
What does the 'cat' command do in Linux?
A) Concatenates and displays the contents of files
B) Changes the attributes of a file
C) Copies files to a directory
D) Changes the permissions of a file

Review Question 10.34
Why is it advised not to directly edit the 'grub.cfg' file?
A) Because it is a binary file
B) Because it is automatically generated based on other files
C) Because it is a system file
D) Because it is a hidden file

10.3.2 File System and Directory Structure

Linux operates on the principle that nearly everything is organized as plain text files, influencing the system's behavior, permissible operations, and accessible objects. Understanding how Linux organizes these files is crucial. Refer to the Filesystem Hierarchy Standard for additional insights (Rankin, 2019). In Linux, a directory corresponds to what the Windows world terms a folder.

To explore the contents of the root directory, launch a terminal and execute 'ls /'. The essential files governing the functioning of your operating system reside within these top-level directories.

/bin: Contains binary files essential for running fundamental Linux programs, encompassing various navigation and file manipulation tools.
/sbin: Holds system binary files, with a focus on binaries used by administrators to manage the system.
/boot: Home to Linux images and boot configuration files necessary for a successful system startup.
/dev: Houses files representing and controlling all physical and virtual devices used by the system.
/etc: Stores configuration files that control the software employed by the system. When configuring services, altering networking, or adjusting core settings, this directory is the primary reference.
/home: Contains directories where owners of user accounts can store their private files.
/lib: Used for software libraries required by binary programs.
/root: Reserved for the root user, though administrators usually avoid logging in as the root user for security reasons.
/usr: Contains non-essential command binaries and the associated data files. Stands for Unix source repository or Unix system resource.

/var: Intended for files likely to be frequently updated, encompassing logs, email messages, and application cache.

In addition to these standard directory resources, Linux employs virtual or pseudo files. These dynamic files, like those in the /proc directory, are created during system boot or in response to a system event. They represent running processes or, in the case of /dev, hardware devices and device drivers. The /sys directory serves as another location for ephemeral pseudo files, containing information about system resources and kernel features. The concept is that processes can access information about the OS environment through /proc, discover available devices in /dev, and learn about those devices and resources via /sys.

Review Question 10.35
What does the '/bin' directory contain in Linux?
A) System binary files
B) Binary files essential for running fundamental Linux programs
C) Directories where owners of user accounts can store their private files
D) Files likely to be frequently updated

Review Question 10.36
What is the purpose of the '/etc' directory in Linux?
A) To store configuration files that control the software employed by the system
B) To house files representing and controlling all physical and virtual devices used by the system
C) To contain non-essential command binaries and the associated data files
D) To hold system binary files

Review Question 10.37
What does the '/usr' directory stand for in Linux?
A) User System Resource
B) Unix Security Repository
C) Unix System Resource
D) User Security Repository

Review Question 10.38
What is the purpose of the '/dev' directory in Linux?
A) To house files representing and controlling all physical and virtual devices used by the system
B) To store configuration files that control the software employed by the system
C) To contain non-essential command binaries and the associated data files
D) To hold system binary files

Review Question 10.39
What is the purpose of the '/var' directory in Linux?
A) To hold system binary files
B) To store configuration files that control the software employed by the system
C) To house files representing and controlling all physical and virtual devices used by the system
D) To contain files likely to be frequently updated

Review Question 10.40
What are pseudo files in Linux?
A) They are files that are stored in the '/usr' directory
B) They are files that are stored in the '/bin' directory
C) They are files that are stored in the '/etc' directory
D) They are files that are created during system boot or in response to a system event

10.3.3 Locale, Navigation, and Timezone Settings

You can enhance your Linux environment for a more comfortable experience with a few commands.

The 'locale' command reveals location settings. 'locale' pertains to the settings reflecting your geographic

location. In my case, I chose Canada during the Ubuntu installation. The 'locale' output indicates that

applications on my computer will assume English communication with Canadian spelling, affecting

spellcheck results in word processors or browsers with text in UTF-8 character encoding. Numeric

representation follows Canadian standards, with decimals presented using a dot instead of a comma.

Additionally, the default paper setting for printing adheres to North American letter dimensions rather than

the European A4.

The actual locale settings are stored in the 'usr/share/locale/' directory.

```
$ cd /usr/share/locale/
/usr/share/locale$ ls
```

To modify how your system applies the locale, edit files in this directory. Most distributions now utilize the

'localectl' command family instead of the 'locales' command for viewing and editing locale settings. For

instance, the command below sets the language to Canadian UTF-8 encoding (assuming the language is

installed):

```
localectl set-locale LANG=en_CA.UTF-8
```

To determine your current position within the file system directory tree, use 'pwd' (present work directory).

```
$ pwd
```

An efficient shortcut for command typing is the 'up' arrow key, which cycles through previous commands in

reverse order. To view the most recent up to 1000 commands issued within this shell, type 'history'.

For one final environment setting, use 'timedatectl' to display your current time zone settings. To list all

available time zones, use 'timedatectl list-timezones'. To make a change, employ 'timedatectl set-timezone'

followed by your preferred setting. You may be prompted for a password.

Review Question 10.41
What does the 'locale' command reveal in Linux?
A) The current directory
B) The history of commands
C) The location settings
D) The timezone settings

Review Question 10.42
Where are the actual locale settings stored in Linux?
A) /usr/share/locale/
B) /usr/bin/locale/
C) /usr/lib/locale/
D) /usr/etc/locale/

Review Question 10.43
What does the 'pwd' command do in Linux?
A) It changes the current directory
B) It displays the current directory
C) It creates a new directory
D) It removes a directory

Review Question 10.44
What does the 'up' arrow key do in the Linux terminal?
A) It moves the cursor up
B) It scrolls the terminal output up
C) It cycles through previous commands in reverse order
D) It moves to the parent directory

Review Question 10.45
What does the 'history' command do in Linux?
A) It displays the history of the Linux system
B) It displays the history of commands
C) It clears the history of commands
D) It saves the history of commands to a file

Review Question 10.46
What does the 'timedatectl set-timezone' command do in Linux?
A) It displays the current timezone
B) It lists all available timezones
C) It changes the timezone
D) It synchronizes the system clock with a remote server

10.4 Configuring the Linux Experience

In this section, we delve into Ubuntu's Advanced Packaging Tool (APT). We'll explore its usage, followed by managing software updates and estimating available applications using APT commands. This knowledge will empower you to customize your Linux experience effectively.

10.4.1 Advanced Packaging Tool (APT)

Linux distributions are equipped with integrated package management systems that provide access to extensive curated repositories of software applications. Beyond offering a convenient method for downloading and installing software, these package managers can be configured to automatically ensure the installation of necessary software libraries and dependencies. Additionally, they keep all installed software up-to-date and secure. In Ubuntu, this system is known as the Advanced Packaging Tool (APT).

Understanding the functionality of the package manager specific to your distribution is a crucial aspect of administering an operating system. To locate desired software, you can initiate a search for applications on Ubuntu using the following command:

```
$ apt search search_term
```

After identifying the desired software, installations and updates are carried out through command-line operations on Ubuntu. The `sudo apt install package_name` command is used to install a specific software package, where package_name is the name of the software package you want to install.

The `sudo apt update` command is used to synchronize the package index files from their sources via the internet, which helps the system know about the newer versions of the packages and their dependencies.

The `sudo apt upgrade` command is used to install available upgrades of all packages currently installed on the system from the sources configured via sources.list file. The 'sources.list' file, residing in the 'etc/apt' directory, contains comprehensive repository information required by the APT system. To view the contents of 'sources.list', you can use the 'cat' command:

```
$ cat /etc/apt/sources.list
```

The file categorizes available software into main, restricted, universe, and multiverse repositories. 'Main' contains officially supported open-source software by Canonical (the publisher of Ubuntu). 'Restricted' includes officially supported packages built with closed-source software. 'Universe' consists of open-source software maintained by the broader community, not Canonical. Lastly, 'Multiverse' is a community repository with software that may be deemed controversial within the open-source community due to restrictive patent protections or complicated legalities.

So, when you run sudo apt update && sudo apt upgrade, it first updates the package lists for upgrades for packages that need upgrading, as well as new packages that have just been released, and then upgrades the installed packages.

If you want to upgrade a specific software package, you can use `sudo apt install --only-upgrade package_name`, where package_name is the name of the software package you want to upgrade. This command will upgrade the package if it is installed and a newer version is available. If the package is not installed or no newer version is available, the command will do nothing.

To check for a list of updated software for Ubuntu, issue the following command:

```
$ sudo apt update
```

The 'sudo' command stands for 'super user do' and allows temporary elevation of the user's account to have root privileges. This practice safeguards the user's computer from potential exploitation. Password entry is required to grant system-based permissions.

Review Question 10.47
What is the command to search for a software package in Ubuntu?
A) sudo apt search package_name
B) sudo apt install package_name
C) sudo apt update package_name
D) sudo apt upgrade package_name

Review Question 10.48
What does the 'sudo apt install package_name' command do?
A) It searches for a software package.
B) It installs a specific software package.
C) It updates the list of available software packages.
D) It upgrades all installed software packages.

Review Question 10.49
What is the purpose of the 'sudo apt update' command?
A) It installs a specific software package.
B) It upgrades a specific software package.
C) It synchronizes the package index files from their sources.

D) It searches for a software package.

Review Question 10.50
What does the 'sudo apt upgrade' command do?
A) It searches for a software package.
B) It installs a specific software package.
C) It updates the list of available software packages.
D) It installs available upgrades of all packages currently installed on the system.

Review Question 10.51
What is the 'sources.list' file?
A) It is a file that contains the list of installed software packages.
B) It is a file that contains comprehensive repository information required by the APT system.
C) It is a file that contains the list of available software packages.
D) It is a file that contains the list of upgraded software packages.

Review Question 10.52
What does the 'Main' repository contain?
A) It contains officially supported open-source software by Canonical.
B) It includes officially supported packages built with closed-source software.
C) It consists of open-source software maintained by the broader community, not Canonical.
D) It is a community repository with software that may be deemed controversial within the open-source community.

Review Question 10.53
What does the 'sudo apt update && sudo apt upgrade' command do?
A) It searches for a software package and then installs it.
B) It updates the package lists for upgrades and new releases, and then upgrades the installed packages.
C) It installs a specific software package and then upgrades it.
D) It updates a specific software package and then removes it.

Review Question 10.54
What does the 'sudo apt install --only-upgrade package_name' command do?
A) It installs a specific software package.
B) It upgrades a specific software package if it is installed and a newer version is available.
C) It removes a specific software package.
D) It searches for a specific software package.

Review Question 10.55
What does the 'sudo' command stand for?
A) Super User Do
B) System User Do
C) Software Update Do
D) System Update Do

Review Question 10.56
Why is password entry required when using the 'sudo' command?
A) To install a software package.
B) To upgrade a software package.

C) To grant system-based permissions.
D) To search for a software package.

10.4.2 Estimate Available Applications

To view a list of upgradable software, use the following command:

```
$ apt list --upgradable
```

To apply updates and patches to all software on Ubuntu, execute the following command:

```
$ sudo apt upgrade
```

It's worth noting that while the 'apt' tool is newer, 'apt-get' is still recommended for use in automated scripting environments.

If you wish to determine the number of available applications, you can estimate it based on the number of lines in the list file. The command below displays this count:

```
$ apt list -a -v | wc
```

Output:

WARNING: apt does not have a stable CLI interface. Use with caution in scripts.

 331838 829695 8813329

In this output:

The first number (331838) represents the total number of lines in the output.
The second number (829695) indicates the total number of words.
The third number (8813329) signifies the total number of characters.

Please note the warning, as apt does not have a stable CLI interface, and caution should be exercised, especially when used in scripts.

Review Question 10.57
What is the command to view a list of upgradable software in Ubuntu?
A) sudo apt upgrade
B) apt list --upgradable
C) apt-get upgrade
D) apt list -a -v
Review Question 10.58
What is the command to apply updates and patches to all software on Ubuntu?
A) sudo apt upgrade
B) apt list --upgradable

C) apt-get upgrade
D) apt list -a -v

Review Question 10.59
Which tool is still recommended for use in automated scripting environments?
A) apt
B) apt-get
C) apt list
D) apt upgrade

Review Question 10.60
What does the command 'apt list -a -v | wc' display?
A) The list of upgradable software.
B) The total number of lines, words, and characters in the output.
C) The list of installed software.
D) The list of available software.

Review Question 10.61
In the output of the 'apt list -a -v | wc' command, what does the first number represent?
A) The total number of characters.
B) The total number of words.
C) The total number of lines.
D) The total number of available applications.

Review Question 10.62
Why should caution be exercised when using the 'apt' command in scripts?
A) Because 'apt' does not have a stable CLI interface.
B) Because 'apt' is a newer tool.
C) Because 'apt' is not recommended for use in automated scripting environments.
D) Because 'apt' can only be used to view a list of upgradable software.

10.5 Chapter Summary

In this chapter, you gained insights into open-source software, exploring various licensing models that underscore the diverse interpretations of 'free' in different contexts. A brief overview of operating systems provided foundational knowledge. The central focus of the chapter was on the installation of Ubuntu in Azure, and practiced fundamental command-line instructions.

10.6 References:

Goldstein, A. (2021). Open Source Licenses Explained. White Source. January 24.
https://www.whitesourcesoftware.com/resources/blog/open-source-licenses-explained/
Intel. (2021). Defining the Interface Between the Operating System and Platform Firmware.

https://www.intel.com/content/www/us/en/architecture-and-technology/unified-extensible-firmware-interface/efi-homepage-general-technology.html

Kappos, D. J. (2016). Open Source Software and Standards Development Organizations: Symbiotic Functions in the Innovation Equation. Colum. Sci. & Tech. L. Rev., 18, 259.

Kim, B. (2021). "Open Technologies for Open Knowledge." Online Searcher. May/Jun2021, Vol. 45 Issue 3, p34-36. 3p.

McHoes, A., & Flynn, I. M. (2018). Understanding operating systems. 8th edition. Cengage Learning.

Oracle. (2021). Oracle VM VirtualBox Overview Version 2.0. Oracle White Pager.
https://www.oracle.com/assets/oracle-vm-virtualbox-overview-2981353.pdf

Rankin, K. (2019). Filesystem Hierarchy Standard. Linux Journal, June 17.
https://www.linuxjournal.com/content/filesystem-hierarchy-standard

Ravi, S. Subramaniam, C. Nelson, M. L. (2008). "Determinants of the Choice of Open Source Software License." Journal of Management Information Systems. Winter2008, Vol. 25 Issue 3, p207-239.

Verma, A. (2018). 10 Reasons to Use Ubuntu Linux. FossBytes. April 6, 2018.
https://fossbytes.com/reasons-to-use-ubuntu-linux-advantage/

Wang, P. S. (2018). Mastering Modern Linux 2nd edition. CRC Press.

10.7 Solutions to Review Questions

10.1 B; 10.2 B; 10.3 D; 10.4 B; 10.5 B; 10.6 A; 10.7 B; 10.8 A; 10.9 C; 10.10 A; 10.11 B; 10.12 D; 10.13 D; 10.14 B; 10.15 A; 10.16 A; 10.17 A; 10.18 D; 10.19 C; 10.20 A; 10.21 C; 10.22 A; 10.23 A; 10.24 C; 10.25 A; 10.26 B; 10.27 C; 10.28 A; 10.29 B; 10.30 C; 10.31 A; 10.32 B; 10.33 A; 10.34 B; 10.35 B; 10.36 A; 10.37 C; 10.38 A; 10.39 D; 10.40 D; 10.41 C; 10.42 A; 10.43 B; 10.44 C; 10.45 B; 10.46 C; 10.47 A; 10.48 B; 10.49 C; 10.50 D; 10.51 B; 10.52 A; 10.53 B; 10.54 B; 10.55 A; 10.56 C; 10.57 B; 10.58 A; 10.59 B; 10.60 B; 10.61 C; 10.62 A;

Chapter 11: Linux Command Line

Chapter Learning Outcomes

11.1 Demonstrate an understanding of how to navigate and manipulate data within the Linux filesystem.
11.2 Explain the principles and techniques involved in testing and troubleshooting network connectivity.
11.3 Create Bash scripts to automate routine tasks and solve specific problems.

11.1 Linux Command Line Basics

In this section, we will learn the advantages of command line in system administration, explore Linux commands, understand shell sessions and configuration files, and patterns in Linux system administration.

11.1.1 Command Line Advantage

Graphic user interfaces (GUI) are widely embraced by business users due to their intuitive design and visual appeal. However, the landscape changes when it comes to serious system administrators who predominantly favor the command line interface (CLI). The shift toward the CLI is driven by two primary factors: efficiency and infrastructure automation.

Efficiency is a critical consideration for system administrators dealing with complex configurations and repetitive tasks. While GUIs provide a visual interface, the efficiency of navigating through layers of admin configuration pages can be time-consuming. In contrast, the command line allows administrators to execute precise and swift commands, making it a preferred choice for those who value time and precision.

Infrastructure automation has become a cornerstone in modern IT operations, especially with the rise of virtualization and cloud computing. These technologies present opportunities for deploying robust, multi-tiered server workloads at scale. Automation is essential for managing and maintaining these intricate infrastructures. Scripting, a powerful tool for automation, finds its sweet spot in the command line environment. System administrators leverage scripting languages to create reusable and efficient automation scripts.

Moreover, the synergy between remote login sessions and command-line scripting is a key enabler for efficient infrastructure management. System administrators often find themselves remotely connecting to servers for maintenance, updates, and troubleshooting. Command-line scripts facilitate seamless automation of these remote tasks, enabling administrators to exert control over their infrastructure from any location.

Review Question 11.1
What are the two primary factors driving the shift towards the command line interface (CLI)?
A) Visual appeal and intuitive design
B) Efficiency and infrastructure automation
C) Complexity and repetitiveness
D) Virtualization and cloud computing

Review Question 11.2
Why is efficiency a critical consideration for system administrators?
A) Because it allows them to execute precise and swift commands
B) Because it enables them to navigate through layers of admin configuration pages
C) Because it helps them to create reusable and efficient automation scripts
D) Because it facilitates seamless automation of remote tasks

Review Question 11.3
What has become a cornerstone in modern IT operations?
A) Graphic user interfaces (GUI)
B) Infrastructure automation
C) Command line interface (CLI)
D) Remote login sessions

Review Question 11.4
What is the role of scripting in the command line environment?
A) It is used for navigating through layers of admin configuration pages
B) It is used to create reusable and efficient automation scripts
C) It is used for deploying robust, multi-tiered server workloads at scale
D) It is used for executing precise and swift commands

Review Question 11.5
How do command-line scripts facilitate system administration?
A) They allow administrators to navigate through layers of admin configuration pages
B) They assist administrators in executing precise and swift commands
C) They help administrators to deploy robust, multi-tiered server workloads at scale
D) They enable administrators to exert control over their infrastructure from any location

11.1.2 Linux Commands

In Linux system administration, the volume of core commands, each with potentially numerous command-line arguments, presents a daunting challenge for memorization. With hundreds of commands and countless variations, it's a Herculean task to commit them all to memory.

A pragmatic approach acknowledges the inevitability of encountering unfamiliar commands and embraces the reliance on documentation as a valuable resource. In the vast landscape of Linux, the internet stands out as an excellent external reference, offering a wealth of guides, forums, and tutorials.

Linux itself provides built-in support systems to aid administrators in their endeavors. Many programs store documentation and sample configuration files in the /usr/share/doc directory tree. A helpful exercise involves navigating to this directory using the cd command and listing its contents with ls.

```
$ cd /usr/share/doc
$ ls
```

Additionally, a quick and effective resource for understanding command functionalities is to append --help to a command. This simple addition provides a concise overview of the command's usage and available options.

```
$ wget --help
```

As Linux administrators navigate the vast array of commands, recognizing the importance of external documentation, leveraging the built-in support systems, and utilizing the --help option can collectively enhance their proficiency and problem-solving capabilities.

Review Question 11.6
According to the author, what is a significant challenge in Linux system administration?
A) The volume of core commands and their variations
B) The lack of documentation
C) The complexity of the GUI
D) The absence of support systems

Review Question 11.7
What is a pragmatic approach to encountering unfamiliar commands in Linux?
A) Ignoring them
B) Memorizing all commands
C) Relying on documentation
D) Using only familiar commands

Review Question 11.8

Where do many programs store documentation and sample configuration files in Linux?
A) /usr/bin/doc
B) /usr/share/doc
C) /etc/share/doc
D) /home/share/doc

Review Question 11.9
How can you get a concise overview of a command's usage and available options in Linux?
A) By using the man command
B) By appending --help to the command
C) By looking at the /usr/share/doc directory
D) By searching the internet

Review Question 11.10
What can enhance a Linux administrator's proficiency and problem-solving capabilities?
A) Recognizing the importance of external documentation, leveraging built-in support systems, and utilizing the --help option
B) Memorizing all commands and their variations
C) Ignoring unfamiliar commands
D) Relying solely on the internet for help

11.1.3 Shell Sessions and Configuration Files

When you open a terminal in Linux, a new shell session is initiated, utilizing the default settings stored in a special hidden file in your home directory known as .bashrc. To view all files, including hidden ones, within the directory, execute ls -a.

The dot at the beginning of the filename signifies its hidden status, making it invisible in regular ls command output. The ls -a command, however, reveals all files, including those hidden. Proceed by opening the .bashrc file with the cat command.

.bashrc governs crucial aspects such as the content displayed in the command line prompt, color display preferences, and the availability of aliases in the command line environment. Should you wish to modify shell values, this is the file to edit. It specifically applies to non-login shell sessions, meaning there's no need for a second login after accessing the GUI desktop.

For a login shell, which is created upon your initial login and may read its values from different files, including .profile, you can explore the .profile in a manner similar to reading the .bashrc. In cases where a .bashrc file exists, its settings will influence the shell environment.

Furthermore, the /etc directory houses a profile file where system-wide shell settings are configured. Utilize the cat command to examine the system-wide .bashrc.

This book delves into the intricacies of the Bash shell, emphasizing its case-sensitive nature for commands and object names. Most commands are executed in lowercase, forming a consistent convention in the Linux environment.

Review Question 11.11
What happens when you open a terminal in Linux?
A) A new GUI session is initiated
B) A new shell session is initiated
C) The .bashrc file is automatically edited
D) The system-wide .bashrc file is opened

Review Question 11.12
How can you view all files, including hidden ones, within a directory in Linux?
A) Use the ls command
B) Use the cat command
C) Use the ls -a command
D) Open the .bashrc file

Review Question 11.13
What does the .bashrc file govern in Linux?
A) The content displayed in the command line prompt, color display preferences, and the availability of aliases
B) The values for a login shell
C) The system-wide shell settings
D) The case-sensitivity of commands and object names

Review Question 11.14
What does a login shell in Linux read its values from?
A) The .bashrc file
B) Different files, including .profile
C) The /etc directory
D) The cat command

Review Question 11.15
Where are system-wide shell settings configured in Linux?
A) In the .bashrc file
B) In the .profile file
C) In a profile file in the /etc directory
D) In the command line prompt

11.1.4 Command Patterns

Understanding common usage patterns is crucial for efficient navigation of Linux commands. Every command begins with the command name, and in many cases, additional arguments and parameters enhance its functionality.

Consider the 'ls' command, which can be executed as-is or with the '-a' argument to display hidden files. Alternatively, '--all' achieves the same result. Offering alternatives accommodates diverse user preferences, with some individuals preferring detailed descriptions while others favor concise single-letter arguments.

Short arguments often have longer equivalents introduced by two dashes. Exceptions exist, such as the 'ip' command for networking administration, which uses 'addr' without a dash for showing IP addresses. The shorter version, 'a,' is also valid.

Commands can combine multiple short arguments for comprehensive functionality. For instance, 'ls -l' lists directory contents in long form, while 'ls -lh' displays human-readable file sizes. Adding 't' organizes objects in descending chronological order ('ls -lht').

Most commands accept properly formatted parameters. For instance, 'ls -l /etc' lists the full contents of the 'etc' directory from the current location in the filesystem.

Mastering the autocomplete feature enhances command-line efficiency. Bash anticipates commands based on user input, facilitating quicker command entry. Autocomplete works best when there's a single matching possibility in the directory. Suppose you are at the root (/) directory and want to see what is in swapfile (it is a binary file), type ls to view the content in this directory. Then type less s and push the Tab key once, it cannot show anything. But if you tab twice, you will see there are more than one directory begins with letter "s". Next, try "cat sw" and Tab, you will see the "less swapfile" in the command line. If you want to open it, just push the Enter key. Bash understands the context of the command. Autocomplete will only work like this when there's only one matching possibility in the directory. You might sometimes need to provide a few more characters to get a good match.

Review Question 11.16

What does the 'ls' command do in Linux?
A) Lists directory contents
B) Shows IP addresses
C) Displays hidden files
D) Autocompletes commands

Review Question 11.17
What does the '-a' argument do when used with the 'ls' command?
A) Lists directory contents in long form
B) Displays hidden files also
C) Shows IP addresses
D) Autocompletes commands

Review Question 11.18
What does the 'ip addr' command do in Linux?
A) Lists directory contents
B) Displays hidden files
C) Shows IP addresses
D) Autocompletes commands

Review Question 11.19
What is the purpose of the autocomplete feature in Bash?
A) Lists directory contents
B) Displays hidden files
C) Shows IP addresses
D) Facilitates quicker command entry

11.1.5 Operations and Regular Expressions

The up-arrow key cycles through recent commands, and the 'history' command displays the 1,000 most recent commands stored in 'bash_history.' Understanding regular expressions is crucial, as certain characters may not be interpreted as expected. Characters such as space, dot, square brackets, asterisk, and question mark might be interpreted by Bash as command instructions.

Creating and navigating directories can illustrate potential pitfalls. For example, creating a directory named 'exercise' and moving into it might lead to unintended outcomes with the 'touch' command. Proper cleanup using 'rm *' resolves issues, and the use of quotation marks or an escape character (\) prevents misinterpretation of characters. A naming convention, such as dashes or underscores, enhances readability and consistency.

In your home directory, create a new directory called 'exercise' by issuing the 'mkdir exercise' command.

Then, move to the 'exercise' directory by issuing the 'cd exercise' command. Use the 'touch' command to create a new file called 'new file' by issuing the 'touch "new file"' command. If you use the 'ls' command to check, you will see two empty files have been created instead of one. The two files are 'file' and 'new.'

What happened? The 'touch' command figured you wanted to create two separate files. To correct the errors, first remove all content in the 'exercise' folder by issuing the 'rm *' command. To see if the content is gone, issue the 'ls' command. Now type 'touch "new file"'. A new empty file called 'new file' is created. To check it, issue the 'ls' command. Another way to solve the problem is by using an escape character (\) right before the character you want to be treated like a normal character. A command of 'touch new\ file\ 2' will create a new file called 'new file 2'. The convention is to use dashes or underscores between words, such as 'new_file' or 'new-file.'"

Review Question 11.20
What does the 'history' command do in Bash?
A) Displays the 1,000 most recent commands
B) Creates a new directory
C) Creates a new file
D) Removes all content in a directory

Review Question 11.21
What is the purpose of regular expressions in Bash?
A) To create new directories
B) To create new files
C) To interpret certain characters as command instructions
D) To change the color of the terminal

Review Question 11.22
What does the 'touch' command do in Bash?
A) Displays the 1,000 most recent commands
B) Creates a new directory
C) Creates a new file
D) Removes all content in a directory

Review Question 11.23
What does the 'rm *' command do in Bash?
A) Displays the 1,000 most recent commands
B) Creates a new directory
C) Creates a new file
D) Removes all content in a directory

Review Question 11.24
What is the purpose of using an escape character (\) in Bash?

A) To display the 1,000 most recent commands
B) To create a new directory
C) To create a new file with spaces in its name
D) To remove all content in a directory

11.2 The Linux File System

In this section, we delve into the intricacies of navigating and manipulating the Linux file system. We'll explore file management techniques and text operations, equipping you with the skills to efficiently interact with Linux's hierarchical file system.

11.2.1 File System Navigation and Manipulation

To navigate through directory trees, use the forward slash (/). For instance, if there's a directory named 'exercise' in my home directory, it would be located at /home/larry/exercise, where 'larry' represents the account name (replace it with your own). You can change your current directory to 'exercise' by using the 'cd' command and verify the change with the 'pwd' command.

```
$cd /home/larry/exercise
$pwd
/home/larry/exercise
```

Create a new directory called 'practice' and generate some practice files. Begin by using the 'mkdir' command to create the directory. Then, list the contents of the parent directory to confirm the addition of the new subdirectory. Finally, change your current location to the newly created subdirectory.

```
$mkdir practice
$ls
file new practice
$cd practice
$ls
```

Note the different color for 'practice' which indicates it is a directory.

Next, launch the 'nano' text editor (it was introduced in Chapter 8) by typing 'nano' followed by the name of an existing or new file. If the file doesn't exist, a new file will be created; if it does, new content will be appended. Before that you may want to install nano:

```
$sudo apt update
```

When the Linux prompt is back, issue the following:

```
$sudo apt install nano
```

You will be prompt for "which services should be restarted?" Pick "3.ssh.service"

Now, you can issue the following to use the nano editor:

```
$nano test1
```

Type text into the editor, and when finished, press 'Ctrl' + 'X' to exit. A dialog will appear at the bottom, prompting you to save the modified buffer.

Press 'Y' to confirm, and another dialog will appear, asking for the file name. Press 'Enter' to save the content to 'test1' in the default Linux format. You can use the 'cat' command to view the content of 'test1'.

```
$cat test1
```

Use the 'touch' command to create additional files for practice. If 'touch' is used on an existing file, it will update the date timestamp, useful for administrative purposes.

```
$touch test2 test3 test10 test11
$ls
test1 test10 test11 test2 test3
```

Create a new directory called 'practice2' within the 'practice' directory. Use the 'cp' command to copy files from the current directory to 'practice2':

```
$mkdir practice2
$cp test1 practice2
$cd practice2
$ls
test1
```

You can copy files with patterns; for instance, 'cp test*' will copy all files starting with 'test'. To copy files with specific characters following 'test'. To practice, first move the current directly back to 'practice'

```
$cd ..
$cp test? practice2
$cd practice2
$ls
Test1 test2 test3
```

To copy all files starting with 'test', regardless of characters following it, first move back one directory:

```
$cd ..
$cp test* practice2
$cd practice2
$ls
```

```
test1 test10 test11 test2 test3
```

To move a file instead of copying it, use the 'mv' command. Create a new directory called 'practice3' inside 'practice' directory and move all 'test' files from 'practice' to 'practice3':

```
$cd ..
$ls
practice2 test1 test10 test11 test2 test3
$mkdir practice3
$mv test* practice3
$ls
practice2 practice3
$cd practice3
$ls
test1 test10 test11 test2 test3
```

Note the use of two dots (..) to refer to the directory above the current one and 'test*' to identify all files starting with 'test'.

While still in the 'practice3' directory, move all 'test' files back to the parent 'practice' directory:

```
$mv test* ..
$ls
$cd ..
$ls
practice2 practice3 test1 test10 test11 test2 test3
```

Next, move 'test1', 'test2', and 'test3' files back to 'practice3':

```
$cd practice3
$mv ../test? .
$ls
test1 test2 test3
```

The single dot (.) indicates the current directory. This command moves all files starting with 'test' followed by a single character from the parent directory (..) to the current directory (.).

To remove all files from the 'practice3' directory, use:

```
$rm *
$ls
$cd ..
$ls
Practice2 practice3 test10 test11
```

Exercise caution as this command will delete all files in the directory. You can also remove a whole directory. For example, remove the 'practice3' directory:

```
$rmdir practice3
$ls
practice2 test10 test11
```

The 'rmdir' command won't remove a directory if it's not empty. If you want to delete the directory and its contents, use:

```
$rmdir practice2
rmdir: failed to remove 'practice2': Directory not empty
$rm -r practice2
$ls
test10 test11
```

The '-r' option indicates recursive deletion.

Review Question 11.25
In Linux, nano is a tool for ________.
A) painting
B) text editing
C) coloring
D) single command

Review Question 11.26
What will the following Linux command do?
```
$ nano test1
```
A) replace a file called test1 if that name is used
B) create a file called test1 if that name exists
C) raise an error if that name exists
D) create a new file called test1 if that name is not used

Review Question 11.27
What will the following Linux command do?
```
$ nano test1
```
A) warm you if that name exists
B) create a new file called test1 if that name exists
C) raise an error if that name exists
D) append content to test1 if that name exists

Review Question 11.28
What will the following Linux command do?
```
$ cp test1 practice2
```
A) copy a file called test1 to practice2 directory

B) copy a file called practice2 to test1 directory
C) compile a file called test1 in practice2 directory
D) compile a file called practice2 in test1 directory

Review Question 11.29
Which file(s) will be copied with the following command?
```
$ cp test? practice2
```
A) test1 or testa only
B) test1 or test10 only
C) testa or testab only
D) test1, test10, testa, or testab

Review Question 11.30
What file(s) will be copied with the following command?
```
$ cp test* practice2
```
A) test1 or testa only
B) test1 or test10 only
C) testa or testab only
D) test1, test10, testa, or testab

Review Question 11.31
What will the following Linux command do?
```
$ mv test1 practice3
```
A) move a file called test1 to practice3 directory
B) move a file called practice3 to test1 directory
C) make a file called test1 visible in practice3 directory
D) make a file called practice3 visible in test1 directory

Review Question 11.32
In Bash, what does two dots (..) mean?
A) two files
B) two directories
C) current directory
D) the directory one level above the current directory

Review Question 11.33
In Bash, what does a single dot (.) mean?
A) current file
B) the directory one level down the current directory
C) current directory
D) the directory one level above the current directory

Review Question 11.34
What will the following Linux command do?
```
$ rm *
```
A) delete all files in the current directory
B) delete all files and directory in the current directory
C) remember all files in the current directory
D) remember all files and directory in the current directory

Review Question 11.35
What will the following Linux command do?
```
$ rmdir practice3
```
A) delete a directory called practice3
B) delete an empty directory called practice3
C) remember a directory called practice3
D) remember an empty directory called practice3

Review Question 11.36
What will the following Linux command do?
```
$ rm practice3
```
A) delete a directory called practice3
B) delete an empty directory called practice3
C) remove a file called practice3
D) remove a file or a directory called practice3

Review Question 11.37
What will the following Linux command do?
```
$ rm -r practice3
```
A) delete a directory called practice3
B) delete a directory called practice3 only if it is empty
C) remember a directory called practice3
D) remember an empty directory called practice3

11.2.2 File Management and Text Operations

To locate files by name in the 'exercise/practice' directory, use the following 'find' command. Issue the following command to search all file names begin with "test" string in the exercise/practice directory.
```
$find exercise/practice -iname test*
```

For finding empty files in the 'exercise/practice' directory, use:
```
$find exercise/practice -empty
```

To search for files based on their access or modification time within the last 5 days, use:
```
$ find exercise/practice -mtime -5
```

Note: 'mtime' refers to modification time. Use 'atime' for access time and 'ctime' for change time.

You can also search for files based on size. Navigate to 'exercise/practice,' use 'nano' to add at least 1000 characters to 'test11,' and then issue the command:

```
$ find -size +1k
```

Only 'test11' should be displayed.

You can also search text in files with the 'grep' Command. The 'grep' command displays filenames containing a specified string. To search for the string 'world' in all files in '/exercise/practice,' use:

```
$ grep "world" *
```

You can also limit the search to a specific file:

```
$ grep "world" test11
```

You use the 'cat' command to view a file previously. The 'cat' Command can also be used to create and concatenate files. For example, you can create a file and input text using:

```
$ cat > test1
Line1 of test1 file
Line2 of test1 file
```

On the keyboard press Ctrl+D to save and exit.

You can view more than one file with the 'cat' command:

```
$ cat test1 test2
```

The 'cat' command can redirect the content of multiple files to one file':

```
$ cat test1 > test3
$ cat test2 > test3
```

The first line above will direct the content from test1 file to test3 file erasing anything inside. The second line above will direct the content from test2 file to test3 file erasing anything inside. As a result, test3 should only contain the content from test2. You can use 'cat' to view the content of 'test3':

```
$ cat test3
```

The solution is to append content with the >> operator:

```
$ cat test1 > test3
$ cat test2 >> test3
$ cat test3
```

The redirection operator can redirect standard error to a file when encountering an error:

```
$ wget www.google.coom 2> errorfile.txt
$ cat errorfile.txt
```

The number 2 is a designation for standard error. Zero is standard in, and 1 is standard out. The commend will redirect the error message to the specified file instead of to the monitor screen. Use the less command to view the content of the errorfile.txt, you will see the exactly same error message in the errorfile.txt.

Review Question 11.38
What will the following Linux command do?
```
$ find exercise/practice -iname test*
```
A) search a file called test in the exercise/practice directory.
B) search a file called practice inside the exercise/test directory.
C) search any files with file name begins with "test" in the exercise/practice directory.
D) search any files with file name includes "test" in the exercise/practice directory.

Review Question 11.39
What will the following Linux command do?
```
$ find exercise/practice -empty
```
A) make the exercise/practice directory empty.
B) search the exercise/practice directory for all empty files.
C) search the exercise/practice directory for all files with empty in the name.
D) search the exercise/practice directory for all files with file name begin with empty.

Review Question 11.40
Which of the following commands searches all files in the exercise/practice directory that are modified within the last 5 days?
A) $ find exercise/practice -atime -5
B) $ find exercise/practice -btime -5
C) $ find exercise/practice -ctime -5
D) $ find exercise/practice -mtime -5

Review Question 11.41
Which of the following commands searches all files in the current directory that are more than 1k in size?
A) $ find -size +1k
B) $ find -size >1k
C) $ find -size more than 1k
D) $ find -size current >1k

Review Question 11.42
What does the following command do?
```
$ sudo apt install locate
```
A) Check the location of installed application called apt.

B) Check the location of installed application called sudo.
C) Check the location of installed application called apt inside the sudo directory.
D) Install the locate program.

Review Question 11.43
What does the following command do?
```
locate -i test10 test11
```
A) Search for a file called test10.
B) Search for a file called test11.
C) Search for files called test10 or test11.
D) Search for a file called test11 in the test10 directory

Review Question 11.44
The locate command reads a precompiled index of all the files and directories on the system. If you look for files just added, _______.
A) you can find it quickly
B) you may not find it
C) you can find it as long as it is in the hard drive
D) you can always find it by using an index

Review Question 11.45
The locate command is _______ than the find command.
A) faster
B) slower
C) neither faster nor slower
D) less used

Review Question 11.46
The locate command has _______ than that of the find command.
A) more options
B) fewer options
C) neither more nor fewer options
D) one option less

Review Question 11.47
The _______ command allows you to display the names of files that contain a particular string of characters that matches your search query.
A) find
B) locate
C) grep
D) search

Review Question 11.48
What does the following command do?
```
$ cat > test1
```
A) categorize the test1 file
B) put the text "cat" in the test1 file
C) move the file test1 inside the cat directory
D) create a file called test1 and await keyboard input for the content of the file.

Review Question 11.49
What does the following command do?

```
$ cat test2 > test3
```

A) Categorize test2 file in the test3 directory.
B) Append the content of test2 file to the test3 file.
C) Replace the content of test2 file with the content of test3 file.
D) Replace the content of test3 file with the content of test2 file.

Review Question 11.50
What does the following command do?

```
$ cat test2 >> test3
```

A) Categorize test2 file in the test3 directory.
B) Append the content of test2 file to the test3 file.
C) Replace the content of test2 file with the content of test3 file.
D) Replace the content of test3 file with the content of test2 file.

Review Question 11.51
What does the following command do?

```
$ wget www.google.coom 2> errorfile.txt
```

A) The number 2 is an error.
B) Output the first two errors to the errorfile.txt.
C) Output the two paragraphs of error to the errorfile.txt.
D) Instead of displaying errors on the screen, it redirects any errors generated by the command to the errorfile.txt.

11.3 Linux Network Connectivity

Seamless network integration requires each device to have a unique IP address. It's crucial to understand your machine's assigned IP address and the default router's IP address. IPv4 addresses are 32-bit integers often expressed in hexadecimal notation or the more common dotted quad format (x.x.x.x), where each 'x' ranges from 0 to 255. For instance, 192.0.2.16 is a valid IPv4 address. A newer version, IPv6, uses 128-bit addresses represented as:

xxxx:xxxx:xxxx:xxxx:xxxx:xxxx:xxxx:xxxx

Each 'x' represents a hexadecimal digit (0-9, a-f). For example, 2607:f8b0:4009:81c::2004 is a valid IPv6 address. With its expansive address space, IPv6 provides superior security features compared to IPv4.

The ip command is a powerful tool for managing network configuration on a Linux system. It's part of the iproute2 package, which comes pre-installed on all Ubuntu systems.

To access your Azure Ubuntu VM, you'll need to use SSH (Secure Shell). From your local machine, open a terminal and type:

```
ssh your_username@your_vm_ip
```

Replace your_username with your username on the Azure VM, and your_vm_ip with the public IP address of your VM.

The ip command is used to display or manipulate routing, devices, policy routing, and tunnels. The basic syntax of the ip command is:

```
ip [ OPTIONS ] OBJECT { COMMAND | help }
```

- `OPTIONS` are optional and alter the behavior of the command.
- `OBJECT` is the type of object to manage. It can be address, route, link, etc.
- `COMMAND` is what you want to do to the object. It can be add, delete, show, etc.

To display the IP addresses of all network interfaces on your system, use the ip addr show command:

```
ip addr show
```

This command will display a list of all network interfaces along with their IP addresses. To explore and verify your network setup, use the terminal and execute the following command:

```
ip route show
```

Review Question 11.52
What is the size of an IPv4 address?
A) 16-bit
B) 32-bit
C) 64-bit
D) 128-bit

Review Question 11.53
How is each 'x' in an IPv6 address (xxxx:xxxx:xxxx:xxxx:xxxx:xxxx:xxxx:xxxx)represented?
A) Decimal digit (0-9)
B) Binary digit (0-1)
C) Octal digit (0-7)
D) Hexadecimal digit (0-9, a-f)

Review Question 11.54
What command is used to display the IP addresses of all network interfaces on a Linux system?
A) ip addr show
B) ip addr display
C) ip show addr
D) ip display addr

Review Question 11.55
What command is used to access your Azure Ubuntu VM?
A) ssh your_username@your_vm_ip
B) connect your_username@your_vm_ip
C) login your_username@your_vm_ip
D) access your_username@your_vm_ip

Review Question 11.56
What does the 'ip' command manage in Azure Ubuntu VM?
A) Routing, devices, policy routing, and tunnels.
B) Files, directories, and permissions.
C) Processes, memory, and CPU usage.
D) Users, groups, and access rights.

11.4 Linux Scripting

In Linux, Bash scripts function like programming code, using Bash commands as instructions.

Consolidating learned commands into a script file allows for their automatic execution in a single run.

Besides standard commands, scripts can encompass added functionality akin to programs, integrating user

inputs, variables, and flow controls.

To initiate a new file named script1.sh, utilize nano. The ".sh" extension designates it as a script, aiding in

file management:

```
$ cd exercise
$ nano script1.sh
```

Input the following lines into script1.sh:

```
#!/bin/bash
echo "Enter your name: "
read name
echo "Welcome to Ubuntu, $name"
exit 0
```

The initial line of each script declares it as executable and specifies the shell interpreter—in this case, Bash in the bin directory. Subsequently, commands like "echo" display messages on the monitor, while "read" waits for and accepts user input. The variable "name" stores the entered value, utilized in the subsequent line. The "$" before a variable name retrieves its value. The concluding "exit 0" line isn't necessary, signaling a successful script execution.

Save and exit script1.sh by pressing Control+X, then Y, followed by the "Enter" key.

To execute script1.sh, make the file executable (covered in the next chapter) using:

```
$ chmod +x script1.sh
```

Run the script by entering:

```
./script1.sh
```

The output prompts: "Enter your name:". For instance, typing "Larry" results in "Welcome to Ubuntu, Larry" on the monitor.

Encountering error messages? Don't fret. Copy the code or error messages, paste them into your browser, and seek help. Most importantly, embrace the learning process—it's not frustrating; it's learning.

Start another script file called script2.sh with nano. This script will prompt the user for a new directory name. Create the directory. Then it prompts the user for a file name, create the file inside the directory. And finally, it prompts the user for a sentence. Save the sentence in the file.

Use the following code for script2.sh:

```
#!/bin/bash
# prompt user for directory and file names
echo "Enter a new directory name:"
read mydirectory
echo "Enter a new file name:"
read myfile
# create the directory and file
mkdir $mydirectory
touch $mydirectory/$myfile
# prompt user for content of the file
echo "Enter a sentence for the file:"
read sentence
echo $sentence >> $mydirectory/$myfile
exit 0
```

The # sign comments out the line. Recall the >> is a redirect operator and it will allow the content on the left side to append to the file on the right.

Save and run the code the same way as you do for script1.sh. In the output prompt, "Enter a new directory name:", Enter "practice2" for directory name. Next, it prompts for a file name, enter "file1". When prompted for a sentence. Then enter a sentence for the file. Change to the new directory to view the file and its content.

Now, go one directory up and run script2.sh again. But this time enter practice2 again for directory name. Since the practice2 directory was created last time you ran the script2.sh. An error will be displayed:

```
mkdire: cannot create directory 'practice2': File exists.
```

To fix the problem, nano script2.sh to update it so that it will only accept a non-existing directory name. Enter the following lines of code right after the "read mydirectory" line:

```
while [ -d $mydirectory ]
do
  echo "Directory exists."
  echo "Enter a new directory name:"
  read mydirectory
done
```

The while loop will repeat the instructions inside the "do … done" block as long as the condition in square bracket is true. The "-d $mydirectory" basically asks if $mydirectory is a directory. If yes, return true. Otherwise, return false. The updated script2.sh is shown below:

```
#!/bin/bash
# prompt user for directory and file names
echo "Enter a new directory name:"
read mydirectory
while [ -d $mydirectory ]
do
  echo "Directory exists."
  echo "Enter a new directory name:"
  read mydirectory
done
echo "Enter a new file name:"
read myfile
# create the directory and file
mkdir $mydirectory
touch $mydirectory/$myfile
# prompt user for content of the file
echo "Enter a sentence for the file:"
```

```
read sentence
echo $sentence >> $mydirectory/$myfile
exit 0
```

Run script2.sh again. This time it will keep prompting the user for a directory name until a non-exist

directory name is entered.

In addition to the "while" loop, Bash also has a "for" loop. One version of the "for" loop is similar to the "for each" loop in other languages. Make a new directory called practice3 inside the exercise directory. Then add three empty files called file1, file2, and f3 to the practice3. You can use touch for the task.

```
$mkdir practice3
$cd practice3
$touch file1 file2 f3
$ls
f3 file1 file2
```

Back to the exercise directory, create a new bash file called script3.sh with the following content.

```
#!/bin/bash
Cd practice3
files="file*"
for file in $files
do
   echo "Renaming $file to udated$file"
   mv $file "updated"$file
done
ls
exit 0
```

The third line put all files with file name begin with "file" (note the wild card *). The "for" loop go through each element in the "files" variable and use the "mv" command to change file name to updatedfile name. For example, file1 will become updatedfile1.

Save and exit script3.sh. Run it and you will see only file1 and file2 are renamed while f3 is still the same. Because f3 does not match the pattern "file*" and thus is not updated.

```
$./script3.sh
Renaming file1 to updatedfile1
Renaming file2 to updatedfile2
f3 updatedfile1 updatedfile2
```

Another popular flow control approach is "if statement". Create a script called script4.sh that can be used to delete a file in a subdirectory of exercise where all our practice scripts located. The script prompts the user for a directory name. If that directory exists, it will prompt the user to enter a file name for deletion. If the file name exists, it will be deleted. Otherwise, user will receive a feedback. You need a nested if statement to accomplish the task. Enter the following code in nano.

```
#!/bin/bash
echo "This script allows you to delete a file"
echo "Enter the name of the directory:"
read mydirectory
if [ -d $mydirectory ]
then
   echo "Enter a file to delete:"
   read myfile
   if [ -f $mydirectory/$myfile ]
   then
     rm $mydirectory/$myfile
     echo "$myfile deleted."
   else
     echo "$myfile does not exist in $mydirectory."
   fi
else
   echo "$mydirectory directory does not exist."
fi
exit 0
```

The if condition is similar to the while condition. The "-d $mydirectory" checks if the directory exists. The "-f $mydirectory/$myfile" checks if the file exists inside the directory. Note that an if statement is terminated with "fi".

Save and run script4.sh. Enter practice3 for directory and f3 for file name as shown in Figure 6.86. The f3 file will be deleted.

```
$ls practice3/
f3 updatedfile1 updatedfile2
$./script4.sh
This script allows you to delete a file
Enter the name of the directory:
practice3
Enter a file to delete:
f33
f33 does not exist in practice3.
$./script4.sh
This script allows you to delete a file
Enter the name of the directory:
```

```
practice3
Enter a file to delete:
f3
f3 deleted.
$ls pracitce3/
updatedfile1 updatedfile3
```

Review Question 11.57
On Linux, Bash _______ is (are) like programming code with Bash command as instructions.
A) code
B) file
C) commands
D) scripts

Review Question 11.58
Which of the following is always the first line of code in Bash script files?
A) #!/bin/bash
B) !#/bin/bash
C) #!/bash/bin
D) !#/bash/bin

Review Question 11.59
What does the following command do?
$ chmod +x script1.sh
A) Add an x to the script1.sh.
B) Add an x to the chmod command of script1.sh file.
C) Make the script1.sh file executable.
D) Make the script1.sh file contain chmod.

Review Question 11.60
Suppose script1.sh is executable. Which of the following command will run the script?
A) run script1.sh
B) run ./script1
C) run ./script1.sh
D) ./script1.sh

Review Question 11.61
For "while" loop or "if" statement, where do you put the testing condition?
A) Inside a pair of parentheses ().
B) Inside a pair of square brackets []
C) Inside a pair of curly braces {}
D) No special characters, just immediately follow the while or if keyword.

Review Question 11.62
In Bash scripts, how do you terminate an if statement?
A) end if
B) endif

C) fi
D) a closing curly brace "}"

11.5 Chapter Summary

In this chapter, you were introduced to several valuable help documentation resources available in Linux. You gained insights into command line syntax patterns, including the method of passing command arguments to programs. Additionally, you acquired foundational file and directory administration skills. The Linux networking segment covered IPv4 and IPv6 addressing, along with instructions on utilizing the SSH secure shell protocol to establish secure and dependable connections with remote servers. Finally, you delved into the architecture of Bash scripts, examining practical example scripts for a better understanding.

11.6 Solutions to Review Questions

11.1 B; 11.2 A; 11.3 B; 11.4 B; 11.5 D; 11.6 A; 11.7 C; 11.8 B; 11.9 B; 11.10 A; 11.11 B; 11.12 C; 11.13 A; 11.14 B; 11.15 C; 11.16 A; 11.17 B; 11.18 C; 11.19 D; 11.20 A; 11.21 C; 11.22 C; 11.23 D; 11.24 C; 11.25 B; 11.26 D; 11.27 D; 11.28 A; 11.29 A; 11.30 D; 11.31 A; 11.32 D; 11.33 C; 11.34 A; 11.35 B; 11.36 C; 11.37 A; 11.38 C; 11.39 B; 11.40 D; 11.41 A; 11.42 D; 11.43 C; 11.44 B; 11.45 A; 11.46 B; 11.47 C; 11.48 D; 11.49 D; 11.50 B; 11.51 D; 11.52 B; 11.53 D; 11.54 A; 11.55 A; 11.56 A; 11.57 D; 11.58 A; 11.59 C; 11.60 D; 11.61 B; 11.62 C;

Chapter 12: Linux System Administration

Chapter Learning Outcomes

12.1 Explain the significance of monitoring a Linux system.
12.2 Demonstrate an understanding of user and group management in Linux
12.3 Illustrate the purpose and methods of socket port scanning.

12.1 Optimizing Linux System

In this section, we explore two critical topics: Monitoring and Performance Analysis (using tools like top, free, and /proc to understand system state) and Troubleshooting Processes (tracking down misbehaving processes using commands like ps, grep, and journalctl).

12.1.1 Monitoring and Performance Analysis

To make informed decisions about improving your system's performance, you need a clear understanding of its current state and any areas that require attention. Linux provides powerful tools that offer quick and accurate insights into various aspects of your system. Let's explore these monitoring techniques:

Navigate to the /proc directory and list its contents:

```
$ cd /proc
$ ls
```

Key system information resides in virtual files within the /proc directory. These files are dynamically created during system boot and in response to events.

View system memory information using the meminfo file:

```
$ cat meminfo
```

The meminfo file contains information about the capacity and usage levels of the system memory. The output shows how much physical memory you have and how much of it is not currently being used.

Inspect CPU specifications via the cpuinfo file:

```
$ cat cpuinfo
```

These files provide insights into CPU capacity and specifications, aiding in understanding system specification.

Monitor current hardware utilization with the top command:

```
$ top
```

The top command provides an automatically-updating screen with data on processes consuming the highest percentages of CPU and memory resources. It's especially useful when your system slows down, helping you identify the cause. The most common culprit for slowdowns is inadequate system memory availability.

Check memory utilization (including swap) using the free command:

```
$ free
$ free -h // Display results in MB and GB for readability
```

Observing low available memory might indicate the need for an upgrade.

Inspect storage devices and file system space usage with the df command:

```
$ df
```

In the networking analysis, one critical aspect involves testing internet speed. This entails utilizing multiple websites dedecated to assessing upload, download, and latency performance. Such tests serve the purpose of verifying and evaluating the performance of the Internet Service Provider (ISP), ensuring that the expected speeds and overall network performance align with anticipated standards.

Consider using iftop to monitor processes consuming excessive bandwidth. But before that you need to install iftop if not available by default:

```
$ sudo apt update
$ sudo apt install iftop
```

Check Network Interface and run iftop.
Identity the designated network interface using:

```
$ ip addr
```

Look for the active interface, e.g., enp0s3. Issue the following command:

```
$ sudo iftop -i enp0s3
```

Observe the constantly updating screen for network utilization.

Review Question 12.1
What directory contains key system information in Linux?
A) /var
B) /etc
C) /proc
D) /sys

Review Question 12.2
Which file provides information about system memory capacity and usage levels?
A) meminfo
B) cpuinfo
C) top
D) df

Review Question 12.3
Where can you find CPU specifications in Linux?
A) /var
B) /etc
C) /proc/cpuinfo
D) /sys/cpu

Review Question 12.4
Which command provides real-time data on processes consuming CPU and memory resources?
A) meminfo
B) top
C) free
D) df

Review Question 12.5
What is the most common cause of system slowdowns?
A) Inadequate CPU capacity
B) Insufficient storage space
C) Low available memory
D) Network congestion

Review Question 12.6
Which command checks memory utilization, including swap space?
A) meminfo
B) top
C) free
D) df

Review Question 12.7
What does the df command help you inspect?
A) CPU specifications
B) Network interfaces
C) Storage devices and file system space
D) System uptime

Review Question 12.8
What purpose do internet speed tests serve in networking analysis?
A) Evaluate ISP performance
B) Diagnose CPU issues
C) Monitor memory usage
D) Assess network security

Review Question 12.9
Which tool can monitor processes consuming excessive bandwidth?
A) top
B) iftop
C) meminfo
D) df

Review Question 12.10
Before using iftop, what step is necessary?
A) Install iftop using apt-get
B) Check network interface using ip addr
C) Verify system uptime
D) Run top command

12.1.2 Troubleshooting Processes

To track down misbehaving processes on your Linux system, you need access to event notifications. Here are the steps and commands to help you:

The ps command without any arguments displays processes running within the current shell:

```
$ ps
```

In your Ubuntu system, you'll see Bash itself and the ps command.

To see all active processes across the entire system, add the aux argument:

```
$ ps aux
```

This provides a comprehensive list of processes. You can even count the lines using wc:

```
$ ps aux | wc
```

To focus on specific processes, use grep. For example, to check the SSH daemon (sshd):

```
$ ps aux | grep sshd
```

The usr/sbin/sshd entry shows the precise command used to launch the process. If a process should be running but doesn't appear in the ps output, investigate further. You might have a typo or an issue. Search system logs for helpful error messages. Many Linux distros now use the journald logging system.

The journalctl command reads log messages processed by journald. To view messages generated in the last 15 minutes:

```
$ journalctl --since "15 minutes ago"
```

If needed, rely on text-only log files managed by syslogd.

```
$ cd /var/log
$ls
```

These logs are saved in the /var/log directory and organized by category. For example, authentication-related events are logged in auth.log, package management logs in dpkg.log, and kernel issues in kern.log. Compressed files (ending in .gz) contain older messages and are eventually deleted to manage disk space.

Review Question 12.11
What does the ps command without any arguments display?
A) Processes running within the current shell
B) All active processes across the entire system
C) Specific processes using grep
D) System logs

Review Question 12.12
Which argument should you add to the ps command to see all active processes across the entire system?
A) aux
B) grep
C) wc
D) journalctl

Review Question 12.13
What does the journalctl command do?
A) Displays a list of all processes
B) Reads log messages processed by journald
C) Investigates system errors
D) Manages disk space

Review Question 12.14
How can you view log messages generated in the last 15 minutes using journalctl?
A) journalctl --since "15 minutes ago"
B) journalctl --last 15m
C) journalctl --recent
D) journalctl --time 15m

Review Question 12.15
Where are text-only log files managed by syslogd stored?
A) /var/log/auth.log
B) /var/log/dpkg.log
C) /var/log/kern.log
D) /var/log/syslog

Review Question 12.16
Which type of log files contain older messages and are eventually deleted to manage disk space?
A) Compressed files (ending in .gz)
B) Authentication-related logs
C) Package management logs
D) Kernel issue logs

12.2 Working with Users and Groups

In this section, we explore essential aspects of user management in Ubuntu. Topics include enhancing IT security through best practices and gaining system insights. Learn how to add users, configure permissions, and maintain a secure environment.

12.2.1 Enhancing IT Security

The weakest link in IT security often lies with people. Some individuals use weak passwords, while others unwittingly click on suspicious links in spam emails. Additionally, innocent users may inadvertently disclose their authentication credentials when falling victim to phishing attacks.

Linux provides tools and processes to minimize these risks. Here are some key practices to enhance security:

Avoid Administrator or Root Logins: Never log in with administrator or root powers. By doing so, even if your session becomes compromised and hijacked by hackers, the damage they can inflict will be limited.
Leverage Sudo: User accounts that belong to the sudo system group can invoke admin powers for a single command. After execution, the user automatically reverts to a regular user. This approach balances convenience and security.
Separate User Accounts: Create separate accounts with unique authentication for each user. This containment strategy helps mitigate damage from an attack on one account.

Precise Administration Powers: Assign administration powers precisely to users who absolutely need them. Avoid granting excessive privileges.

Now, let's delve into system files:

The /etc/shadow File: This file contains encrypted versions of all user passwords. It's inaccessible using commands like cat or less. To view it securely, use:

```
$ sudo cat /etc/shadow
```

Your password is required to access this file. The shadow file's protection prevents unauthorized access. Decrypting its contents would grant full system access, so exercise caution.

User Account Data in /etc/passwd: The passwd file no longer contains password information but holds account data for each user and system account. Use less to examine it:

```
$ cat /etc/passwd
```

Look for the line corresponding to your account. For example:

```
larry:x:1000:1000:Ubuntu:/home/larry:/bin/bash
```

Here, larry is the username, x indicates a password in the shadow file, and other fields provide essential details.

Group Information in /etc/group: The group file serves a similar purpose for groups. For instance:

```
$ cat /etc/group
```

Note that larry is a member of the sudo group, enabling admin powers via sudo.

User Privileges with id: Quickly check privileges associated with specific users:

```
$ id larry
```

This displays user and group IDs, as well as group memberships (including sudo).

Monitoring Logged-In Users:

`$ who` // Shows currently logged-in users, session start times, and origins.

`$ w` // Provides details on active users and their activities.

`$ last` // Lists system logins since the beginning of the month.

Stay vigilant, and ensure that access aligns with intended authority levels. If unusual logins occur, investigate promptly.

Review Question 12.17
What is the primary focus of IT security practices?
A) Protecting system files
B) Enhancing user convenience
C) Minimizing risks associated with people
D) Encrypting network traffic

Review Question 12.18
Why should you avoid logging in with administrator or root powers?
A) To prevent unauthorized access to system files
B) To limit potential damage if your session is compromised
C) To improve system performance
D) To enhance user convenience

Review Question 12.19
What does the sudo system group allow users to do?
A) Access encrypted password files
B) Execute admin commands for a single task
C) Create separate user accounts
D) Decrypt system logs

Review Question 12.20
What is the purpose of separate user accounts with unique authentication?
A) To improve system performance
B) To enhance convenience
C) To mitigate damage from attacks on one account
D) To simplify user management

Review Question 12.21
What does the /etc/shadow file contain?
A) Encrypted user passwords
B) System logins since the beginning of the month
C) Group membership details
D) User account data

Review Question 12.22
Why is the /etc/shadow file inaccessible using commands like cat or less?
A) To prevent unauthorized access
B) To improve system performance
C) To encrypt its contents
D) To simplify user management

Review Question 12.23

What information does the /etc/passwd file contain?
A) Encrypted user passwords
B) User account data
C) Group membership details
D) System logins

Review Question 12.24
What does the line "larry:x:1000:1000:Ubuntu:/home/larry:/bin/bash" in /etc/passwd represent?
A) Larry's password
B) Larry's user ID
C) Larry's group ID
D) Larry's home directory and default shell

Review Question 12.25
What purpose does the /etc/group file serve?
A) Contains encrypted user passwords
B) Holds account data for each user
C) Provides group membership information
D) Lists system logins

Review Question 12.26
How can you check user privileges using the id command?
A) id larry
B) id sudo
C) id /etc/shadow
D) id passwd

12.2.2 Adding Users and Managing Permissions

To add a new user named "bob" with a home directory at /home/bob, use the following commands:

```
$ sudo useradd -m bob
$ sudo passwd bob
```

The first command creates the user and the -m option ensures that a home directory is created for the user.

The second command sets a temporary password for "bob."

Once "bob" logs in for the first time using the temporary password, he can change it to a permanent one using (switch user):

```
$ su bob
```

The default files for new users are copied from the /etc/skel directory, also known as skeleton directory.

You can explore its contents using:

```
$ cd /etc/skel/
$ ls -a
```

This directory acts as a template for new users' home directories.

You can create a group and assign permissions to the whole group. To limit user access, create a new directory called "cs101" inside the /var directory:

```
$ sudo mkdir /var/cs101
```

Next, create a new group called "cs101-group":

```
$ sudo groupadd cs101-group
```

Make "cs101-group" the owner of the "cs101" directory:

```
$ sudo chown :cs101-group /var/cs101/
```

Add "bob" to the "cs101-group":

```
$ sudo usermod -a -G cs101-group bob
```

Finally, grant write permission to group members:

```
$ sudo chmod g+w /var/cs101
```

Now "bob" will have full control over the contents of the "cs101" directory.

Remember to replace "bob" with the desired username and adjust directory paths as needed.

Review Question 12.27
What does the -m option do in the useradd command?
A) Creates a new user.
B) Sets a temporary password.
C) Ensures a home directory is created for the user.
D) Copies default files from the /etc/skel directory.

Review Question 12.28
What does the command (sudo passwd bob) do?
A) Creates a new user.
B) Sets a temporary password.
C) Changes the user's password.
D) Copies default files from the /etc/skel directory.

Review Question 12.29
What command can "bob" use to log in for the first time using the temporary password and then change the temporary password to a permanent one?
A) su bob
B) sudo passwd bob
C) sudo usermod -a -G cs101-group bob

D) sudo chmod g+w /var/cs101

Review Question 12.30
What is the purpose of the /etc/skel directory?
A) It contains default files for new users.
B) It stores temporary passwords.
C) It acts as a template for system configuration.
D) It is the home directory for all users.

Review Question 12.31
Which directory should you explore to see the contents of the skeleton directory?
A) /etc/skel
B) /home/bob
C) /var/cs101
D) /etc

Review Question 12.32
What command creates a new group called "cs101-group"?
A) sudo chmod g+w /var/cs101
B) sudo usermod -a -G cs101-group bob
C) sudo chown :cs101-group /var/cs101/
D) sudo groupadd cs101-group

Review Question 12.33
How can you make "cs101-group" the owner of the "cs101" directory?
A) sudo groupadd cs101-group
B) sudo usermod -a -G cs101-group bob
C) sudo chown :cs101-group /var/cs101/
D) sudo chmod g+w /var/cs101

Review Question 12.34
What command adds "bob" to the "cs101-group"?
A) sudo useradd -m bob
B) sudo passwd bob
C) sudo usermod -a -G cs101-group bob
D) sudo chmod g+w /var/cs101

Review Question 12.35
How can you grant write permission to group members for the "cs101" directory?
A) sudo groupadd cs101-group
B) sudo usermod -a -G cs101-group bob
C) sudo chown :cs101-group /var/cs101/
D) sudo chmod g+w /var/cs101

12.3 Linux Server Security

In this section, we focuse on safeguarding your Linux server. It delves into the intricacies of permissions and attributes, explores file attributes and permissions, and elucidates the concept of directory permissions and symbolic links, providing a robust foundation for secure server management.

12.3.1 Permissions and Attributes

In the previous section, we set up a cs101 directory with restricted access, ensuring that only members of the cs101-group could edit its contents. Additionally, we added our user, bob, to this group. Now, let's observe these permissions and attributes in action.

First, change to the cs101 directory and switch to the bob user:

```
$ cd /var/cs101
$ su bob
```

The su command allows us to switch users, and now we're logged in as bob.

Next, we'll have bob create a new file called homework.txt using the touch command. This action demonstrates that if bob weren't a member of the cs101-group or if the cs101 directory weren't owned by that group, creating the file would have been impossible:

```
$ touch homework.txt
$ ls
```

To further illustrate the importance of group associations, let's try creating a file in the var/log directory, which is owned by root. We'll issue the touch command to create a file named assignment.txt. However, this won't work, as bob lacks the necessary permissions:

```
$ cd /var/log
$ touch assignment.txt
```

The output will be: "Touch: cannot touch 'assignment.txt': Permission denied." This example highlights the value of associating groups with specific objects like directories.

Review Question 12.36
What is the purpose of setting up the cs101 directory with restricted access?
A) To demonstrate the use of the su command
B) To ensure that only members of the cs101-group can edit its contents
C) To create a new file called homework.txt
D) To switch users to bob

Review Question 12.37

What does the su command allow us to do?
A) Create new files
B) List directory contents
C) Switch users
D) Change file permissions

Review Question 12.38
What does the output "Touch: cannot touch 'assignment.txt': Permission denied" indicate?
A) The touch command was successful
B) The file assignment.txt was created
C) The user has necessary permissions
D) The user lacks permissions to create the file

12.3.2 File Attributes and Permissions

Switch back to the /var/cs101 directory and run ls -l to display the file attributes of the contents, which currently include only one file. The -l option stands for the long version. Additionally, using ls with the -d option will list the attributes of the /var/cs101 directory:

```
$ cd /var/cs101
$ ls -l
$ ls -dl
```

Every object in a Linux file system, whether it's a file or a directory, has unique metadata associated with it. This metadata is represented by 10 characters that indicate the permissions of the object.

Let's break down what those two commands reveal. First, consider the file homework.txt. The initial 10 characters on the line consist of four blocks: file type, owner permissions, group permissions, and others' permissions. Here's what each part represents:

File Type: The first character indicates the file type. A dash (-) means it's not a directory.
Owner Permissions: The next three characters (rw-) represent the ways the object's owner can interact with the file. In this case:
The r: The owner can read the file contents.
The w: The owner can write or edit the file (including deletion).
The -: The owner does not have execute rights.
Group Permissions: The following three characters represent the permissions for members of the owning group (in this case, bob's group):
The rw-: All group members have both read and write authority but lack execute permissions.
Others' Permissions: The final cluster of three characters (r--) indicates the rights of all other non-root users:
The r: Others can read the file.
The --: Others cannot write or execute.

Additionally, the output shows that the file owner is bob, and its group is also bob.

Now let's examine the cs101 directory using ls -dl. The first character (d) indicates that it's a directory. The subsequent groups represent permissions as follows:

Owner's Rights, rwx: The owner has full permission (read, write, and execute).

Group's Rights, rwx: The group (cs101-group) also has full permission.

Others' Rights, r-x: Others can read and execute but not write.

The owner of the cs101 directory is root because it was created by Larry using sudo. The group associated with it is cs101-group.

To modify an object's attributes, you can use chmod. For instance, let's add execute permissions to homework.txt for others:

```
$ chmod o+x homework.txt
$ ls -l
```

In this command: o refers to others (see table below), + indicates that we're adding a permission, x signifies execute rights. Notice that the last character changes from a dash (-) to x.

Character	Represent	Example
u	The file owner	u+x add owner execute right.
g	The members of the group	g+r add group read right.
o	All other users	o+w add other users write right.
a	All users, identical to ugo	a+r add all users read right.

Another way to represent object attributes is using numeric notation. Each permission (read, write, execute) corresponds to a numeric value: 4 for read, 2 for write, and 1 for execute. By adding these values together, we get the total numeric equivalent. For example: rw- would be 6, r-x would be 5, and so on. The highest possible permission level is 7 (read, write, and execute).

For homework.txt, where both the user and group have read and write permissions while others have read and execute, the notation is 6, 6, 5. Meanwhile, the cs101 directory would be represented as 7, 7, 5.

You can apply this notation with chmod. For instance, granting full permissions to all users:

```
$ chmod 777 homework.txt
$ ls -l
```

Review Question 12.39

What does the -l option do when running ls in the /var/cs101 directory?
A) Lists the attributes of the /var/cs101 directory
B) Displays the file contents in a long format
C) Switches to the cs101 directory
D) Creates a new file called homework.txt

Review Question 12.40
What does the first character in the file attributes represent for homework.txt?
A) File type
B) Owner permissions
C) Group permissions
D) Others' permissions

Review Question 12.41
Which permissions are associated with the owner of homework.txt (-rw-rw-r--)?
A) Read and write
B) Write and execute
C) Read and execute
D) Read, write, and execute

Review Question 12.42
What does the -d option do when running ls in the /var/cs101 directory?
A) Lists the attributes of the /var/cs101 directory
B) Displays the file contents in a long format
C) Switches to the cs101 directory
D) Lists the attributes of the /var/cs101 directory itself

Review Question 12.43
What permissions do others have for homework.txt (-rw-rw-r-x)?
A) Read and write
B) Write and execute
C) Read and execute
D) Read only

Review Question 12.44
What numeric value represents full permissions (read, write, and execute)?
A) 4
B) 5
C) 6
D) 7

Review Question 12.45
What does the command chmod o+x homework.txt do?
A) Adds read permissions for others
B) Adds execute permissions for others
C) Removes write permissions for others
D) Changes the owner of the file

Review Question 12.46

What does the numeric equivalent 6 represent in permission notation?
A) Read and write
B) Read and execute
C) Write and execute
D) Read, write, and execute

Review Question 12.47
What is the highest possible permission level using numeric notation?
A) 4
B) 5
C) 6
D) 7

Review Question 12.48
What notation represents the permissions for the cs101 directory (drwxrwxr-x)?
A) 7, 7, 5
B) 6, 6, 5
C) 7, 7, 7
D) 6, 6, 6

12.3.3 Directory Permissions and Symbolic Links

Another important attribute that can be added to a directory is the sticky bit. This is particularly useful for directories like cs101, where all members of the cs101-group have editing privileges. The sticky bit ensures that group members can only delete their own files within the directory.

To illustrate, let's change the directory to cs101 and display its permissions for comparison. Then, we'll use the chmod command to add the sticky bit and display the updated permissions.

```
$ cd /var/cs101
$ ls -l
$ sudo chmod +t .
$ ls -dl
```


Note that the x for others is now replaced by t.

Another useful attribute is symbolic links. These are handy when you need access to specific directories or files from multiple locations. Instead of creating multiple copies of a file (which can become complicated if the source file is frequently updated), you can create a symbolic link to the source file at the required location. This link can be used just like the original file.

For instance, let's say you have a script.sh file in the /home/larry/exercise directory (replace larry with your account name). If you don't have this file, you can create one with nano and include any command in it. Then, use the ln command to create a symbolic link in the /var/cs101 directory.

```
$ nano /home/larry/exercise/script.sh
$ sudo ln -s /home/larry/exercise/script.sh /var/cs101
```

The ln command creates a link, and the -s option specifies that the link should be symbolic. The first location is the absolute path of the original script, and the second location is where you want the symbolic link created. You'll need to use sudo because you're creating the link in a directory that your user doesn't own.

Finally, change the directory to /var/cs101 and view the symbolic link that was created there.

```
$ cd /var/cs101
$ ls -l
```

Review Question 12.49
What is the purpose of the sticky bit in a directory?
A) It allows all members of a group to delete any file in the directory.
B) It ensures that group members can only delete their own files within the directory.
C) It prevents anyone from deleting files in the directory.
D) It allows users to stick files to the directory for easy access.

Review Question 12.50
How is the sticky bit added to a directory?
A) Using the chmod +s command.
B) Using the chmod +t command.
C) Using the chmod +x command.
D) Using the chmod +r command.

Review Question 12.51
What does the ln -s command do?
A) It creates a hard link.
B) It creates a symbolic link.
C) It removes a symbolic link.
D) It updates a symbolic link.

Review Question 12.52
What is the purpose of a symbolic link?
A) To create a shortcut to a file or directory from another location.
B) To duplicate a file or directory.
C) To hide a file or directory.
D) To lock a file or directory.

Review Question 12.53
What happens when the sticky bit is added to a directory?
A) The x for others is replaced by t.
B) The x for others is replaced by s.
C) The r for others is replaced by t.
D) The w for others is replaced by t.

Review Question 12.54
What command is used to view the permissions of a directory?
A) ls -l
B) ls -a
C) ls -d
D) ls -dl

Review Question 12.55
Why might you need to use sudo when creating a symbolic link?
A) Because you're creating the link in a directory that your user doesn't own.
B) Because creating a symbolic link requires root privileges.
C) Because the ln -s command always requires sudo.
D) Because sudo makes the symbolic link stronger.

Review Question 12.56
What is the first location in the ln -s command?
A) The location where the symbolic link should be created.
B) The location of the directory that contains the file.
C) The absolute path of the original file.
D) The relative path of the original file.

12.4 Chapter Summary

In this chapter, we delved into the monitoring, optimization, and security of Linux systems. We gained insights into performance management by controlling processes using tools such as systemctl. We addressed security concerns by managing access through the configuration of users, groups, and permissions. We further enhanced control over file system objects through the application of the sticky bit and symbolic links.

12.5 Solutions to Review Questions

12.1 C; 12.2 A; 12.3 C; 12.4 B; 12.5 C; 12.6 C; 12.7 C; 12.8 A; 12.9 B; 12.10 B; 12.11 A; 12.12 A; 12.13 B; 12.14 A; 12.15 D; 12.16 A; 12.17 C; 12.18 B; 12.19 B; 12.20 C; 12.21 A; 12.22 A; 12.23 B; 12.24 D; 12.25 C; 12.26 A; 12.27 C; 12.28 B; 12.29 A; 12.30 A; 12.31 A; 12.32 D; 12.33 C; 12.34 C; 12.35 D; 12.36 B; 12.37 C; 12.38 D; 12.39 B; 12.40 A; 12.41 A; 12.42 D; 12.43 C; 12.44 D; 12.45 B; 12.46 A; 12.47 D; 12.48 A; 12.49 B; 12.50 B; 12.51 B; 12.52 A; 12.53 A; 12.54 D; 12.55 A; 12.56 C;